SAVE
the
EARTH

JONATHON PORRITT

FOREWORD
HRH THE PRINCE OF WALES

INTRODUCTION
DAVID SUZUKI

McClelland & Stewart Inc.
TORONTO

A DORLING KINDERSLEY BOOK

Published in Canada in 1991
by McClelland & Stewart Inc.
The Canadian Publishers,
481 University Avenue,
Toronto, Ontario, M5G 2E9

First published in Great Britain in 1991
by Dorling Kindersley Limited,
9 Henrietta Street, London WC2E 8PS

PROJECT EDITOR *Douglas Amrine*
ART EDITOR *Peter Luff*

SENIOR EDITORS *Josephine Buchanan, CWF McDonald*
SENIOR ART EDITOR *Caroline Murray*
ASSISTANT EDITOR *Candida Ross MacDonald*
ASSISTANT ART EDITOR *Tina Vaughan*
ASSISTANT DESIGNER *Mustafa Sami*
PROJECT ADMINISTRATOR *Gillian Harvey*

ENVIRONMENTAL RESEARCHER *Donna Rispoli*
PICTURE RESEARCHER *Suzanne Williams*

MANAGING EDITOR *Carolyn King*
MANAGING ART EDITOR *Nick Harris*

Canadian Cataloguing in Publication Data
Porritt, Jonathon
    Save the earth
Includes index.
ISBN 0-7710-7021-7
    1. Conservation of natural resources.
    2. Environmental protection. I. Title.
S936.P67 1991   333.7'2   C91-094172-6

Computer page make-up by the Cooling Brown Partnership,
Hampton-upon-Thames, Middlesex
Reproduced by Colourscan, Singapore
Printed and bound in Italy by Arnoldo Mondadori, Verona, Italy

PUBLISHER'S NOTE

We have made every effort to produce this book using environmentally friendly materials. The paper was pulped and bleached using acid-free chemicals. Only oxygen was used in the bleaching process, to avoid the use of chlorine and the production of dioxins, and minimizing the discharge of harmful effluents. The boards were manufactured from 100 percent recycled materials, and the lamination on the jacket is from a cellulose-based resin.

By buying this book, you have already helped to support the work of Friends of the Earth International: this book's royalties are going to a special *Save the Earth* fund. Please see page 203 for details of how this money will be spent. If you wish to make a further contribution, write to your local Friends of the Earth organization, whose address is on page 202, and ask for membership details.

The views expressed in this book do not necessarily reflect those of Friends of the Earth International or any of its member groups.

CONTENTS

FOREWORD 6
HRH The Prince of Wales

INTRODUCTION 10
David T. Suzuki

1 • AWAKENING 14

TAKING STOCK
Is This the Last Chance? 20
Jonathon Porritt

A NEW INTERNATIONAL ORDER
One World and Beyond 32
Jonathon Porritt

2 • EARTH 40

RAINFOREST
**The Disappearing
Forests 46**
Norman Myers

GRASSLANDS
Defending the Open Range 56
David Hall and Jonathan Scurlock

CROPLANDS
Blowing in the Wind 62
Lester Brown

BIODIVERSITY
The Richness of Life 70
The Importance of Diversity
Peter Raven
A Wealth of Species 74
Ghillean Prance

MOUNTAINS
Losing the High Ground 80
David Pitt and Denis Landenbergue

3 • AIR 88

GLOBAL WARMING
Climate at Risk 94
Stephen Schneider

AIR POLLUTION
Living Dangerously 102
Michael Walsh

4 • FIRE 110

POPULATION
Crunching Numbers 116
Jonathon Porritt

TOWNS AND CITIES
Empowering People 122
*Jorge Hardoy and
David Satterthwaite*

RURAL RESOURCES
Relearning Civilization 130
Anil Agarwal

TRIBAL PEOPLES
Honoring Wisdom 136
Robin Hanbury-Tenison

5 • WATER 142

OCEANS AND SEAS
Failing Fisheries 150
John Beddington

SHORELINES AND ESTUARIES
Turning the Tide 158
Robert Earll

RIVERS AND LAKES
Damming the Flow 166
Philip Williams

WETLANDS
Draining the World Dry 174
David Bellamy

6 • HEALING 182

ACCEPTING RESPONSIBILITY
Ecology Begins at Home 188
Jonathon Porritt

THE WAY FORWARD
Celebrating the Earth 196
Jonathon Porritt

Useful Books and Addresses 202
Friends of the Earth
International 203
Index 204
Acknowledgments 208

FOREWORD

HRH The Prince of Wales

🌍

A T A TIME WHEN it was not particularly fashionable to talk about environmental matters – when they were very much at the bottom of the list of most people's priorities – I rather rashly found myself raising them in public. Rashly, because I then discovered that I was considered mildly dotty or, at worst, a relatively harmless crank for doing so! But I raised these issues because I had felt for some time that the developments we were seeing, and the warnings that were being advertised by certain scientists, were symptomatic of a form of industrial, technological, and social progress being pursued without sufficient thought to the long-term consequences of such progress.

When all is said and done, we have only this one planet to inhabit. No other life-supporting planet has, as yet, been discovered. Until one is found, and the means to colonize it have been perfected, it makes sense, as far as I am concerned, to nurture our only life-support system. We are, or *should* be, more than anything else, the stewards of this unique oasis in an otherwise apparently barren and inhospitable universe.

It is, of course, easy to fall into the trap of imagining that in the romantic, distant past our ancient ancestors lived in a kind of pastoral Utopia, totally in harmony with nature and their surroundings. Conservationists and environmentalists are frequently accused of wanting to revert to the unrealistic vision of a pre-industrial past.

While the images of the past are, of course, romanticized, I do believe that our headlong rush for so-called "progress" has meant that we have ignored some of the humbling lessons that our ancestors learnt over thousands of years of hard-won experience. (An old Chinese philosopher had a neat comment on those so eager for progress. He said: "They drown in what they do.") I believe that our Western, Greco-Roman heritage contains some fundamental truths about the universe and about man as the

microcosm of the universe, which we have lost and would do well to recover. In the East, the reverse is true. They tend to pay attention predominantly to the spiritual aspect of life, and regard the everyday world as "maya," pure illusion. As a result, the everyday world gives them a disastrous jolt now and then in the form of droughts and famines. What both East and West are lacking is balance between the outer and inner worlds.

Every ancient society seems to have been governed and influenced by mythology. While to the modern way of thinking the myths of the past may seem primitive and irrelevant to a technological society, I would contend that it is precisely because we have lost sight of those myths, and failed to see their true significance in unconscious terms, that our whole approach to life and to our natural surroundings has become so unbalanced.

It is perhaps worth recalling what a myth is. It is a narrative or fable having a meaning attached to it other than that which is obvious when it is taken literally. The term itself is a Greek one meaning "word," and hence a tale or story. The inner aspects of truth, when presented in literal language, are liable to be misunderstood, and therefore all great religions and philosophies have made use of myth and allegory for veiling (and at the same time revealing to those who have eyes to see) their profoundest truths. Our ancestors may not have developed a sophisticated technology, but their insight into the hidden, unconscious aspects of the laws of nature was simple and profound and in one sense more sophisticated than our own.

Greek mythology, in the symbolic language of gods and goddesses and strange creatures, is telling us about some of the eternal truths we need to understand in order to redress the balance in our lives and to meet the challenges the world faces. The story of what happened to Prometheus, who stole fire from the gods, should remind us that modern technological man has assumed a godlike quantity of power and is in danger of destroying his world with it. Man's power now *is* awesome. How can he manage this power to his and nature's advantage?

Another myth which tells us a similar kind of story is that of Phaethon, the vainglorious child of the sun god Helios, who insisted on driving his father's sun-chariot across the sky. Too late he realized he was neither old enough nor strong enough to control its mighty team of untamed horses. They drove the sun-chariot too near the Earth with the result that crops, forests, and towns began to burn, and even the

seas started to boil, threatening all marine life. To avoid destruction of all that lives, his own father was forced to have his beloved son struck down by a thunderbolt and cast flaming into the sea.

To many modern rationalists, myths such as these are merely a synonym for fiction. "It's only a myth," people say, meaning there is no truth in it. However, in India, where these things are better understood, the famous philosopher Gomara Swamy has said, "Myth embodies the nearest approach to absolute truth that can be stated in words." And C. G. Jung said at the very end of his life, "A myth is the revelation of the divine life in man."

In Western terms, one of the underlying factors which may have contributed (by being taken literally) to the desire to dominate nature, rather than live in harmony with it on a sustainable basis, is to be found in the Book of Genesis where it records that, "God said unto man, be fruitful and multiply, and replenish the Earth and *subdue it: and have dominion over the fish of the sea and over the fowl of the air and over every living thing that moveth upon the Earth.*" To me, that Old Testament story has provided Western man, accompanied by his Judeo-Christian heritage, with an overbearing and domineering attitude towards God's creation. It may not have been a conscious realization, but it has contributed, nevertheless, to a feeling that the world is somehow entirely man's to dispose of – as income, rather than a capital asset which needs husbanding. By contrast, the Koran specifically mentions the fact that the natural world is loaned from God.

What I am trying to say, rather haltingly, is that now we have begun to realize we need to make adjustments to our "conventional" outlook on things such as accepted economic theory, and on what we mean by progress, we also perhaps need to make room once more for that unconscious element in our lives which has been displaced by the march of rationalism, a process which has increasingly led to misunderstanding and resentment on the part of the more traditional societies of the developing world. Making such adjustments will not be easy – I am not sure how I am going to, either! – but in order to tackle the future global challenges it is my own personal belief that we need to combine technological ability with, for want of a better description, spiritual readjustment and a realization that certain truths are eternal and not merely subject to the whims of late 20th century fashion.

In this way, I feel sure we will rediscover that ancient art of husbandry: of stewardship of the land which always recognized what is now known by the latest fashionable description of "sustainability." We will discover, too, that it really *is* possible to avoid unnecessary waste and, what is more, that man's ingenuity and inventiveness, fueled by the incentive provided by necessity, can provide some remarkable methods of tackling the various problems that we recognize have to be addressed.

Much is written and said about the problems of the developing world, and there is a kind of fashionable jargon used in relation to it. We have to be very careful not to impose our Western concepts or solutions onto the people of developing countries. Just because we have all the technological know-how and the economic theories does *not* mean that we have all the answers.

Above all, we need to operate within the framework of the culture and religion of each country. For example, in Indonesia (which is predominantly Muslim), they are operating one of the more successful family planning policies in the developing world largely because great efforts have been made to persuade the Imams in each community to accept the policies as part of the Muslim religion. Without such efforts, the policies would have foundered at once.

In such countries you will find that they think we, in the developed world, should rediscover the kind of non-material values which enable a proper balance to be struck between the outer world of nature and the inner world. Such a balance permits us to understand better the law of eternal opposites which means that every apparent advantage always has a disadvantage and that certain limitations need to be accepted. Inevitably this is an uncomfortable truth, but until there is a gradual acceptance of our fallibility in this regard I think it will be difficult to achieve the kind of "sustainability" that is now being talked of.

In this important new book, Jonathon Porritt's own distinctive and challenging message is augmented by contributions from many other eminent environmentalists, each with a slightly different perspective on the world's environmental problems, and a host of other contributors. Their combined wisdom indicates, to me at least, just how pressing is the need for a change in our attitudes if we are to be serious about our long-term survival on this planet.

Charles

INTRODUCTION

David T. Suzuki

Canada as a political entity was only invented by the Europeans who arrived in North America within the past few centuries. But long before this land was "discovered" by Europeans, plants, animals, and aboriginal peoples had flourished here for thousands of years. If there was a paradise on Earth, it would surely have been Canada. The First Nations of Canada recognized the immensity and complexity of nature, they were grateful for the generous fecundity of the Earth, and they felt humility before the incomprehensible mysteries of the world. The boundaries of the territories within which they lived were shaped by the ecological realities of the areas – watersheds, mountain ranges, prairies, foothills, and river basins.

The land and all of its occupants were sacred. The people could not be separated from the land; it made them what they were. The land embodied their history, culture, and purpose. What were they if they did not have the land?

Europeans arrived as part of the great wave of exploration around the world after the Dark Ages had given way to the Renaissance, the birth of science, and the Industrial Revolution. They came ebullient with a sense of confidence and cultural superiority. Their attitude was based in the Judeo-Christian belief that they had been created in the image of a God and enjoined to populate the Earth and tame it.

In the eyes of those conquerors, Canada held vast "resources" just waiting to be exploited for economic benefit by the superior technology of Europe. They set out to tame the land and transform it with the imprint of human technology and power. Within two centuries, the bison and passenger pigeons were gone; aboriginal people, flora, and fauna were under assault everywhere.

This attitude and pattern persist to the present time. Air, water, and land continue to be used as a repository for household wastes, industrial effluent, and agricultural runoff. Consumption in Canada results in a disproportionate use of resources and production of pollution per capita, in comparison with the poor countries of the world.

At the same time, the prairie soils that accumulated over millennia to make Canada a breadbasket of the world are being mined of organic matter at a staggering rate of centimeters per year. Within a century the prairies will be reduced to a dustbowl.

Canada leads the industrial world in per capita energy consumption and output of greenhouse gases. Acid precipitation from industries in the eastern states of the United States as well as Ontario and Quebec industries has already sterilized thousands of lakes and threatens the deciduous forests of southern Ontario and Quebec.

Canada's unique and envied wilderness is being destroyed and degraded by the inexorable demands for "development." Massive clearcut logging sites, immense hydroelectric dams, urban sprawl, and mining operations reduce wilderness to small isolated pockets.

The severity of Canada's ecological destruction has stimulated the rapid growth of environmental groups. In the early 1970's, Greenpeace was formed in Vancouver and went on to become a global force. In Ontario, Pollution Probe was created by academics and activists to pressure the government on pollution, and it remains a potent group today.

The Acid Rain Coalition has lobbied effectively for a US Clean Air Act. Probe International is investigating the impact of Canadian aid and industries on Third World countries. Canadian branches of international groups like Friends of the Earth, the Sierra Club, and Cultural Survival have developed their own Canadian agendas. The Environmental Youth Alliance, an umbrella group for high school environmental clubs, grew explosively from a few hundred members to 20,000 members in two years.

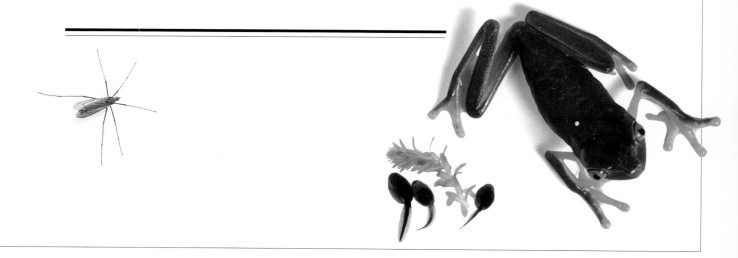

The other significant group is Native people, who have begun to reassert their culture and to push for recognition of their sovereignty. Across Canada, non-Native environmentalists are recognizing Native spirituality and their connection with the land as the key part of reaching a new contract with nature, and are rallying behind the landclaims of Canada's First Nations.

One of the first coalitions came about in the Queen Charlotte Islands, in the early 1970's. Environmentalists and the Haida people launched a 15-year battle to save the southern part of the islands which are considered to be sacred by the Haida. They were successful in 1988, and this campaign has served as a model for other joint efforts.

But as people concerned with the environment attempt to fight skirmishes over local issues, the underlying cause of the problems continues to generate yet more crises. The core of the problem resides in the beliefs, values, and attitudes of people today. These were handed down to us by the original colonizers of the New World and have infiltrated the entire planet.

● Human beings are superior to all other life forms, and it is our right to exploit all other species just as we wish.

● We lie outside the bounds of nature, create our own environment, and by virtue of the limitless capacity of human intellect, are no longer subject to the constraints of the natural world.

● Science and technology provide more than enough knowledge to understand and the tools to control all of nature.

● Economics must be the major priority and preoccupation at all levels of society.

● "Success" and "progress" are measured by the extent to which we can participate in the global marketplace and economy, and by the extent to which we can generate ever higher levels of economic growth.

● Human boundaries and borders make more sense than ecological delineations.

● The ecological costs of human activity, like dams, farms, clearcut forests, and housing, can be "mitigated."

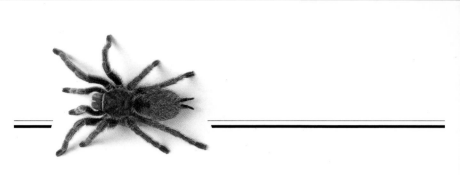

We are blinded by these deeply held assumptions because we never bother to question them. So our destructive activities continue unabated: we fight brushfires while the source of the conflagration – our beliefs – continues to send out sparks to generate more problems. To begin the profound changes that are needed, we must re-examine the very values by which we live. We must think beyond the next paycheck or stock dividend to reflect on the kind of world we are leaving for our children and their children.

Stanford University ecologist Paul Ehrlich has said that the solution to the ecocrisis is not scientific but quasi-religious. Harvard University tropical expert Edward O. Wilson points out that we must discover a new spiritual relationship with the rest of the biosphere. Leading scientists are recognizing the importance of a spiritual connection with nature that lies outside science and is congruent with the attitudes of aboriginal peoples around the world.

Each of us begins the change by redefining our personal values, needs, and priorities. As animals, we have absolute requirements for clean air, water, soil, and biodiversity. We must also have food, clothing, and shelter. But we are also social animals who are fulfilled by the opportunity for love, family, community, social justice, meaningful work, and the experience of wilderness.

In meeting these needs, it is *not* retrogressive to rediscover the values from the past that could deflect us from the dangerous path we are now on. Indeed, our future depends on it.

David T. Suzuki is a Canadian geneticist, journalist, and environmentalist.
He presents the television program *Man Alive*.

I

AWAKENING

Alone in space, alone in its life-supporting systems, powered by inconceivable energies, mediating them to us through the most delicate adjustments, wayward, unlikely, unpredictable, but nourishing, enlivening, and enriching in the largest degree – is this not a precious home for all of us earthlings? Is it not worth our love? Does it not deserve all the inventiveness and courage and generosity of which we are capable to preserve it from degradation and destruction and, by doing so, to secure our own survival?

From **Only One Earth** *by* BARBARA WARD *and* RENÉ DUBOS

DAWN ON THE SHORES OF MARYLAND

Save the Earth is a call to arms, a cry from the Earth, a simple celebration of its fragile beauty. It is also a tribute to the Earth's friends, to all those who have told us for so long that caring for the Earth is not some optional extra, but the greatest challenge we face.

There are many different voices within this book. Eighteen of the world's leading scientists and environmental experts have provided an overview of the continuing pressures on the Earth's ecosystems. More than 100 political and religious leaders, artists, authors, and campaigners, from every corner of the Earth, have added their personal comment on the state of the world as they see it today.

Though there may be many voices, there is little dissonance between them. It is clear that the damage we're doing to the Earth still outstrips today's new-found intentions of doing something about it. Time *is* running out. For many people, and for many species, it already has.

The Earth is at risk as never before. We have contaminated lands and rivers with poisons, fouled shorelines and oceans with massive spills of oil, and altered the chemistry of the air on

FLYING IN THE FACE OF PROGRESS (opposite)
A tern skims low over its North Dakota marshland home. All over the world, much "unproductive" land of this kind has been drained for agriculture.

VICTIMS (above) *Displaced Somalis trudge towards a refugee camp. The causes of war and famine in the Third World often lie in the unequal relationship between the rich North and the poor South.*

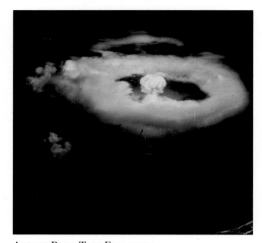

ATOMIC BOMB TEST EXPLOSION
CONTAMINATES BIKINI ATOLL, 1946

which life depends. No wonder people ask questions about the way we are continuing to exploit the planet.

The intention of this book is simple: to make some small contribution to finding the answers by weaving together sound science and powerful emotions. We depend on our increasing knowledge of the workings of planet Earth, and must allow that knowledge to inform our political and economic systems. Yet change cannot be an entirely rational and intellectual process. The transformation of today's society is as much about people's hearts and souls as it is about their minds.

This is not an easy balance to get right. Having endured years of criticism for being "too emotional," most environmental organizations have learned to stick rigorously to the facts, to get the science right as a precondition for their successful campaigning. But that in turn has sometimes led to a lack of balance; science and technology cannot help us out of our problems if our values become warped and distorted. Unless our emotions are stirred and our spirit challenged, no amount of rational analysis can do the job. The scale of this challenge is truly daunting, and the readiness of most politicians to take it

A LONDON "PEA-SOUPER": SMOG KILLS
HUNDREDS IN THE 1940'S AND 1950'S

on is questionable. As ever, the determining factors are political will, money, and the power of those vested interests that stand to lose in the process.

DDT RESULTS IN THIN-SHELLED
PEREGRINE EGGS IN THE 1950'S

Eastern Europe provides us with more object lessons in this respect than we could possibly want. Communism unleashed on those countries and their people an environmental assault of unprecedented ferocity. It is still not possible to quantify the damage done, but huge sums of money will be required simply to bring Eastern Europe up to the environmental standards of Western Europe, let alone to improve further on those standards as we now know that we are all going to have to do.

In many cases, it will cost far more to clean up or refit factories in Eastern Europe than it would to level them to the ground and start all over again. The social and economic costs of catching up in this way, and putting right the accumulated wrongs of 40 years of mismanagement and corruption, will be hard to bear. But borne they must surely be. East or West, North or South, these are not avoidable costs.

THE TORREY CANYON OFF THE CORNISH COAST:
FIRST OF THE BIG OIL SPILLS, 1967

They can either be paid now (as Western economies have at least endeavored to do to some extent) or they can be put off until tomorrow (as Eastern Europe and many Third World countries were and still are attempting to do). One way or another, these natural debts must be paid, and the longer the payment is deferred, the greater the interest that accrues and will be owed. Future generations will curse us when they come to total the ecological debts that we have passed on to them.

We have done, and continue to do, terrible things to the Earth in the name of "progress." We also do terrible things to each other – both consciously, through war, violence, racial intolerance, and the continuing suppression of basic human rights, and unconsciously,

NO LESSONS LEARNED: IN 1978, OIL FROM THE AMOCO CADIZ SMOTHERS THE FRENCH COAST

through a world economic order that systematically keeps the Third World poor, and grants privilege and power only to those who have learned to wink at such glaring injustice.

Most people in the rich countries of the North have learned to ignore levels of global suffering and poverty that should make our hair stand permanently on end. For every one of the 40,000 children that die every day of the year from preventable diseases, there must be 10,000 in the North who manage to sleep every night of their lives in the knowledge that

this nightmare shows no sign of coming to an end.

Finally, there is not a single problem referred to in this book that won't be exacerbated in one way or another by the massive increases in human population that lie inevitably ahead of us.

I believe it is still very much in the balance, whether we can succeed in rescuing ourselves and the Earth from the consequences of our arrogance and folly. There's no room for the

IN 1984, A FACTORY EXPLOSION KILLS THOUSANDS AT BHOPAL

unbelievable complacency of those who claim that we have already done enough, and that our economic prospects will be undermined if we make too much of a song-and-dance about the environment. The truth is that there will be no singing and no dancing if we don't take far more drastic measures than we have to date.

The wounds we have inflicted can be healed; the Earth can be "saved" from further destruction. But if it is to be done, it must be done now. Otherwise, it may never be done at all.

RADIATION FROM CHERNOBYL SPREADS ACROSS EUROPE IN 1986

PER GAHRTON

66 *I live in the countryside of Skåne, between the artificial pinewood plantations further north and the chemicalized grain plains southwards. Here is a last refuge from industry's conquest over nature.*

Crucial to this little paradise are the cows, who keep the meadows open by their grazing and provide the milk for farmers with no more than 100 to 200 acres (40 to 80 hectares) of land. These cows are soon to disappear. Parliament has decided to slaughter 140,000 milking cows and divert 1 million acres (400,000 hectares) of grain land to pinewood plantations. There will be tight pinewood 'armies' standing to attention all over the place. A devastating monoculture will evolve, a prelude to the coming chemical desert.

And the milk? A Swedish professor of molecular biology has the solution. He reports that cows are very inefficient 'machines,' converting a mere 0.004 percent of the solar energy they receive. But this can be changed by science! We shall soon be able to construct more efficient machines that can be fed with energy, water, carbon dioxide, nitrogen, and minerals, and deliver milk at the other end.

I know it is 'irrational,' but I want to preserve stinking, dirty, ruminating, inefficient black-and-white lowland cows on the meadows. The professor believes that even paper pulp could be made directly by machines, without the detour through pinewood trunks. So mankind really might circumvent nature altogether, living without cows and trees, substituting machines for photosynthesis.

I may be completely out of my mind, but that prospect makes me mad with fear. 99

MAPLE SEEDS
Acer rubrum

Per Gahrton is a Member of the Swedish Parliament for the Green Party.

SURFACE-MINING BROWN COAL IN GERMANY

MICHEL BATISSE

66 *Every human society attempts to get organized within its own house. Each house rests on four pillars: the number of people, the level of available natural resources, environmental quality, and the intensity of economic development. If some pillars rise disproportionately (be it the number of inhabitants in poor countries or material consumption of goods in rich countries), the house becomes unbalanced. Today the whole planet is our common house, and it is high time to get it back in balance.* 99

Michel Batisse is the former Assistant Director General (Sciences) of Unesco, and the President of Mediterranean Blue Plan.

IVAN LACKOVIC CROATA

WINTER LANDSCAPE IN CROATIA

66 *Where are the placid landscapes of my childhood? Where are the forests, full of birds? Where is the silence of my homeland? Are we the last romantics who yearn for the beauty of the changing seasons? Where are the flowers we gathered near stream waters when we were children? Where is the whiteness of the snow? Does it live on only in paintings? Remember! The face of the Earth is similar to that of a human being. Don't forget that you are but a traveler on this planet and nothing belongs to you.* 99

Ivan Lackovic Croata is a Yugoslav painter.

DAVID SUZUKI

" *It is time to redefine our place on Earth. The evolutionary path followed by our species was the development of a massive and complex brain which gifted us with memory, curiosity, imagination, and inventiveness. The vast panorama of human history and countless cultures were expressions of that brain.*

All life forms share the same fundamental cellular make-up. Every living being can trace its lineage back to the same primordial cell. Furthermore, 99 percent of the genes found in human beings are identical with those in our nearest relatives, the chimpanzees and orangutans, while the ancestry of all human races goes back to a single female along the Rift Valley of Africa some 200,000 years ago. Thus, we emerged from the web of life on Earth and in the company of many other species.

As animals, we are totally embedded in the natural world and dependent on the rest of life and its support systems for our well-being and survival. Over 70 percent of our bodies is water that came from the canopy of the Amazon rainforest, the icesheets of Antarctica, and all of the world's oceans. And every bit of our nutritional needs must be derived from other living beings.

The human brain now holds the key to our future. We have to recall the image of the planet from outer space: a single entity in which air, water, and continents are interconnected. That is our home. **"**

David Suzuki

David T. Suzuki is a Canadian geneticist, journalist, and environmentalist. He presents the television program *Man Alive*.

FARMS IN EASTERN WASHINGTON, USA

MARIO SIGNORINO

" *Putting ecological politics into action means approaching life with imagination and intelligence, knowledge and emotion, responsibility and culture. It fights against bureaucracy and ideology, uniformity, authoritarianism, and any attempt to eliminate diversity and autonomy. And to everyone it offers a new friend: the Earth.* **"**

Mario Signorino

Mario Signorino is the Founder and President of *Amici della Terra Italia* (Friends of the Earth, Italy).

JAMES LOVELOCK

" *Everyone these days is a manager. We even talk of 'managing' the whole planet, with all of us as the stewards of the Earth. I think it's arrogant even to talk in such terms. Originally, a steward was the keeper of the sty where the pigs lived; this was too lowly for most humans, and the status of the 'styward' was gradually raised as he was put in charge of men as well as pigs. Are humans now to be made accountable for the smooth running of the climate, the composition of the oceans, the air, and the soil?*

I would suggest that our real role is more like that of the proud trade union functionary, the shop steward. We are not managers or masters of the Earth, we are just workers chosen as representatives for the others, the rest of life on our planet. All living things are members of our union, and they are angry at the diabolical liberties taken with their planet and their lives by people. **"**

James E Lovelock

James Lovelock is the President of the Marine Biology Association, a Fellow of the Royal Society, and the creator of the Gaia Theory.

KARAN SINGH

" *We must shed the quaint superstition that ours is a race in some special way entitled to exploit this planet ad infinitum for its own selfish purpose. Rather, as in the concept of the ancient Vedas, we must realize that this planet of ours is the Earth Mother – Bhawani Vasundhara in the Hindu tradition, Gaia in the Greek – which has nurtured consciousness up from the slime of the primeval ocean for thousands of millions of years and brought it to where it now stands. Humanity in a way represents the collective brain of Mother Earth. Human consciousness, which contains unlimited potential for spiritual growth, must now move beyond the narrow confines of race and nationality, creed and ideology, and increasingly reflect global concerns.* **"**

Karan Singh

Karan Singh is the former Maharaja of Kashmir, and was a member of Indira Gandhi's cabinet.

PURPLE-THROATED
WOODSTAR
Philodice mitchellii

TAKING STOCK
IS THIS THE LAST CHANCE?
JONATHON PORRITT

The vision of progress that has driven the world economy since the Second World War has enriched many but impoverished the Earth, leaving us no more than a decade to put things right.

People today tend to measure progress almost exclusively in materialistic terms, with the odd token reference to such eccentric ideas as "quality of life." This vision of progress has gradually assumed such overwhelming dominance that it is now almost beyond discussion, let alone criticism. Woe to any environmentalist who dares to suggest that we have hitched our horses to the wrong progressive wagon! No sooner are such heretical words uttered than one is instantly reviled as a Stone Age reactionary. Alternative models of progress are treated with absolute contempt.

But I believe there is now an unanswerable case that such a "vision" of progress, if pursued to its logical conclusion, must inevitably destroy that which it sets out to achieve. The aspiration to go on getting richer, year after year, come what may in ecological terms, must inevitably destroy the natural resources and life support systems on which we depend.

Politicians today are caught in a terrible trap. They can see that the merry-go-round they have helped to create is getting noisier, dirtier, and always riskier. But egged on as they are by teams of unworldly economists unable to tell the difference between a clod of earth and a lump of concrete, they do not dare get off it. This represents an astonishing lack of both vision and common sense.

The speed with which such destruction will bite has been greatly accelerated by the export of this very Western vision of progress to every corner of the Earth. Inequitable and perverse though it may have been, the Earth has just about coped with roughly 1 billion people living out their materialistic fantasies in this way. There's not a hope in hell that it will cope with 5 or 6 billion, let alone 10 or 11 billion, subscribing to a similar fantasia.

We must all confront this one truth: that what may be possible for a minority of humankind, albeit at great cost, simply cannot work for the whole of humankind. Our kind of progress depends on lacerating the Earth, on gouging out its

SONG OF FAREWELL (inset above) *Gurney's pitta is on the brink of extinction as a result of the destruction of lowland forests in Thailand and Burma.*

IRREVOCABLY SCARRED (opposite) *This copper mine at Cuajone in Peru is a glaring example of the brutal way in which human "progress" is wounding the Earth.*

POACHERS' PLENTY (left) *In many parts of southern Africa, poachers have ruthlessly slaughtered elephants and rhinos for their tusks and horns. A worldwide ban on the sale of ivory has largely proved effective, but the rhino remains at risk, owing to the Far East's faith in the non-existent "medicinal" properties of its powdered horn.*

INDICATORS OF DECLINE

We know the damage we have already done to the Earth in the name of progress: how we have polluted its atmosphere, destroyed its forests, poisoned its rivers, and caused the extinction of species we did not even know existed. We know we must change our attitudes on the consumption and pollution of our natural resources by industrialized societies. We know that, despite scientific advances in agriculture, it is becoming harder and harder to feed the world's growing population. Yet all the indicators show that these destructive trends, which have accelerated so dramatically over the last 40 years, are set to continue until well into the next century.

TRIBAL PEOPLES
(right) *For many indigenous peoples around the world, it is not a question of decline, but of extinction. Those that have not already been exterminated now face eviction from their lands and the destruction of their culture* (see page 140).

POPULATION (above)
If present attitudes to family planning do not change, the world's population could nearly triple by the year 2100 (see page 120).

AIR-
POLLUTION
MONITORING
DEVICE

AIR POLLUTION (left)
The number of motor vehicles in the world is set to increase steadily by 15 million a year until at least the year 2010. The corresponding rise in CO_2 emissions will accelerate climate changes caused by the greenhouse effect (see pages 98 and 106).

CROPLANDS (left)
Despite the use of pesticides and fertilizers, the world's per capita grain production has fallen every year since 1985 (see page 65).

BIODIVERSITY (below)
Each day 50 to 100 species of animals and plants become extinct, as the habitat of animals like these Madagascan sifakas is destroyed (see page 76).

OZONE DEPLETION (above)
The ozone in the upper atmosphere protects life on Earth from harmful ultraviolet radiation. The levels of ozone fluctuate monthly, but chemicals have caused the yearly average to decrease considerably (see page 91).

FAILING FISHERIES
(below) *Uncontrolled fishing has reduced stocks of almost all commercial species, some to less than one-tenth of their former numbers* (see page 154).

RAINFORESTS (above)
The world's tropical rainforests are being burned and bulldozed so fast that half of those remaining may vanish in the next 40 years (see page 52).

riches, on stripping its life-sustaining skin of soil and forest, on poisoning its pure air, on defecating copiously in its pure water.

For some people, such language may be a little "emotive." Yet you will find the self-same truth "scientifically rendered" in each of the succeeding chapters. The argument is whether or not it is necessary, not whether or not it is happening.

In this context the single most important indicator of environmental decline is the extent to which the damage done is reversible. The most heinous ecological crime of all is for any one generation so seriously to assault the web of life that the damage done is literally irreversible for every generation that follows.

The extermination of thousands of life forms before we have even managed to record their existence *(see page 76)* is by far the most tragic consequence of humankind's "march of progress" across the face of the Earth.

ASSESSING THE LOSS

Understandably, concern about this is usually expressed in terms of our own potential loss, by way of possible new drugs, or genetic material for agricultural and industrial uses. It seems easier for most people to measure wealth (even natural wealth) in monetary terms or as a function of the amount of profit that can be realized.

Such things are indeed important, especially for politicians struggling to find ways of using this natural wealth to improve the living standards of their people. But they are not sufficient in themselves. Regardless of the potential value of any species to us humans, its loss is even more important in itself, representing an avoidable erosion of diversity, a small but significant diminution in the Earth's natural wealth.

It isn't just the loss of species that accounts for irreversible damage. Whole habitats are sometimes lost: once cut down, ancient woodlands or old-growth forests will only be restored to their former richness after hundreds of years; damage to wetlands through drainage or "development" is often entirely irreversible. And it is of little consolation to those living in affected areas to know that similar habitats survive elsewhere or in other countries. For people who suffer the loss most immediately of a treasured wildflower meadow or a muddy shoreline, the damage done is still irreversible.

ON THE GREEN FRONT
RIGHT LIVELIHOOD AWARD

The Right Livelihood Award was introduced in 1980 to honor and support work that faces up to the problems of environmental degradation, social injustice, poverty, and war. Since then, more than 40 people and projects have received Right Livelihood Awards, chosen from 300 nominations from some 50 different countries.

The collective message of these initiatives is one of hope and reassurance. Today's problems are not insoluble, nor are their solutions beyond the resources of individuals and small groups of people acting locally and collectively, mobilizing the energies and talents of others and working for the common good.

An important purpose of the Award is to project this hopeful message. As Jakob von Uexkull, the founder of the Award, puts it: "We live in a period of global confusion and doubt. Practical, replicable projects dealing with the challenges facing us are few and far between. This Award is for such projects, the cornerstones of a new world which we can enjoy living in."

The Awards have often been controversial, free of the Western prejudice which assumes that everything worth knowing has been discovered in Western universities and laboratories. Several Award winners have contributed to *Save the Earth*, and others are featured on page 54 (COICA), page 69 (Dr. Melaku Worede), page 129 (Self-Employed Women's Association), page 134 (The Six S Association), page 139 (Survival International), and page 169 (Dr. Akililu Lemma).

UPROOTED
When the trees are gone, the wells are dry, and the soil has been worn away, life for people in villages and small towns can become impossible. They have no option but to pack up their few possessions and get on the road. The phenomenon of the "environmental refugee" is becoming increasingly commonplace, especially in Africa.

JOE MILLER

If the Earth
were only a few feet in diameter,
floating a few feet above a field somewhere,
people would come from everywhere to marvel
at it. People would walk around it marveling at its
big pools of water, its little pools and the water flowing
between. People would marvel at the bumps on it and the
holes in it. They would marvel at the very thin layer of gas
surrounding it and the water suspended in the gas. The people
would marvel at all the creatures walking around the surface of
the ball and at the creatures in the water. The people would
declare it as sacred because it was the only one, and they would
protect it so that it would not be hurt. The ball would be the
greatest wonder known, and people would come to pray to
it, to be healed, to gain knowledge, to know beauty and to
wonder how it could be. People would love it and defend
it with their lives because they would somehow
know that their lives could be nothing
without it. If the Earth were only
a few feet in diameter.

Joe Miller

Joe Miller is an artist who lives in the State of Washington.

CLEAN CHIP
There is a chance that the much heralded new technology will help repair the damage done by the old. For example, the essential components of this standard microchip (right) are made of silicon, one of the Earth's most abundant elements. Microchips have already made a significant contribution to the improvement of energy efficiency and the reduction of pollution. Yet we must not lose sight of the fact that, though clean and efficient in themselves, microchips are used in many of the industries most responsible for polluting the planet.

Often unknowingly, the relationship we have with the environment is underpinned by contact with familiar landmarks, by the presence of a certain tree on the skyline, or by the reassuring reappearance of the early crocus in an inner city park. When these go, the connections between us and the Earth are further weakened.

There are subtler forms of irreversibility to which we pay little attention. Every time another acre of farmland goes under concrete or asphalt for new housing and roads, the productive capacity of that patch of topsoil is lost forever. Given the huge uncertainties that now hang over a future constrained more and more by global warming, it seems folly to be talking of land being "permanently surplus to agricultural requirements." Who are we to identify "permanence" in this way, as we live out our few split seconds of existence?

FINITE RESERVES

The use we make of those resources that are both finite and impossible to reuse or recycle, particularly our reserves of fossil fuels, can also be described as irreversible. Refining a barrel of oil to produce gasoline for immediate use means that you can't use that barrel of oil in the future as a "chemical feedstock" or for any other purpose. However bullish we might be about proven oil reserves (which have indeed increased massively over the last 20 years), there is still a legitimate question to be asked about our use of oil today. Is it really right that we should squander so huge a share of so important a natural legacy on propelling millions of lumps of metal over millions of miles to produce millions of tons of pollution?

Fortunately, however, most environmental damage *is* reversible. Rivers can be cleaned; buildings can be renovated; topsoil can be replenished; forests can be replanted. With care, whole habitats can be restored, and species returned to their rightful place. But such activities are little more than "holding measures", relieving the worst symptoms of damage but doing nothing to address the underlying causes of the damage. And these can all be traced back to that same unsustainable vision of progress that now dominates our lives.

There are, of course, other models of progress for us to refer to. Some we can only acquaint ourselves with at second hand, for they are as irreversibly dead as the dodo. Some are still actively pursued at the "margins" of our industrial society: by indigenous people who have not yet been finally exposed to the "benefits" of industrial progress; by so-called "drop-outs" who have totally renounced industrial society, collectively or individually; and by a much more recent surge of Greens who endeavor to pursue alternative values within the very belly of the industrial beast.

They all have one thing in common: their overriding goal is to live more in harmony with the Earth and to help in a process of healing by giving the Earth time and space to heal itself. Our very existence and dominance over other forms of life make it impossible to reconstitute some notional Garden of Eden; the aim must be a practical, hard-headed symbiosis, learning to live in mutual dependence with the rest of life on Earth.

SELF-DELUSION

Let me repeat that this alternative vision of progress is not anti-technological. The problem is not technology itself, but the uses to which we put it. By single-mindedly gearing technological development to the pursuit of profit (in the hope that the ensuing wealth will somehow trickle

POWER FOR THE FUTURE (right) *These solar collectors in the Australian outback are just one example of a worldwide investment program in increasingly sophisticated solar energy technologies. Costs are falling and technical problems are being overcome.*

FRICTIONLESS MOTION (left) *Train systems based on magnetic levitation, like this 1987 Japanese prototype, will improve operating efficiency and cause minimal pollution. Smaller versions of the "maglev" train are already in operation in several countries.*

SUPERCONDUCTIVITY (below) *Discovered in 1986, superconducting ceramics are expected to lead to a technological revolution. In this experiment, a magnet floats above a superconducting ceramic base, cooled by nitrogen to the temperature at which the material has no electrical resistance.*

TRANSPORTABLE SOLAR POWER (right) *In this African village, the power required to run a refrigerated medicine chest is provided by photovoltaic cells.*

FIBRE OPTICS (below) *Optical fibers made of glass are cheaper, more efficient, and far less damaging to the environment than the copper cables they are replacing throughout the world.*

down to all), we have disregarded the environmental and distributional impacts of such technologies. We have even learned to live with the grim anomaly of being able to put a human being on the moon even as millions of people continue to eke out the barest of existences.

TOOLS FOR SUSTAINABILITY

Most of the technologies that will ensure a dignified and secure future for each and every one of us on Earth – without destroying its beauty and diversity – are already in existence or being developed. Renewable energy technologies; energy efficient stoves; micro-processor control systems; comprehensive recycling schemes; selective plant breeding; magnetic levitation; fiber optics; high temperature ceramics; waste-into-wealth systems from both animal and human sewage; advance telecommunications; durable, reliable pump and irrigation systems: the list is long and impressive. It may not conform to the strictest definition of sustainability (taking no more from the natural world than can be replenished naturally), but it offers a vast improvement on where we are today.

But beware the green technofix! Some of these technologies are just as likely to cause unanticipated problems and regrettable side-effects as their environment-hostile predecessors did. Technical fixes of any variety can only provide part of the answer: halving the exhaust pollution from one automobile is great, but not if the number of automobiles on our roads doubles during the same period! Only a combination of new technologies and changing values can offer any serious hope.

The principle of "One World" sounds great in theory, but how can it be put into practice? The agencies, institutions, treaties, and funding arrangements that will be needed to give it real substance barely exist. If these cornerstones of practical sustainability are not laid very soon, then the prospects for the rest of this decade are poor indeed.

SWORDS INTO PLOWSHARES *This statue outside the United Nations building in New York symbolizes the hopes of all those who want a massive redirection of resources toward providing sustainable development for all.*

ANDY RUSSELL

"One fine spring morning in 1989, I spoke to a crowd of high school students in Calgary, Alberta. They were forming a new environmental organization, and my role was to give them encouragement and advice. But as I stood there looking at those bright, hopeful faces, I was fully aware that at best we were passing them a heavy legacy of great trouble. Not one of these kids would ever enjoy the treasures of nature that I had been blessed to know.

As a boy, I grew up rambling and reveling in the wildness of great reaches of country on the east of the Canadian Rocky Mountains, where the slopes were covered with trees, the meadows rich with flora and abundant wildlife, and the clear, cold streams were pure and teeming with trout and other fish. We boys took pride in being able to go where we wished on horseback or on foot, living very much like the bears, deer, and other life around us.

But now even the springs bubbling from the rock near the top of the continental divide show traces of lead from car exhaust fumes. Down the slopes, industrial wastes have impregnated the ground water from the grassroots to bed-rock with chlorides, sulphates, heavy metals, and other chemical pollutants. In many places it is so concentrated that it is dangerous for people and animals to drink.

It was this contrast that filled my mind in front of those young people. My generation had let them down, and even if they are willing to work and fight until their sweat burns their eyes, they will not know what I knew. I was so choked up that I am afraid I did not make a very good speech – not nearly adequate to match the hope, enthusiasm, and courage of those youngsters."

Andy Russell is a Canadian author and environmental campaigner.

DAVID MACAULAY

"It has been said that while a single murder is a tragedy, a million deaths is a statistic. Even the most frightening statistics can be ignored so long as they remain numbers, and are almost guaranteed to be ignored if they presage dire consequences. While we may not be able or even wish to comprehend fully the implications of the population figures to the right, it is information that should remind us that, for the moment at least, we still have choices to make. We need not choose the upper road to ruin. But, if we overlook our responsibility and make no decision, our course, and that of all mankind, will be chosen for us."

David Macaulay teaches illustration at the Rhode Island School of Design. He has been creating books, such as *Cathedral* and *The Way Things Work*, since 1973.

ROAD TO RUIN? *World population in the year 2100*

14 BILLION

11 BILLION

7 BILLION

THREE WAYS TO GO *The Earth's population is now 5 billion. The figures above are three UN projections (see pages 120-121) of the number of people who may be competing for our planet's stretched resources in 2100.*

THE EARTH SUMMIT

The Earth Summit, convened by the United Nations General Assembly, is a unique attempt to confront many of today's most pressing environmental and development concerns. The United Nations Conference on Environment and Development, as it is also known, will be held in Rio de Janeiro, Brazil, in June, 1992. It is predicted to be the largest international summit to date.

As Maurice Strong, the Earth Summit Secretary-General, explains on the opposite page, this is an opportunity that will not easily be repeated, and that must not be squandered. Before, during, and after the Summit, those world leaders attending have to appreciate that the longer we delay in addressing the basic issues of poverty, sustainability, and justice, the harder it becomes to offer any prospect of a secure future for humankind.

Placing the Key Issues on the Agenda

Six major themes make up the substance of the Conference's deliberations: conventions on climate change, forests, and biodiversity; an "Earth Charter," which defines principles of conduct to promote a sustainable future; "Agenda 21," which specifies the actions necessary to implement the Charter in the 21st century; ways to ensure developing countries the necessary financial resources for promoting sustainable development; ways to ensure affordable access to environmentally sound technologies; and the strengthening of existing international environmental institutions.

Hundreds of thousands of us are determined to make the Earth Summit an historic event that we will be proud to look back on. Every citizen of this planet must pour on the pressure on all world leaders, leaving them with no choice but to play an active and constructive part in establishing a new agenda for North/South relations and for the future of planet Earth itself.

HALTING EXTINCTIONS (inset, above) *These yellow-headed parrots (Amazona ochrocephala) are just one of many endangered species. The Earth Summit must work toward a convention on the conservation of biodiversity.*

DEFENDING VENICE (right) *Climate change is a topic at many conferences. For the people of Venice, Italy, global warming is not just a subject for discussion, but a daily concern as rising sea levels threaten the city.*

SOUTH AMERICAN RAINFOREST (above) *The world's leaders must address their attention to the ongoing destruction of the tropical rainforests, which play such a crucial part in regulating regional climate patterns.*

MAURICE STRONG

66 *Twenty years ago in Stockholm, the United Nations Conference on the Human Environment placed environmental issues on the world's agenda. In June 1992, the leaders of all the nations of the world will gather together in Rio de Janeiro for an unprecedented 'Earth Summit' to agree on a series of measures which could determine the future of our planet as a hospitable home for human and other forms of life. Despite progress made on many fronts since the Stockholm Conference, the environment has deteriorated alarmingly during the past 20 years.*

The ecological imperatives – and opportunities – so clearly and cogently presented in this book demonstrate that we must now effect a major shift in our priorities and in our time horizons. We must act wisely and responsibly to produce a future that will be more secure and sustainable for those who come after us.

As Jonathon Porritt says, poverty is one of the greatest threats to the environment. The day-by-day struggle for survival drives the poor of the world to undermine and destroy the resources on which their future depends. The prospect of breaking out of the vicious circle of poverty and environmental destruction thus depends on development.

This is why the 1992 Earth Summit is about environment and development. Its primary purpose is to move the environment issue into the center of economic policy and decision-making – to ensure that both developing and industrialized countries can make the transition to the more environmentally sound and sustainable development pathways that are the key to our common future.

To effect this transition will take a major shift in political will and corresponding changes in aspirations and priorities. There are hopeful signs in the growing environmental concerns of governments, industry, and people, often mobilized through non-governmental organizations.

The success of the Earth Summit in providing the basis for the transition to sustainability will depend on the concrete measures it adopts. These are expected to include conventions to limit climate change and preserve biodiversity; an 'Earth Charter' setting out the principles of sustainability; an agreed agenda for the 21st century incorporating specific actions to give effect to these principles; and agreement on means to ensure their implementation through financial resources, technology transfer, and institutional change.

In the final analysis, the response of the world leaders at the Earth Summit will depend largely on the political will of their own people. This, in turn, will rest on their level of awareness and understanding of the decisions to be taken. 99

Maurice F. Strong is the Secretary-General of the United Nations Conference on Environment and Development: the Earth Summit.

JOSÉ LUTZENBERGER

66 *We are all aware of the historic importance of the 1992 Conference on Environment and Development hosted by Brazil. Never before have the heads of state of almost all the countries in the world come together to discuss a common goal.*

How are we to reverse the present suicidal course of modern industrial societies? How are we to give up our predatory forms of development in favor of development that can be sustained, that puts our species back in harmony with the rest of Creation?

We constantly use the word 'development,' and we constantly insist that we need more development. But we almost never define precisely what we mean. As long as we don't define it, development will continue to be what it is now – fundamentally destructive and unsustainable. 99

José Lutzenberger is the Special Secretary for the Environment in Brazil.

CARLO RIPA DI MEANA

66 *I believe it is important to reaffirm the virtues of a gradual reform of the existing system. We should not fall prey to the 'all or nothing' illusions of today's green fundamentalists. Such fundamentalism has shown itself incapable of offering rational, practicable solutions to real problems.*

What must be proposed instead is to act concretely, preserving prosperity and technological development, but adapting them, or rather forcing *them to comply with the demands of sustainability.*

Environmental organizations have won battles in a way that would have been unimaginable only a few years ago. Their strength and passion have been the determining factor in raising the awareness of Italian people, not just about domestic issues, but also about the threat to the global commons posed by disappearing rainforests and global warming.

This build-up of awareness is an essential element in finding solutions to the environmental problems we are all facing. Only vigorous pressure from public opinion can bring about more environmentally sound practices, both in individual behavior and in the running of national economies. 99

Carlo Ripa di Meana is the Minister for the Environment of the European Economic Community.

HALINA SCHIWUJOWA

*❝ The Silesian landscape has been making me sad
and melancholic for many years. Silesian pyramids – slag heaps,
mostly enveloped in clouds of smoke. Silesian trees – carrying their time
of history, shining sometimes with gold over violet shadows in the glare
of the sunset, motionless, as if they would like to soak in the last
sunbeams, apprehending their own annihilation.
As far back as 1955, the whisper of my heart and mind
was to defend our Earth against annihilation. Nobody was
interested then, but they are now.
This is 'my ecological shout' for the defense of our Earth. I wish
I could have even the smallest share in stopping the threat of annihilation
of our globe. Our Earth can wait no more for help. ❞*

Halina Schiwujowa

Halina Schiwujowa is a Polish artist.

HENRI CARTIER-BRESSON

*❝ In the present race forward of technology,
'save the Earth' cannot be separated from
'save mankind' – but how? ❞*

Henri Cartier-Bresson

French photographer Henri Cartier-Bresson was one of the founders
of Magnum Photos, established in 1947.

DAVID PUTTNAM

*❝ For years, I've attempted to record the emotions and experiences
that formed the basis for my overwhelming belief in an 'ordered universe.'
I recently stumbled across this entry in the diary of the great
American explorer, Admiral Byrd. Dated 14 April 1934, he writes
from a weather station deep in the Antarctic: ❞*

Took my daily walk at 4 p.m. today in 89 degrees of frost.
. . . I paused to listen to the silence. . . . The day was dying,
the night being born – but with great peace. Here were
imponderable processes and forces of the cosmos,
harmonious and soundless. Harmony, that was it! That
was what came out of the silence – a gentle rhythm, the
strain of a perfect chord, the music of the spheres, perhaps.
It was enough to catch that rhythm, momentarily to be
myself a part of it. In that instant I could feel no doubt
of man's oneness with the universe. The conviction
came that that rhythm was too orderly, too harmonious,
too perfect to be a product of blind chance – that,
therefore, there must be purpose in the whole and that
man was part of that whole and not an accidental off-
shoot. It was a feeling that transcended reason; that
went to the heart of man's despair and found it
groundless. The universe was a cosmos, not a chaos;
man was as rightfully a part of that cosmos as were the
day and night.

David Puttnam is an independent British film producer. He has been the
President of the Council for the Protection of Rural England since 1985.

BARRY COMMONER

*❝ By 1970, it was clear that changes in the technology of
production are the root cause of modern environmental pollution. Now
this conclusion has been confirmed by the sharply divergent results of the
effort to clean up the environment. Only in the few instances in which the
technology of production has been changed – by eliminating lead from
gasoline, mercury from chlorine production, DDT from agriculture,
PCBs from the electrical industry, and atmospheric nuclear explosions
from the military enterprise – has the environment been substantially
improved. When a pollutant is attacked at the point of origin – in the
production process that generates it – the pollutant can be eliminated;
once it is produced, it is too late. This is the simple but powerful lesson
of the two decades of intense but largely futile effort to improve the
quality of the environment. ❞*

Barry Commoner

Environmentalist and author Barry Commoner directs the Center for
the Biology of Natural Systems at Queen's College in New York.

NIKOLAI VORONTSOV

66 *For most countries, a 'man-centered' world view (anthropocentrism) has been the dominant philosophy. Christianity inherited it from Judaism, and the atheist, communist countries inherited it from them. Its influence pervades every corner of our lives.*
Now that we have come to recognize that humanity is just one part of the biosphere, as dependent on it as all the rest, ecology must be made a major priority in all economic systems. We must start by assessing the carrying capacity of each and every territory, accepting that the biosphere recognizes no manmade borders.
The transition from an anthropocentric world view to a biocentric world view is inevitable, and will in due course prove even more influential than the transition between the teaching of Ptolemy (that the sun went around the Earth) and the teaching of Copernicus (that the Earth goes around the sun). 99

Nikolai Vorontsov is the Chairman of the USSR State Committee on Nature Conservation.

ERNST VON WEIZSÄCKER

66 *Prices should tell the ecological truth. Only in that way can the efficiency of the market economy be harnessed for the environment. And the most elegant instrument to make prices tell the ecological truth is an ecological tax reform. Prices for energy and other resources would be raised slowly but steadily, while taxes on human labour, added value, and corporate profits would be reduced.* 99

Professor Dr. E. U. von Weizsäcker is the Director of the Institute for European Environmental Policy in Bonn.

TRADING MERCANTILES IN CHICAGO

HOLDING BACK THE DESERT IN MAURITANIA

VIRGINIA MCKENNA

What is the Earth?

What is the Earth?
A ball in space?
A little paradise?
Planet of melting ice
And inner fires?

Under my hand
Its surface crumbles
Crushed underfoot
Its myriad flowers.

Forests lie trembling
Under my sword
The ocean darkens
Weeping black tears.

Death of sweet rivers
Death-giving rain
Silent and secret
Invisible pain.

A gift from heaven
This little world
Each bird a jewel
Each tree a mother.

What is the Earth?
A fragile heart.
Tender my touch
To save its life –
And mine.

British actress Virginia McKenna is a founder of Zoo Check, which campaigns for new attitudes towards captive wild animals.

RICHARD BRANSON

66 *We simply have to stop taking the Earth for granted. It is, after all, the only home we've got. It's already late in the day, and the need is more urgent than ever for all of us who live together on this planet to work together seriously in order to repair the damage we've done, and to deepen our understanding of what went wrong and why.* 99

Richard Branson is the Chairman of the Virgin group of companies.

A NEW INTERNATIONAL ORDER
ONE WORLD AND BEYOND
JONATHON PORRITT

To protect our children's future, we must work together as a true family of nations. Such cooperation cannot be achieved unless there is a more just and equitable distribution of the world's wealth.

In the autumn of 1989, even as the collapse of the Berlin Wall and the simultaneous cry of freedom from Eastern Europe reverberated around the world, I attended a high level conference at which various international experts openly speculated about the need to build a new wall. Not between East and West, but between the industrialized countries of the North and the developing nations of the South. A wall made up of economic defenses (against cheap imports from the Third World); psychological defenses (against painful reminders of the terrible poverty and suffering in so many countries in the South); and military defenses (against the day when that suffering reaches such a pitch that people simply march on the rich North).

According to the experts' provocative hypothesis, this wall would be erected when the benefits that the North still derives from the South were outweighed by the costs. Such costs would include growing unemployment in the North; ever higher levels of immigration, and unmanageable numbers of refugees; and demands for increased and possibly "punitive" aid flows, involving real transfers of financial resources from North to South. If this were to coincide with a period of shrinking prosperity in the North, which is perfectly possible, it would simply be considered "politically unacceptable" to reduce domestic public expenditure in order to assist the South in the manner required. North and South would then become "de-linked." The South would be left to stew in its own polluted juices, while the North defended its relative affluence and well-being.

Other speakers at the conference were as horrified as I at such a diabolical prospect. Set against it was not just the voice of shared humanity, but the powerful refrain of interdependence – the extent to which all countries in the modern world

DIGNITY IN DESPAIR (opposite) *The 1984 famine in Ethiopia shocked people the world over into a global spasm of charity. But since then, despite the best efforts of aid and development organizations, little has been achieved in terms of removing the underlying causes of poverty and famine. Much of the blame lies with the corrupt and vicious government in Ethiopia, which wastes millions of dollars every year on the arms it needs to crush the independence movements in Eritrea and Tigray.*

WRONG SIDE OF THE DIVIDE (left) *For as long as there have been wars, there have been refugees, like this young Cambodian in a camp in Thailand. But in the 1980's a new phenomenon began to emerge – large numbers of people on the move, displaced not by war, but by environmental degradation. There comes a point when the Earth will give no more, when the trees are gone and the inhabitants can no longer scratch a living from the eroded soil.*

SUSANNAH YORK

❝ If Ibsen's 'Enemy of the People' were alive today, he would recognize the ethic that has informed capitalist and communist countries alike – economic growth before public health and well-being. The true enemies of the people are those who continue to sacrifice our long-term interests for short-term gains. But perhaps we should all look in the mirror. ❞

Susannah York

Susannah York is a leading British actress in films, television, and on the stage.

BRINGING HOME THE WATER
Boys of the Dogon tribe in Mali carry pots of water back to their village. As numbers of humans and livestock increase, pressure grows on the already limited water supplies in the Sahel and East Africa. By the year 2000, Kenya will have only half as much water for each of its citizens as they currently have.

are now inextricably linked together. That interdependence is partly commercial, as the business activities of the world's companies become literally global; partly rhetorical, as we subscribe, in theory at least, to the notion of "One World;" and partly cultural, as the modern communications and information industries bind us all into a new global village. To talk of "de-linking" in such a context sounds almost fantastical.

Although the industrialized North provides development aid to the Third World, far more money travels from South to North than vice versa each year. The developing countries are an immense market for manufactured goods, food, and armaments; they are also heavily in debt to Northern banks. Even after subtracting the development aid spent by Northern governments, US$40 billion net travels from the South to the North each year.

What's more, we are now far more aware of the basic pattern of ecological interdependence that regulates life on Earth: the carbon cycle, the oxygen cycle, global weather patterns and so on. In our former state of ignorance, we believed that we humans existed somehow outside or beyond the influence of these great life forces, inhabiting a parallel but quite independent world of our own.

We now know rather better. A sequence of ecological jolts over the last 20 years (acid rain, ozone depletion, deforestation, global warming, toxic poisoning) has demonstrated that our human affairs can only be successfully pursued as a living part of this natural world, not divorced from it.

Yet few people have woken up to the strategic and political consequences of this realization. Our efforts to protect these global commons will be defined by our ability to achieve consensus on the measures required. Perhaps the most pertinent example of this is that if China were to achieve the same per capita energy consumption rates as the United States, total global emissions of carbon dioxide would be tripled. The reductions that smaller countries could achieve in CO_2 emissions would become all but irrelevant.

Poverty is one of the greatest threats to the environment today. It is poverty that drives people to overgraze, to cut down trees, to adopt ecologically damaging short-cuts and lifestyles, to have larger families than they would otherwise choose to have, to flee from rural areas into already over-burdened cities – in short, to destroy the very foundation on which the future depends in order to stay alive today.

It's about time people in the developed world began to think more logically about the implications of extreme poverty. To protect the environment, we must improve living standards in the Third World. To reduce population growth rates, we must improve living standards in the Third World. To do right by future generations, we must improve living standards in the Third World.

There is a powerful element of self-interest in aiding developing countries. This kind of self-interest is not the kind promoted in the 1970's ("if the South gets richer, we all get richer, because they'll have more money to purchase our goods and services"), but the self-interest of "all being in it together" in building a sustainable future. In an unprecedented way, the rich North is now dependent on the Third World if we are to achieve many of our most cherished goals.

SYMPATHY AND OUTRAGE

Frankly, most people reading this book would probably prefer it if self-interest had nothing to do with it. Most of us would prefer that the simple knowledge of the grotesque injustice of today's economic order (with around US$40 billion net moving from South to North every year) would be sufficient to persuade people throughout the developed world of the need for change.

Such was the feeling at the time of Live Aid and Band Aid in the mid-1980's, when a profound sympathy and anger moved millions of people to help raise millions of additional aid dollars. It just wasn't right that so many in the South should be dying of malnutrition and easily preventable diseases, when so many in the North were dying of over-consumption and the equally preventable "diseases of affluence."

It was a time of genuine enlightenment. The notion of "One World" began to look more like a working reality than a less than honest banality. But the inertia and the inherent injustice of today's trading relations and Third World indebtedness quickly despatched even that extremely powerful upswelling down memory lane. Many

HEAT HUDDLE
Boys in Mexico City huddle together over a warm air outlet. By the year 2000, three out of four Latin Americans will live in urban areas, often in conditions of great poverty and hardship. In many cities there are already thousands of young people living and sleeping on the streets. Amid escalating levels of crime and drug abuse, many disappear without trace every year. Overworked police forces are unable to offer any protection.

SUFFER THE CHILDREN

Every year 14 million children under the age of five die unnecessarily in the developing world. That's just in an ordinary year; whenever there is famine or drought, the figure is worse.

FOOD AID *Is this the only future for starving children?*

Four million die of diarrheal diseases, mostly from drinking polluted water. Five million die of diseases such as measles, tetanus, and whooping cough, which have long since been brought under control in the West. More than a million die of malaria. The rest are struck down by a combination of illnesses, mostly exacerbated by malnutrition.

The means of preventing these deaths are not expensive. Oral rehydration (ORT), for instance, is a mixture of salt, sugar, and clean water. The World Health Organization

estimates that more than half the children who die of diarrheal diseases would be kept alive by ORT. It has been around for centuries, and is as simple as it sounds. Most of the other problems could be solved with vaccination programs and wider use of antibiotics.

UNICEF argues that the cost of providing these three life-savers (ORT, vaccination, and antibiotics) would be around US$2.5 billion a year and provides some chilling comparisons: this sum is equal to 2 per cent of the Third World's expenditure on arms; the cost of 5 Stealth bombers; the annual advertising budget of the US tobacco industry; what the Third World pays every week to service its debts. What a world we live and they die in.

ON THE GREEN FRONT
IIED
International Institute for Environment and Development

The International Institute for Environment and Development (IIED) has always been ahead of its time. It was founded in 1971 (largely through the inspiration of pioneer environmentalist Barbara Ward) at a time when environmental and development organizations tended to plow quite separate furrows.

IIED's approach – that there can be no real development unless it is in sympathy with the local environment – has always been in accord with the concept of "sustainable development," which has dominated the development agenda since 1987. The organization's strength lies in its close work with local people in South-East Asia, Africa, and Central and South America. Both rural and urban issues are addressed.

IIED was also one of the first organizations to recognize the importance of environmental economics, setting up the London Environmental Economics Centre together with University College. Its *Blueprint for a Green Economy* was as near to a runaway success as an economics book is ever likely to be. With its publishing operation (Earthscan) producing some 30 titles a year, it is easy to see why IIED remains one of the most quietly influential organizations in this area.

people's lives were saved, but the political and economic systems that put them at risk, both North and South, remained largely untouched.

Just how many deaths will it take to break this stranglehold of callous indifference?

Casualties of uncaring political and economic systems can be seen much closer to home. For all the material progress we have made in the West, there seems to be just as much human suffering as ever. Those who seek to escape through drugs, alcohol, violence and even suicide, are just the most visible manifestation of a purposelessness and alienation that distorts so much of our society. Accounts of life in downtown New York, and many other large Western cities, where the down and out live in perpetual desperation and poverty, reveal a form of destitution that no amount of money will ever remove.

What at first looks like a crisis of finite biological systems exposed to infinite human demands, is in reality a crisis of human values. Our efforts to enrich ourselves by dominating the Earth have impoverished the planet and our spirit alike. Many

LAND OF PLENTY (above)
Indonesian villagers display the fruits of their rice harvest. Over the last 30 years, Indonesia has seen massive increases in agricultural productivity.

LAND OF POVERTY (right)
These two youngsters stripping firewood off one of the few surviving trees make a telling point about the future of Mali and other countries in the Sahel. Around 80 million people now subsist there on severely degraded land. In Mali, the desert has spread about 220 miles (350 kilometers) in just 20 years, yet wood remains by far the most important energy source, for both cooking and heating.

people are now utterly convinced that the answers to this crisis can only come through a rediscovery of spiritual values. For without a readiness to forego some of the "instant gratification" currently on offer, in the interest of different and deeper rewards, no politician on Earth will be able to offer an honest version of sustainable development and "green wealth creation."

These are some of the broader issues that must be taken up by conferences such as the United Nations Conference on the Environment, also known as the Earth Summit. It's no good discussing global warming and bio-diversity, unless such concerns are linked to the fate of the Earth's poor. Interdependence may sound like a cosy ticket to go to the polls on, but it endures little compromise on questions of justice and basic humanity.

That, of course, was the most powerful challenge of the Brundtland Report, *Our Common Future*, published in 1987. This report first brought to the world's attention the fundamental concept of sustainable development, defined as the kind of

PEACE DIVIDEND

The end of the Cold War and the democratization of Eastern Europe have raised great hopes for massive reductions in military spending. The nations of the world currently spend about 6 percent of their combined gross national product on arms. Despite the tragic war in the Gulf, halving that figure in order to realize a lasting "peace dividend" has become an achievable target rather than a pious dream.

Even a straightforward reduction in arms spending, with no subsequent reallocation of the funds saved to promote sustainable development in the Third World, would bring enormous benefits, in terms of the tons of steel, barrels of oil, megawatts of energy, and depletion of precious metals that will no longer be poured down the global drain in the futile pursuit of military superiority.

Given the political will, the peace dividend could be many times greater – cuts in arms spending could be redirected in full to the business of healing the Earth and providing sustainable livelihoods for the world's poorest people.

The billions of dollars a year that would become available could and should be used as the means of converting dreams into reality. The peace dividend is the one potential source of cash that can support the programs of international cooperation that we now know to be necessary.

HOLDING BACK THE SAND
This field of millet, planted on the edge of a sand dune in Niger, may look frail, but it is all that stands between these local villagers and the onward march of the desert. Deserts can be turned back – through appropriate tree-planting projects and better agricultural and land management techniques, but Western governments have been notoriously stingy in their funding of anti-desertification programs, despite the terrifying droughts of recent years.

CLIVE PONTING

66 *The Western view of history as the onward march of scientific, economic, and industrial progress is a dangerous delusion. There are instances of earlier societies that destroyed themselves by destroying their environment – the cities of Sumer, of the Indus valley, of the Mayas and Aztecs.*

The apparently remote example of Easter Island offers a grim warning. European voyagers in the 18th century found a few miserable survivors living a squalid and barbaric life in a barren, treeless landscape. They were at a loss to explain the hundreds of massive carved stone statues and other traces of what had evidently been an advanced and complex society.

The Polynesians who first settled this isolated, well-wooded island had cut down all the trees – for fuel, to make huts and canoes, but especially to enable them to transport the huge statues to the ceremonial centers of the various clans. When the island was deforested, their whole complex society, which had lasted for a thousand years, collapsed within a few decades.

It seems incredible that they could build up a civilization against great odds, but couldn't bring themselves to change their ways enough to ensure its survival. How different are we? 99

British author Clive Ponting is a Research Fellow at the University of Swansea.

JESSE JACKSON

66 *We have entered a new world order.*

The Cold War that hung over our heads and hearts for decades is over. Europe is dismantling its missiles and rebuilding its economy. Nelson Mandela is leading the fight for a free, non-racial, democratic South Africa.

But the promise of the new world order is threatened by the twin injustices of poverty and environmental destruction. Environmental destruction falls most heavily on the shoulders of the disadvantaged, and this is a threat to democracy itself. What is democracy, after all, if your air is too polluted to breathe? What is economic development if your land is too poisoned to farm? What is international law if rich countries dump their toxic wastes on the shores of poorer nations?

Environmental justice is fundamental to the new world order. The United States is proud of Liberty's promise to the world: 'Give me your tired, your poor, your huddled masses, who yearn to breathe free.' We must now extend the right to breathe free to every nation and every individual, for the right to breathe free is the most basic human right of all. 99

Reverend Jesse L. Jackson, the President and founder of the National Rainbow Coalition, is now lobbying Congress to grant statehood to Washington, D.C.

WALTER CRONKITE

66 *There is one maxim and a corollary that must underlie all of our thinking about saving the Earth.*

The maxim is that no private interests – neither rights to property nor profit – can get in the way of the human right to clean air and clean water and an atmosphere that will permit continuation of life on Earth. The corollary is that the costs of saving the Earth must be shared by us all. Polluters need not be compensated for ending their pollution, but we must understand that industry and governments have the right in future to include the cost of non-polluting into the price of their products or services. 99

Former anchor of CBS News, Walter Cronkite is now a Senior Correspondent and member of the Board of Directors at CBS.

SAND DUNES IN THE KALAHARI

GEORGE HARRISON

Save the World
We've got to save the world
Someone's children, they may need it.
So far we've seen
The big business of extinction bleed it.
We've got to save the world.

We're at the mercy of so few,
With evil hearts determined to
Reduce this planet into hell,
Then find a buyer and make a quick sale.

We've got to save the world
Someone else may want to use it.
It's time you knew
How close we've come.
We're gonna lose it – we gotta save, we gotta save, we gotta save the world.

Former Beatle George Harrison is now a film producer as well as a musician and song-writer.

development that allows us to meet our current needs without trespassing on the rights of future generations to enjoy the same access to the world's natural wealth as we do today.

Sustainable development is an important and pioneering concept. It raises a huge question mark over current trading relations and the whole "aid business," which until now has seen huge sums of money squandered on inappropriate development projects, on shady deals with corrupt politicians in Third World countries, on undermining rather than underpinning the basic life-support systems of Third World countries, and on centralized bureaucracies rather than grass-roots self-reliance. If sustainable development means anything, it means not only that a higher percentage of Western gross domestic production should be devoted to aid programs, but that it should support quite different models of development.

DOUBLETHINK

It is therefore very worrying to a lot of environmentalists that the debate about sustainability is hedged with half-truths and deliberate ambiguities. What kind of game do politicians think they are playing when they talk of "sustainable economic growth," knowing full well that a 3 percent annual growth rate actually means a doubling of production and consumption in just 25 years?

All that the concept of sustainability seems to mean to most politicians is being able to go on subscribing to the literally unsustainable – namely, infinite growth on a finite planet. By a piece of linguistic manipulation worthy of George Orwell's *1984*, sustainability can be interpreted as sustaining the patently unsustainable. Given how many environmentalists are taken in by this, it is hardly surprising that most of the public are too.

For the Third World, much of today's new green awareness and much of the chit-chat about sustainability seems somewhat academic. How nice for the European Community to be able to spend billions of dollars reducing nitrate levels in water supplies, when so many millions of people in their countries still do not have regular access to clean water of any description.

Sustainable development will remain "a nice idea" until basic issues of equity and per capita consumption levels are far more honestly addressed by the affluent nations of the North.

FAMILIARITY BREEDS CONTEMPT
At what point will images like this scene at the Korem refugee camp during the 1984 Ethiopian famine cease to stir charitable impulses in the West? There is evidence that "compassion fatigue" *is already setting in. But the developed world must understand that its own future depends on giving more in real terms to the Third World, helping to create genuinely sustainable livelihoods.*

II

EARTH

*The phrase "conquest of nature" is certainly one of the most objectionable
and misleading expressions of Western languages. It reflects the illusion that all natural forces
can be entirely controled, and it expresses the criminal conceit that nature is to be considered
primarily as a source of raw materials and energy for human purposes.*

From **A God Within** *by* RENÉ DUBOS

MAGNOLIA, SHOWING
THE FORM OF THE FIRST
FLOWERING PLANTS

Planet Earth is 4.6 billion years old. If we scale this inconceivably vast timespan down to a more manageable 46 years, then modern man has been around for four hours, and the Industrial Revolution began a minute ago. During those 60 seconds of biological time, man has multiplied his numbers to plague proportions, ransacked the planet for fuels and raw materials, and caused the extinction of countless species of animals and plants.

In his "Gaia hypothesis," the British scientist James Lovelock puts forward the revolutionary idea of the Earth as a living organism, responding to any threat against it in such a way as to maximize the chances for the survival of life on the planet. He also suggests that the role of humankind in all this could be pretty insignificant. In evolutionary and geological terms, we are indeed little more than a blip on the surface of the Earth.

So does that give us an excuse not to worry about the damage we are doing to the Earth? I certainly hope not. However brief our tenure on Earth, it brings with it responsibilities, not just to other humans, but to the profusion of life-forms with which we share this evolutionary moment. One of the primary purposes of humankind must be to protect the soil and to

GEOLOGICAL TIME (opposite) *Each colored
band of rock in Arizona's Painted Desert records
the passing of millions of years, making man's brief
time on Earth pale into insignificance.*

LIONESS AND CUB (above) *Powerful as it is, the
lion's position in the cycle of life on the Serengeti
plains is highly vulnerable, depending on the grass,
the grazing animals, and the seasonal rains.*

BIODIVERSITY: RED MAPLE SEEDS AFTER A
RAINFALL, WISCONSIN

maintain forest cover and habitat diversity. Since the late 1960's, it has become customary for sceptics to accuse environmentalists of permanently "crying wolf." Why, these sceptics ask, is it all so urgent now, given the relative ease with which the Earth *seems* to have withstood most of the damage inflicted on it over the last 20 years? From what does the Earth need to be "saved?"

It is often easier to deny the truth than to confront it. Let's be thankful that we have indeed got through the last 20 years with no more than a handful of appalling environmental disasters. However, let's never forget that for millions of people their environment has already collapsed, as witnessed by the huge increase in "environmental refugees," all those who have been displaced from their homelands by drought, deforestation, and other environmental crises.

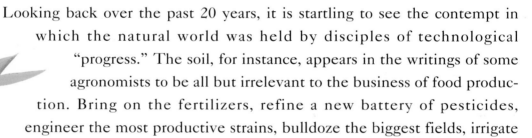

GRASSLANDS: BLACK RHINO
IN NAIROBI NATIONAL PARK

BIODIVERSITY: STRELITZIA
FLOWER, HAWAII

Looking back over the past 20 years, it is startling to see the contempt in which the natural world was held by disciples of technological "progress." The soil, for instance, appears in the writings of some agronomists to be all but irrelevant to the business of food production. Bring on the fertilizers, refine a new battery of pesticides, engineer the most productive strains, bulldoze the biggest fields, irrigate till the drought comes home, and forget the billions of tons of soil that are lost every year. Such was the recipe for modern agriculture. The somewhat humbler business of soil management, fertility building, and erosion control somehow got lost in a man-made world that felt it owed nothing to nature.

The fact that the last 20 years have been characterized more by progressive decline than by vertiginous environmental collapse hardly seems a cause for rejoicing. At the same time, I do believe that the foundations for a more just, compassionate, and sustainable future are now being laid.

GRASSLANDS: SEEDS GERMINATING AFTER
A SHOWER IN THE SAHARA, SUDAN

BIODIVERSITY: RARE THREE-HORNED
CHAMELEON, ZAIRE

Some of this foundation work has a very high profile, ringing resonantly in the fine speeches of world leaders, advocated passionately by the massed ranks of environmental and development organizations, amplified with increasing authority by the world's media. Despite the media's tendency to leap from one fashionable cause to the next (from world hunger to AIDS to the environment), it would be unfair to deny their part in increasing environmental awareness. It is easier to be "green" today than ever before.

But most of the foundation work is being painstakingly put together at the grass-roots level, with very little media attention – reflected in the concerns and lifestyle choices of millions of people who know what they owe to themselves and to the future.

CROPLANDS: HARVESTING THE MAIZE
IN SOUTHERN ILLINOIS

It is this grass-roots base that leads me to believe that the current level of environmental activity will not fade away, but will steadily strengthen. The signs of hope are multiplying, reinforcing the mounting pressure for new approaches and lasting change. We are getting better at shouting out the good news, tempering mounting despair with reminders that solutions do exist, and that many are already viable and capable of being replicated on a much wider scale.

We may, nonetheless, be experiencing a sense of "green fatigue."

ANTARCTICA:
ICE CLIFFS BREAKING
AWAY FROM THE
MAINLAND COAST

Too much talk and not enough action; too much gloom and not enough positive hope; too many depressing economic problems and (as yet) not enough evidence that a green approach would necessarily solve them. The way forward will be neither smooth nor uninterrupted.

Though it is a great deal better than standing still, having to take two steps forward and then one step back is obviously an extremely frustrating way of making progress. The time has come to increase pressure on politicians to accelerate the pace of change. The evidence from the Earth itself demands no less of us.

MOUNTAINS: GLACIAL GROOVES IN ANTELOPE
CANYON, UTAH

SADRUDDIN AGA KHAN

*We need nature more than nature needs us.
It should be looked on with awe and humility.
Sadly, the hubris of* Homo sapiens *is boundless. His record
at 'managing' nature has been dismal. Observing the world around us,
it seems that animals and plants may be more enlightened than man.
They do not self-destruct through drugs, doomsday, and conventional
weapons, or the population explosion. They do not pollute the air
or transform the Earth and the sea into a garbage dump.
Could it be possible that instinct, which we have lost,
is a better guide than logic? We have a lot to learn.
But do we have the time?*

Prince Sadruddin Aga Khan, who was given the United Nations Human
Rights Award in 1978, is the President of the Bellerive Foundation.

GERALD DURRELL

*Some time ago I was in a museum in Los Angeles
and there, in several large drawers, I saw numerous skins
of the California condor. It was dreadful to realize that here,
in front of me, carefully preserved, lay more California
condors than actually existed in the wild.
The great ecosystems are like complex tapestries
– a million complicated threads, interwoven, make up
the whole picture. Nature can cope with small rents in the fabric;
it can even, after a time, cope with major disasters like floods,
fires, and earthquakes. What nature cannot cope with is the steady
undermining of its fabric by the activities of man.*

British author and naturalist Gerald Durrell is the founder
and Honorary Director of the Jersey Wildlife Preservation Trust.

AUSTRALIAN OUTBACK, KIMBERLEY, WESTERN AUSTRALIA

JACK ABSALOM

*Of all the great places I've seen, I believe the spectacular gorge country of the Kimberley region, in the far north of Western Australia,
is one of our most magical areas. Because of its remoteness and comparatively tiny population, this ancient area is still almost the same as it would
have been before white settlement. I believe this is one of the world's greatest treasures, and my wish is that it remains that way.*

Australian painter Jack Absalom specializes in scenes of the outback.

YOKO ONO

Earth Piece (Spring 1963)
Listen to the sound of the Earth turning.

Earth Piece (Summer 1990)
The Earth is giving us so much. We should listen to the Earth and its heartbeat, and live in harmony with this beautiful planet.

[signature]

Yoko Ono is an artist.

JOHN FOWLES

"*My unhappiness is not over this Dorset I inhabit, nor indeed over anywhere else in particular, but, above all, over how blindly and selfishly our species goes on living everywhere, seemingly stuck between suicide and senility. Crystal-clear what is wrong, and equally clear that as a species we cannot face doing anything about it. We are now far too many, beyond restraint, and multiplying like an uncontroled virus.*

My thoughts are of all the animals, plants, birds, insects we poison out of this world, and how they have been a chief consolation and delight of my six decades of life. Such a loss may hardly seem to matter; I grow old, I shall soon be gone. What does matter is that for the majority, the younger, loss now becomes the rule.

It is like some insane fiat: 'Nature will shortly cease to exist. It is henceforth strictly forbidden to mean anything to anyone.' It won't quite happen so, of course. Such a situation will creep slowly upon us and our confused intelligences, stuffed with conflicting values and notions.

But then one day the death of nature will be unopposably real, irreversible. There will be no more green.

So I felt this burning summer. In form I might belong to humankind; in reality I seemed one of a ravenous self-destroying horde of rats. I am glad there is no god. If there were, I cannot imagine that we rampant, myopic, and insatiably self-centered creatures should be allowed to survive a single day more."

[signature] John Fowles

British novelist John Fowles is the author of a number of modern classics, including *The Magus* and *The French Lieutenant's Woman.*

DISPLAY IN A TROPHY SHOP, ZIMBABWE

RICHARD LONG

TOUAREG CIRCLE, THE SAHARA, 1988

In happiness
Or sadness,
Weeds grow and grow.
Taneda Santoka (1882-1940)

[signature]

Richard Long is a British artist who creates "walks" in the landscape. He also sculpts with wood and stone, and creates "mud works" in galleries.

ROBERT REDFORD

"*It is not enough that the scientific community has information that will affect the future of our environment. The baton has to be passed from the scientists to the public and then be translated into political and legislative action. The first two steps have occurred – now it is time for the third. I am afraid we cannot expect our current leadership to do this. We can't wait for leadership on environmental issues to come from the top; it isn't going to happen. The past decade has made that clear. People all over the world are demanding more from their leaders – and getting it. In America, poll after poll tells us that the people are way ahead of the politicians. The most important step we can take is to tell our leaders that if they don't protect the environment, they won't get elected.*"

[signature]

American actor, director, and producer Robert Redford sits on the boards of the Friends of the Earth USA, the Environmental Defense Fund, and the Natural Resources Defense Council. He is also the founder of the Institute for Resource Management.

Cola nitida, A RAINFOREST PLANT USED IN MODERN PHARMACOLOGY

RAINFOREST
THE DISAPPEARING FORESTS

NORMAN MYERS

MALAYAN FROG BEETLE
Sagra buqueti

BIRDWING BUTTERFLY
Ornithoptera croesus

*Of all the world's forests, it is those in
the tropics that face the greatest threat from
the matchbox and the chainsaw.*

Tropical forests are the glory of nature. They are a vivid part of cultures in many lands. Yet many of them are now at risk. We have already lost half of the world's tropical forests, and the deforestation rate has almost doubled during the 1980's. In just another few decades, we could witness the virtual elimination of tropical forests. Think of it, the bright green band around the equator in our school atlases, signifying the most vibrant vegetation on Earth, may have to be recolored dirty brown to denote what has gone forever.

Tropical forests are the finest celebration of nature that has ever graced the face of the planet. Their biotic diversity is legendary. In 125 acres (50 hectares) of Peninsular Malaysia there are more tree species than in the whole of North America. A single bush in Peru may

*Professor Norman Myers
MA PhD has been a consultant
to several UN agencies, the World
Bank, the Organization for
Economic Cooperation and
Development, the World Resources
Institute, and other organizations.
His main interest lies with the
resource relationships between the
developed and developing worlds.*

feature as many ant species as there are in the British Isles. Recent research reveals that the canopies of tropical forests may well contain 30 million insect species. This means that these forests, which cover only 6 percent of the Earth's surface, are home to 70 percent, and possibly as much as 90 percent, of all the Earth's species.

As the forests disappear, so, too, do their species – probably at a rate of several dozen a day right now. Some people argue that if we lost a number of insects yesterday, and the sun still came up today, does it truly matter? They might like to consider the oil-palm plantations of Malaysia. Until ten years ago the pollination of millions of oil-palm trees had to be done by hand, an inefficient and expensive way of performing the task. One day, the plantations'

**CLOUDFOREST
IN VENEZUELA**
(opposite) *Rainforests
higher than 3,000 feet
(900 meters) above sea
level are often referred
to as cloudforests.
Average temperatures
are lower at these
altitudes, and there are
fewer species than in the
lowland rainforests,
but such cloudforests
are among the most
beautiful and evocative
places in the world.*

**JEWELS IN
THE CROWN**
*The hyacinth macaw
(far left) is one of the
most threatened of the
Amazon's many
parrots. A combination
of habitat loss and
trapping (for sale to
ignorant parrot-lovers
in Europe and
America) has driven it
to the edge of extinction.
The red-eyed tree frog
(left) is well established
throughout Central and
South America,
wherever the rainforests
remain intact.*

LONG-TERM BENEFIT
Preserving the rainforest is in our own interest. A weevil (above) native to the Cameroon forest now helps pollinate oil-palms (right) in Malaysia, saving plantation owners millions of dollars each year.

owners asked themselves how the oil-palm pollinated itself in its native habitat of Cameroon's forests, in West Africa. So researchers went to Cameroon, where they found the job was undertaken by a tiny weevil. Stocks of the weevil were taken back to Malaysia, where they were released into the plantations. (There was no problem of ecological complications with other species, since it was known that the weevil confined its attentions to the oil-palm alone.) The pollination is now entirely accomplished by the weevil, with savings of US$140 million per year.

We should all consider this the next time we use margarine, cosmetics, or any of the other palm-oil based products that owe their manufacture in part to the services of a seemingly insignificant insect from Cameroon's forests.

We might also be thankful for the wealth of the tropical forests next time we visit a pharmacist for medicine. There is a one-in-four chance that our purchase will derive from tropical forest plants. It may be an antibiotic, an analgesic, a diuretic, a laxative, a tranquilizer or even just cough drops, among many other products. As a measure of the benefits gained from these plantbased items, commercial sales worldwide are now thought to be worth nearly US$30 billion a year.

SHARING THE PROFITS

The key to sustainable use of the rainforest lies in ensuring that a share of the profits made from its resources is used to preserve those same resources. For instance, the pharmaceutical company that manufactures drugs from the Madagascar periwinkle *(Catharanthus roseus)* to fight leukemia and Hodgkin's disease has made many millions on its original investment. The plant is now grown on a commercial basis in several countries, but Madagascar, from whose forests it first came, has received very little, if anything, for its contribution to human well-being.

Pressure for Land
Madagascar is one of the world's poorest countries, and its remaining rainforest and wildlife are under constant pressure from a growing population desperate for land. Though the government does derive income from tourists coming to see its wildlife, it is hard for politicians to resist pressures to

"develop" the remaining rainforest, given that so many people are in such desperate poverty. It is not a good sign that the North has taken both the benefits and the profits to be made from the Madagascar periwinkle, while the forests that produced it (and which may well hold other equally valuable plants) are threatened with destruction due to economic pressure.

MADAGASCAR PERIWINKLE
This rainforest plant has provided a drug effective in fighting leukemia, one of the most intractable of cancers.

The rainforest of Madagascar contains 12,000 different plant species, over 60 percent of which are unique to the island.

The contraceptive pill was originally manufactured from a wild yam growing in Mexico's forests, and the latest pill comes to us courtesy of a forest plant of West Africa. One of the biggest breakthroughs against cancer in recent decades has stemmed from the Madagascar periwinkle *(Catharanthus roseus)*, the source of two potent drugs used against leukemia and Hodgkin's disease. According to the National Cancer Institute in the United States, tropical forests may well contain at least ten more plants with similar superstar potential against cancer. There is even some hope that a therapy to counter AIDS lies with a plant in Queensland's forests.

Much the same applies to a host of foods and industrial materials. All this represents only a fraction of the forests' potential. Scientists have taken a cursory look at barely 10 percent of the 125,000 plant species found in the world's tropical forests, and a close look at only 1 percent. So we can hope for streams of further products from tropical forests, provided the scientists can get there ahead of the sawmen.

CLIMATE STABILITY

A still more important benefit of tropical forests lies with the part they play in climate control. Deforestation is creating two main problems here. As the green band around the equator becomes transformed into a bald ring, there is an increase in the "shininess" of the Earth's surface. This "albedo effect" will eventually distort convection currents, wind patterns, and rainfall regimes in regions throughout the tropics, and possibly further afield too.

Even more significant is the climatic disruption that would ensue through the build-up of carbon dioxide (CO_2) in the global atmosphere. Emissions of CO_2 account for almost half of the

IRREPLACEABLE MEDICINE CHEST (left) *The rootstocks of the Dioscorea vine provide diosgenin, an important ingredient of contraceptive pills, cortisone, and other drugs. Dioscorea thrives only in the rainforest.*

Dioscorea elata

FUNGI IN A FRAGILE ECOSYSTEM (right) *Most of the fertility of the rainforests is found within their foliage, not in the forest soil. Rainforests therefore depend on a huge number of insects, fungi, and bacteria to accelerate the decomposition of dead animals and plants.*

NORMA ALEANDRO

Us

He is alone
This nesting, suckling animal
That once raised its front legs and stood.
He bends what was rigid
Moves energy, harnessing it
Divides the planet into squares
itemizes everything, and what is not there
He conceptualizes.

I love this animal deeply
because I remember the pain
of when we stood up straight
and how we wept for joy
when we found our way.

Norma Aleandro is an actress and writer from Argentina. This is an excerpt from *Us*, published in her collection *Poemas y Cuentos de Altenazor*.

BRUCE COCKBURN

If a Tree Falls

Rain forest
mist and mystery
teeming green
green brain facing lobotomy
climate control centre for the world
ancient cord of coexistence
hacked by parasitic greedhead scam –
from Sarawak to Amazonas
Costa Rica to mangy B.C. hills –
cortege rhythm of falling timber.

What kind of currency grows in these new deserts,
these brand new flood plains?

If a tree falls in the forest, does anybody hear?
Anybody hear the forest fall?

Cut and move on
take out trees
take out wildlife at a rate of a species
every
single day
take out people who've lived with this for 100,000
years –
inject a billion burgers worth of beef –
grain eaters – methane dispensers –
Through thinning ozone,
waves fall on wrinkled earth –
gravity, light, ancient refuse of stars,
speak of a drowning –
but this, this is something other.
busy monster eats dark holes in the spirit world
where wild things have to go
to disappear
forever

If a tree falls in the forest, does anybody hear?
Anybody hear the forest fall?

Bruce Cockburn is a singer and songwriter, and Honorary Chairman of Friends of the Earth, Canada.

RAINFOREST RANCHING IN BRAZIL (below) *Vast areas in Central and South America have been cleared and burned for cattle ranching – essentially to provide cheap beef for Western consumers.*

SLASH AND BURN IN THAILAND (right) *More rainforest is destroyed by peasant farmers than by anything else. But responsibility for this lies largely with governments who fail to promote land reform and sustainable agricultural practices as an alternative to rainforest clearance.*

greenhouse effect, which threatens to bring about drastic climatic and ecological change through the process of global warming. Every year an additional 4 billion tons of carbon accumulates in the atmosphere, and roughly 30 percent of this surplus is estimated to derive directly from the accelerated burning of tropical forests.

The world's tropical rainforest is burned and bulldozed at the rate of 63,000 square miles (160,000 square kilometers) each year.

While we benefit every day from the existence of tropical forests, we also contribute every day to their destruction. We are not necessarily aware that we are doing it, but many of us are. People in all developed nations stimulate overexploitation of tropical forests through their demand for specialty hardwoods. Consider your own home: it may feature a woodblock floor, fine furniture, or a variety of cabinets and other shelving that contain tropical hardwoods. But the price we pay for our parquet floors does not reflect the full cost of their production, especially the long-term cost of deforestation in remote areas such as West Africa and Borneo.

In a more indirect fashion, but with a similar result, Western consumers are contributing to the loss of tropical forests through our consumerist demand for cheap supplies of livestock feed. For example, the European Community imports millions of tons of calorie rich cassava from Thailand each year, to be fed to the excessively large numbers of cattle, pigs, and poultry in Europe. The cassava is grown on Thai croplands that have been established on deforested land. Again, the price of the cassava fed beef, pork, and chicken does not cover all the costs involved.

Therefore, let's bear in mind that each of us contributes, through our consumerist lifestyles, to the daily decline of the tropical forests.

The "cassava connection" parallels the well-known hamburger linkage between North America and Central America. But there is a good news item: in response to a consumer boycott, Burger King, previously the main importer of Central American beef, has ceased its imports of rainforest beef. This is a reflection of the determination of millions of individual Americans to use their "dollar votes" in defense of the tropical forests.

CASSAVA CONNECTION *Much rainforest has also been lost from growing cassava or manioc (seen here growing together with bananas in Ecuador), which is then used as feed for livestock in Europe and the United States.*

There is further good news emerging in the form of a proposed tree planting campaign for the humid tropics, which could do much to counter the build-up of CO_2 in the global atmosphere. As trees photosynthesize, they absorb CO_2: a tree is half carbon. There is no better place for trees to grow than the tropics with their year-round warmth and moisture. A single acre (less than half a hectare) can soak up four tons of carbon each year for several decades. So 400,000 square miles (1 million square kilometers) can lock away 1 billion tons of carbon.

There are 79 hydroelectric dams planned for Amazonia over the next 20 years, threatening over 58,000 square miles (150,000 square kilometers) of pristine rainforest with flooding.

We can't eliminate all of the accumulation of carbon in the global atmosphere by tree planting, since there isn't enough spare land available. But we could realistically aim to reduce it by half. This would cost around US$80 billion through the decade – a small investment in comparison with some of the eventual costs of not doing anything. For instance, up to $200 billion will be required to redesign irrigation systems so that the world's croplands can cope with the severe climate changes produced by the greenhouse effect.

The funding for this tree planting campaign should be supplied primarily by the industrialized nations, on the grounds that they have long been responsible for the great bulk of the greenhouse effect. If the effort were spread over ten years, the cost would work out at around $8 billion a year – or five times the amount now going into tropical forestry from all sources. Of course, the campaign would have to be accompanied by far greater measures to halt deforestation. There would be no point in planting trees in one area if forests continue to be destroyed in another. However, such a massive injection of funds for forestry might well provide vital incentive for hard-pressed governments in the tropics to become truly concerned about deforestation.

This idea was once regarded by some experts as laughably unrealistic. But the 1990 report of the Inter-Governmental Panel on Climate Change

JOHN HEMMING

66 *My personal love of the tropical forests is older than my realization of their scientific importance. It started when I lived for six months in the cathedral-like splendor of the forests of the upper Iriri in central Brazil, a shadowy world of great beauty without direct sunlight. That was then a region unexplored by Western man, teeming with wildlife, where you could push through dense undergrowth to broad rivers that had never been seen by any non-Indian.*

More recently, on the Maracá Rainforest Project at the northern edge of the Amazon basin, I witnessed the amazing wealth of another uninhabited and undisturbed forest. We found several hundred species of creatures new to science – an indication of the amazing genetic wealth that remains to be discovered, and a reminder of the need to protect all types of forest.

To protect the forests, we must protect the tribal people who have evolved a way of life in sustainable harmony with their habitat. I have studied the tragic history of countless tribes that have fought and suffered and are now extinct. During the two years that I have worked with Brazilian Indians, I have experienced the absolute quiet of sleeping in communal huts, fishing with Mehinaku, trying to keep up with walking Chavante, and the idyllic life in an Asurini village. Their struggle for survival must become our struggle too. 99

John Hemming

John Hemming is Director and Secretary of the Royal Geographical Society in London.

YOICHI KURODA

66 *In just 40 years, Japan has become a major economic power. While the pace of Japan's economic advance has been astonishingly rapid, recognition of its disastrous impact on the global environment has been painfully slow.*

After years of campaigning to stop the wasteful use of tropical timber, local authorities and construction companies have finally begun exploring alternatives. Unfortunately, Japanese trading companies have quickened the pace of their destructive exploitation of rainforests for timber, and Japan's aid agencies and bankers continue to fund large-scale dams, mines, pulpwood plantations, and tourism developments in sensitive environmental areas.

Japan needs nothing less than a completely new economic direction that will reduce production and imports of raw materials, and will respect local economies, native peoples, and the natural world. This is now the real challenge for Japanese citizens, businessmen, and policy-makers in the last decade we have left to us to save the Earth. 99

黒田洋一

Yoichi Kuroda is the Coordinator of the Japan Tropical Forest Action Network.

TIME BOMB: TROPICAL RAINFOREST

Almost half the world's tropical rainforests have already been destroyed. Knowing what we do of their incalculable diversity, their enormous potential benefits, and the consequences of their disappearance for the world's climate, it is insanity to let this destruction continue. Yet an area of rainforest the size of six football fields is still being destroyed every minute of every day. In a few decades, more than three-quarters of the original forests may have disappeared forever. To slow down the rate of destruction, the international community must help rainforest countries develop sustainable management policies and alternative sources of income; too many aid projects merely accelerate the spread of commercial forestry.

FERNS IN CHILEAN RAINFOREST (left)

DEATH OF A FOREST (right) *As in so many other tropical regions, parts of the rainforest in the Malaysian state of Sarawak are being sacrificed for short-term financial gain.*

Nigeria
In Africa's most populated country, demand for land may eliminate the remaining forests by the mid 1990's.

Madagascar
Forests here, with many unique endemic species, are the most threatened in the world.

Brazil
More than a quarter of the world's surviving rainforest is in Brazil, so new threats to the forest from mining, ranching, and settlement make it the focus of international concern.

Côte d'Ivoire
Slash-and-burn and logging are reducing existing forests by 15 percent per year, one of the highest rates in the world.

REMAINING RAINFORESTS (above)
The light green areas indicate where rainforest has already disappeared; the dark green areas show the forest that still stands today.

Papua New Guinea
So far, forests here have suffered relatively little, but they are threatened by logging and clearance for planting cash-crops.

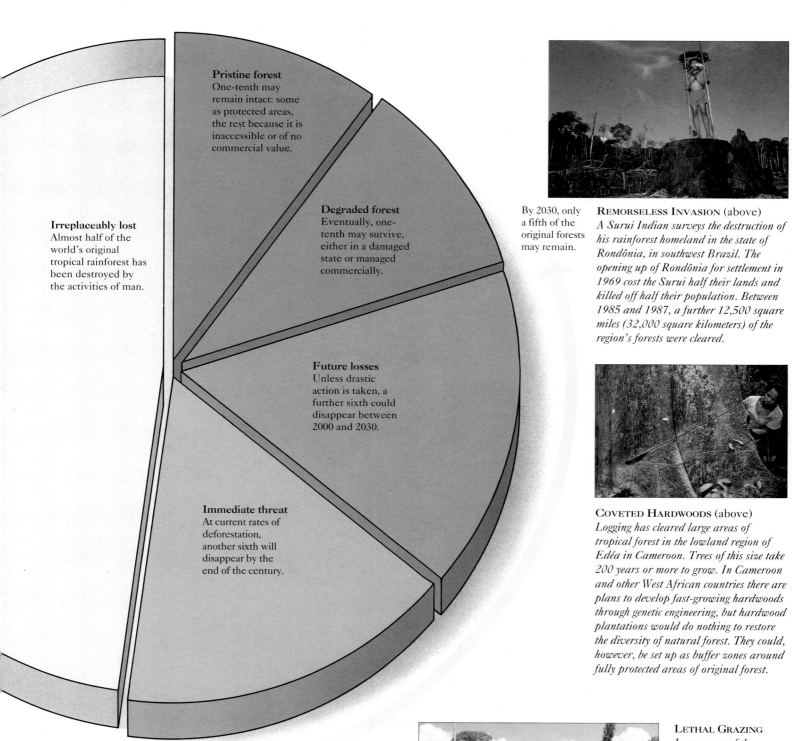

Pristine forest
One-tenth may remain intact: some as protected areas, the rest because it is inaccessible or of no commercial value.

Irreplaceably lost
Almost half of the world's original tropical rainforest has been destroyed by the activities of man.

Degraded forest
Eventually, one-tenth may survive, either in a damaged state or managed commercially.

Future losses
Unless drastic action is taken, a further sixth could disappear between 2000 and 2030.

Immediate threat
At current rates of deforestation, another sixth will disappear by the end of the century.

By 2030, only a fifth of the original forests may remain.

The amount of original rainforest left in 1991.

THE TIMESCALE OF DESTRUCTION (above) *This diagram shows the proportion of the world's tropical rainforest already destroyed, predicted losses over the next few decades, and the small area that may then remain. The original extent of the rainforests was an area of 6 million square miles (16 million square kilometers); today just half of this remains.*

REMORSELESS INVASION (above)
A Surui Indian surveys the destruction of his rainforest homeland in the state of Rondônia, in southwest Brazil. The opening up of Rondônia for settlement in 1969 cost the Surui half their lands and killed off half their population. Between 1985 and 1987, a further 12,500 square miles (32,000 square kilometers) of the region's forests were cleared.

COVETED HARDWOODS (above)
Logging has cleared large areas of tropical forest in the lowland region of Edéa in Cameroon. Trees of this size take 200 years or more to grow. In Cameroon and other West African countries there are plans to develop fast-growing hardwoods through genetic engineering, but hardwood plantations would do nothing to restore the diversity of natural forest. They could, however, be set up as buffer zones around fully protected areas of original forest.

LETHAL GRAZING
Large areas of the Amazon and Central American rainforest have been cleared for cattle ranching. With no tree cover and no tree-roots to retain it, the thin layer of topsoil is almost completely eroded within a few years.

ON THE GREEN FRONT

ON THE GREEN FRONT
EVARISTO NUGKUAG

EVARISTO NUGKUAG
*Winner of the Right
Livelihood Award 1986*

Evaristo Nugkuag is an Aguarunan Indian from Peru. In 1981, he set up an organization which brought together 13 different tribal groups, representing more than half of Peru's 220,000 rainforest Indians. From the very start, this organization was concerned with supporting and protecting its weaker members, and it was largely due to this new-found solidarity that Peruvian Indians were able to hold their ground against many assaults on their basic human rights in the early 1980's.

In 1984 Evaristo Nugkuag initiated a series of agreements with tribal people in other countries to create the Coordinating Organization for Indigenous Bodies in the Amazon Basin (COICA). This organization now has representatives from Colombia, Brazil, Peru, Ecuador, and Bolivia, and speaks for more than half of the Amazon Indians. It is a clear demonstration of their ability to forget internal frictions in order to promote the joint welfare of all Amazonian peoples.

Evaristo Nugkuag explains his belief in the importance of COICA's work: "Ours is a history characterized by the ignorance of oppression from a dehumanized Western capitalist system. Crimes, atrocities, and injustices are too numerous to affect our feeling any longer. Yet our nations have their pride, their history, their heroes, their beliefs, their customs, just like any other.

Defending Rights and Land
"Now through our organizations, we are getting stronger, from village to village, from country to country. Our principal objective is to promote an independent response to our daily problems, and defend our rights from an indigenous perspective without outside interference.

"Our principal line of action is the defence of our land and our resources, as well as our right to our own language, culture, and education, to self-determination and political representation for the security of our people."

proposed the planting of 1 million square miles (2.4 million square kilometers) of trees worldwide during the next 20 years.

HOPE FOR THE FUTURE

There is still hope for the tropical forests. Several countries, notably the Philippines, Thailand, and India, have declared their deforestation a national emergency. The country with the worst deforestation in recent years, Brazil, is getting to grips with the problem, having appointed Dr. José Lutzenberger, one of the world's best known environmentalists, to be Special Secretary for the Environment.

Even more promising is the spread of citizen-activist groups in tropical forest countries. The Indonesian Environmental Forum wields considerable political clout. In India the Chipko Movement and the Silent Valley campaign have achieved remarkable breakthroughs. In Kenya the Green Belt organization has planted more trees in one year than the government achieved in the previous ten years. There has been a similar quantum leap in local tree planting in Colombia. Although these good-news items are still only small bright stars in an otherwise dark sky, we have made light years of advance since the mid-1980's.

At last it is beginning to look possible that the 1990's will be the decade when humankind finally determines to save the most exuberant expression of nature in the written history of life on Earth. If we achieve it, we shall surely be regarded by untold generations of the future as giants of the human condition. We have both the responsibility and the privilege of being able to save all our tropical forests, for all of us, for all time.

HARDWOOD PLANTATION (right) *Teak is one of the few hardwood species that can be grown successfully in plantations, such as this one in southern India. Further investment in similar projects will help to relieve pressure on virgin rainforests.*

OF VALUE IN ITSELF (opposite) *The exotic cotton-topped tamarin, a small squirrel-monkey, has no uses for mankind, and lives only in the northwestern regions of Colombia in South America. Happily, the tamarin is in no particular danger as yet. But how long will it be before man's activities begin to threaten its forest home?*

GRASSLANDS
DEFENDING THE OPEN RANGE
DAVID HALL AND JONATHAN SCURLOCK

Grazing animals and grasslands have evolved together over millions of years. Interfering with the balance between them has far-reaching consequences for the whole planet's ecology.

The wide open prairies of North America, the tree-dotted grasslands or savannas of Africa, and the Russian steppes: they all conjure up visions of unchanging sameness, yet nothing could be further from the truth. These ecosystems support thousands of different species, both above and below the ground, and play a crucial role in maintaining the ecological balance of the world.

Yet the importance of the grassland environment was once recognized only by ecologists and conservationists. However, a growing number of scientists and decision-makers are finally waking up to the complex dilemmas involved in ensuring that the world's grasslands continue to sustain the many communities that are dependent upon them.

Grasslands are one of the most widespread vegetation types in the world, covering nearly one-fifth of the Earth's land surface. The majority of this area is within the tropics: though you'd never know it from reading the popular press, tropical grasslands are more extensive than tropical forests, particularly in Africa. Grasslands are likely to remain roughly constant in area for the foreseeable future; although

TANZANIAN SUNSET (opposite) *These great plains once stretched across East Africa in an almost unbroken blanket. Their range and teeming wildlife, such as the African elephants (inset, above), have been progressively reduced by pressure of human numbers.*

David Hall BSc MSc PhD *is a Professor of Biology at King's College, London. He lectures worldwide on biomass, photosynthesis, and climate change, and edits the journal* Biomass and Bioenergy.

Jonathan Scurlock MA MSc PhD *works on post-doctoral research with Professor David Hall at King's College, London, and is an independent consultant on plant physiology, environment, energy resources, and development.*

some marginal grasslands are turning to desert, conversion of forest to grazing land continues elsewhere. It is crucially important to obtain more information about grassland ecosystems in their present form before they are modified by either the effects of global climate change or increasingly intensive management.

Grasslands occur either where seasonal drought conditions prevent the development of any significant tree cover, or where our predecessors or contemporaries have cleared forest to create grazing land. Natural grasslands include the savannas of Africa, the North American prairies, and the dry steppes of the southern USSR. Semi-natural grasslands, where forest has been cleared away and grass cover is maintained by grazing, cutting or burning, tend to be wetter and more productive. Many of the grasslands of South and South-East Asia fall into this category. A third category of agricultural grasslands or pastures occurs where new grass species or varieties have been introduced and are maintained by methods of cultivation such as

TOWERING TERMITES *Termites that build their mounds on open grasslands have benefited from man's destructive activities in the tropics. Forest clearance for cattle ranching in South America and Africa has considerably extended their range.*

PATTERNS OF MIGRATION (right) *The grasslands of the Masai Mara National Park in Kenya are criss-crossed with the tracks followed year after year by migrating wildebeest. Population pressure on land outside such parks means that migratory animals are often constrained within artificial boundaries. Tensions between the Park's authorities and pastoralists like the Masai are common, but easier to resolve when local people share in the profits of tourism.*

COKE'S HARTEBEEST *(Alcelaphus buselaphus cokei)* **IN KENYA'S NAIROBI NATIONAL PARK** (below)

fertilization and irrigation. European lowland grazing lands are typical examples of this category.

In general, grassland soils contain a great abundance of organic matter, both close to the surface and deep down, but levels of available soil nutrients in tropical grasslands tend to be much lower than in temperate grasslands. This is reflected in the relatively poor nutritional value of tropical grasslands compared with temperate grazing lands, for many tropical grasses have a low protein content.

Grazing lands have long been undervalued as a resource for low-input, sustainable agriculture. It has gradually become clear that two strategies are required for their sustainable management: a minimal management regime for natural grasslands, to avoid excessive disturbance, and the controlled management of semi-natural grasslands depending on the particular regional circumstances. In neither case can one talk of a "hands-off" conservationist approach; good conservation depends on sustainable economic exploitation. This may be a matter of rearing sheep and cattle to maintain the English landscape, or perhaps of raising game animals instead of livestock on the rangelands of Kenya.

In recent decades, Europe's unwieldy Common Agricultural Policy has been responsible for the destruction of much wildlife habitat. With the worthy intention of ensuring European food security, its massive subsidies have encouraged large farmers to convert marginal land to intensive agriculture, but often failed to stop smaller farmers from going out of business. Europe's dry grasslands have been reduced to less than one-tenth of their original area, and often replaced by inappropriate crops. The 1990 agreement to start cutting European farm subsidies provides a chance to redress the balance, so long as the "set-aside" programs of reversion to grassland and woodland are aimed at over-intensive cerealgrowers, rather than at low-input farmers who already find it hard enough to survive.

The Sahara Desert is expanding southwards, engulfing degraded grasslands, at a rate of 30 miles (50 kilometers) every year.

A severe drought from 1973 to 1975 first drew the world's attention to the sub-Saharan region of Africa known as the Sahel. Here, the way of life for many nomadic cattle herders is threatened by population increase, overgrazing, and the conversion of fragile semi-arid grazing land to arable crops, all of which are leading to desertification. Initially, many rehabilitation projects in the Sahel had an inflexible approach based solely on tree-planting, with minimal concern for grassland ecology, and with little or no reference to the local people and the grazing patterns of their livestock.

By the mid-1980's, many such projects had failed, largely because local herders and farmers had little direct interest in growing trees. More recent efforts have concentrated on local management of livestock density, to avoid overgrazing and promote natural regeneration of grass and tree cover. Although grassland management strategies are still subject to controversy, severely degraded areas can be rehabilitated if proper attention is paid to locally sustainable grazing practices.

Some of the serious problems associated with rehabilitation can be seen in the Rift Valley of Kenya, where the semi-arid East African plains have been subjected to 80 years of topsoil erosion on a huge scale. The thorny scrub vegetation is now of little value to people and their livestock unless it is very carefully managed. Yet population

TAMING THE TSETSE FLY

Scientists reckon there are more than 4 million square miles (11 million square kilometers) of central and southern Africa that remain pretty much out of bounds because of the menace of the tsetse fly. This creature is the carrier of the trypanosome parasite, the cause of sleeping sickness in humans and a disease called "nagana" in cattle.

More than US$1 billion have been spent trying to eradicate the tsetse fly by aerial spraying, clearing the trees and bush (in which the flies rest), and slaughtering game. None of this has made much difference.

One of the most successful projects has been in Zimbabwe, where a team of British scientists has developed a technique for sterilizing tsetse flies. In order to catch them, they have to lure them into settling on pieces of dark cloth treated to look and smell like cattle.

Risk of Overgrazing
Restricting the range of the tsetse fly is a desirable goal, but were the fly eradicated, and new grasslands opened up to cattle, it would be all but impossible to prevent rapid and massive overgrazing.

Environmentalists are now beginning to ask whether it might not make more sense to develop systems for "ranching" the indigenous African game animals, most of which are resistant to the trypanosome parasite.

BLOOD-SUCKER *When tsetse flies bite, they can pass on the amoeba-like organism that causes sleeping sickness.*

LAURENS VAN DER POST

66 *When I came back to the world, after ten years of war, ten years of death and killing, I found that I could not face society. I felt a strange instinct to go back to the wilderness of Africa. I went to live in the bush, alone. I remember the first evening in the wild, seeing the first kudu bull as I made camp on the Pafuri River. He came out of the river where he had been drinking, sniffing the air between him and me. He threw that lovely head of his back, and I looked at him with a tremendous feeling of relief. I thought, 'My God, I'm back home! I'm back at the moment when humanity came in, where everything was magical and alive, quivering with a magnetism from the fullness of whoever created it all.' And I lived there for four whole weeks and gradually, through the animals, I was led back to my own human self.* 99

Laurens van der Post.

Laurens van der Post is a South-African born explorer and writer, now living in England. This is an extract from his essay *Wilderness: A Way of Truth.*

RETURN OF THE LARGE BLUE
In 1979, the large blue butterfly was declared extinct in Britain. It has since been reintroduced (with limited success) following the discovery of a complex interdependence between two species. The large blue (Maculinea arion) lays its eggs on wild thyme bushes. When the newborn caterpillar falls to the ground, it is picked up by one particular species of red ant (Myrmica sabuleti), which believes the caterpillar is one of its own grubs. Safe in the ants' nest, the caterpillar gorges itself on grubs for ten months, before emerging as a butterfly. It is now known that this ant – without which the large blue is doomed – can survive only on warm, heavily grazed slopes, so the large blue's survival still rests on a knife-edge.

WANGARI MAATHAI

" As a child I was greatly impressed by a huge wild fig tree near our home. My mother had told me that fig trees are not cut or burnt because they are used for religious ceremonies. I was forbidden even to collect dead twigs from it. Today that tree is no longer standing. When tea-growing was introduced into my area for cash, that huge, ancient fig tree was axed and burnt to make way for tea bushes.

Not too far from the tree was the source of a stream, from which I would fetch water for my mother. I was fascinated by the way the clean, cool water pushed its way through the soft red clay, so gently that even the individual grains of the soil were undisturbed. It then flowed downstream, winding softly between the deep green stems of a little forest of arrowroots. The leaves of the arrowroot are very broad, beautifully green. I would sometimes cut a broad arrowroot leaf to fetch water. The leaf would be so clean and oily that water would dance on it like a large silver ball. I would rejoice at its purity and coolness.

As soon as the fig tree was cut, the stream dried up, and the broad-leafed arrowroots gave way to tea bushes. My children will never see the huge fig tree, nor the broad-leafed arrowroots. They have never seen the source of a spring. When I visit this little valley of my childhood dreams, I feel the tragedy under my feet. Gulleys stare at me, telling the story of soil erosion which was unknown before; the land appears exhausted, the only thing which seems to matter is how many tea leaves can be picked so that the country can earn more foreign exchange. Hunger is on the faces of the local people. Firewood is scarce because every tree has been cut, even those that were forbidden. People are only concerned about today; they do everything to maximize production and income at the expense of tomorrow. "

WMMaathai

Former anatomy professor Wangari Maathai is the head of the Green Belt
Movement, founded by the National Council of Women of Kenya.

pressure continues to force people on to this deteriorating marginal land. Such grasslands were not always barren. In the Baringo District at the beginning of this century, grasses grew shoulder-high, supporting many wild animals. However, as European settlers forced people off the good upland soils, grazing pressure on the lowlands was massively increased. As the grasses dwindled and natural fires (which play an important role in the ecology of tropical grasslands) became rare, thorny acacia scrub started to take over. Now even the acacia trees are at risk, cut down to meet local and urban demand for wood fuel and charcoal.

Against this background of progressive over-exploitation, the Baringo Fuel and Fodder Project (BFFP) stands out as a continuing success story which has reversed the process of deterioration. In the early 1980's, fast-growing young trees were planted to establish vegetation cover, and were protected from the all-consuming goats by thorn-bush and solar-powered electric fences. Low earth embankments were built to catch rain-water running off the land and prevent further soil loss.

In careful consultation with local people, the project has grown over the last ten years, gradually establishing well-managed fields of multi-purpose trees and grasses that provide sustainable sources of livestock fodder, fuel wood, and thatching grass. Compared with the many failed development projects instigated by governments and international organizations, the BFFP has succeeded because it really is a "grass-roots" project.

MISSING CARBON

Whether they are in temperate or tropical zones, we are only just beginning to realize the important role grasslands play in transferring carbon between the atmosphere, vegetation, and soil. Scientists have calculated that the amount of carbon dioxide, the major greenhouse gas, in the atmosphere is not increasing as fast as human activity is adding to it through fossil fuel burning and deforestation. Somewhere on Earth, there must be a "sink" for the excess carbon released into the atmosphere, but we do not know whether the missing carbon is taken up in grassland soils or forest trees.

What we do know is that the annual burning of many tropical grasslands is a significant factor in the global carbon cycle. This means that a net loss of carbon and nutrients may result if the pressures of fire and grazing become so intense that they result in deterioration and serious erosion.

As yet, there is barely enough statistical information to develop proper management options. However, a project coordinated by the United Nations Environment Program, based on work in Mexico, Thailand, and Kenya, shows that grasslands account for more than a quarter of worldwide carbon turnover on land. Previous estimates put the amount at less than a tenth.

We can now construct computer models of grassland productivity and carbon cycles, using data from all over the world, including prairies, steppes, and savannas, from the plains of Mexico to the inundated grasslands of the Brazilian Amazon. This unique collaboration will help predict how the world's grasslands will cope with increased carbon dioxide in the atmosphere and resulting changes in rainfall and temperature.

There is an urgent need to understand our grasslands better, and plan their management accordingly, both for the sake of their unique animals and plants, and to ensure the future of the world's human population and its livestock.

ON THE GREEN FRONT
AMAZON RESEARCH

Philip Fearnside, an ecologist working at the National Institute for Amazon Research in Manaus, Brazil, has dedicated more than ten years of his life to studying cattle ranching in the deforested areas of the Amazon basin.

Working with local scientists under adverse circumstances, since long before Amazon rainforest destruction was a fashionable research topic, he has highlighted the environmental bankruptcy of converting forest to low-quality pasture, a cheap way of obtaining legal title to the land. Large-scale ranchers received up to 70 percent subsidies for "land improvement," yet half this grazing land has already been abandoned after only a few years of beef production.

Because so little attention had been paid to sustainable grazing practices, it is doubtful how much benefit the Amazonian and Central American countries have gained from ranching on tropical forest soils. The cost to the environment is huge, with little forest regeneration taking place on abandoned grazing land, and the self-sustaining rainfall cycle of the entire Amazon area now under threat due to piecemeal forest destruction.

The meticulous research and campaigning work of Fearnside and others has drawn the world's attention to the problems and conflicts of this region, and the Brazilian government has since reduced the financial incentives it offers for unsustainable ranching in the Amazon basin.

FINAL REMNANTS (left) *North America's grasslands once teemed with millions of bison. Now only a few remain, in reserves and National Parks, and even here their survival is not guaranteed.*

THE PARTY'S OVER (above) *A windpump lies abandoned in the Australian bush, where overgrazing has turned productive land into semi-desert. Millions of tons of topsoil are lost every year.*

CROPLANDS
BLOWING IN THE WIND

LESTER BROWN

As the world's croplands are eroded, while populations continue to increase, the prospect of frequent famines grows ever more serious.

BARN OWL
Tyto alba

As the 1990's progress, the world's farmers are being faced with the daunting task of feeding some 93 million more people every year, but with 24 billion fewer tons of topsoil than the year before. At some point, either the loss of topsoil from the world's croplands will have to be checked by effective soil conservation practices, or the growth in the world's population will be checked by hunger and starvation.

For 10,000 years, since agriculture began, the area of the Earth's land surface that was devoted to raising crops expanded more or less continuously. As populations increased, farmers moved from valley to valley and from continent to continent, extending the area under cultivation. But in 1981, with one-tenth of the Earth's land surface under the plow, this increase in the area of agricultural lands finally came to a halt. Human populations, however, have continued to swell.

Historically, as demand for food outstripped local supplies, farmers devised ingenious techniques, such as irrigation, terracing, and fallowing, for extending agriculture on to new lands. Irrigation enables crops to grow where rainfall is low or unpredictable. Terracing permits farming on steep slopes, even mountainsides. Centuries of laborious effort shaped elaborate, picturesque systems of terraces in Japan, China, Nepal, Indonesia, and the Andean highlands of South America, which the Incas once inhabited.

In semi-arid regions where the level of rainfall is not sufficient to sustain continuous cultivation, such as the Great Plains of North America, the Anatolean Plateau of Turkey,

Lester Brown MSc MBA
is the founder of the State of the World *reports,* World Watch *magazine, and the Worldwatch Institute in the USA, of which he is President. He is also a UN Environment Prize winner.*

and the drylands of the Soviet Union, farmers learned to let their fields accumulate moisture by leaving them fallow between crops. Under the system of "alternate-year cropping," land is left fallow every other year. Cultivators destroy all vegetation on the land that is to lie fallow, then cover it with a dust mulch to curb any evaporation of water from the soil. Where fallowing leaves the soil vulnerable to erosion by the wind, farmers plow their fields in strips, alternating cropped strips with fallow ones, so that the cropped plots serve as windbreaks. Such practices permitted production of wheat to bounce back in the American Great Plains after the dustbowl years of the 1930's.

In the humid tropics, more nutrients are stored in vegetation than in the soil itself. Stripped of their dense vegetative cover, soils in parts of sub-Saharan Africa, the Amazon basin, the outer islands of Indonesia, and other tropical regions quickly lose their nutrients. But fallowing the land slowly restores soil fertility. Tropical farmers have mastered "shifting cultivation," whereby they clear land and crop it for three or four years, then systematically abandon it and move on as the crop yields decline. When the exhausted soils have revived, after some 20 to 25 years, the shifting cultivators return to repeat the cycle.

Irrigation, terracing, fallowing, and shifting cultivation have enabled farmers to raise crops where conventional agriculture could not survive. In doing so, they have greatly increased the Earth's capacity to

WIND OF DESTRUCTION (opposite) *It looks beautiful, but the real beauty of this grain field is just blowing away in the wind. Studies in the USA show that for every 1 inch (2.5 centimeters) of topsoil lost, yields fall by around 6 percent.*

EARS OF BARLEY
Hordeum vulgare

EVA MOBERG

❝ I find it pathetic that man has called himself Homo sapiens, *'intelligent man.' Man is incredibly innovative, but he is definitely not very intelligent.*
We regard our civilization as the most developed to date.
With just as much reason, if not more, you could call it the most stupid. If, for the last thousand years, all cultures had behaved and reasoned the way we do, then we would not exist today. The biological prerequisites for life on Earth would have collapsed long ago.
We are incapable of seeing more than one possible way of being and thinking, and continue to work against our own interest in the firm belief that we are promoting it. We are even stupid enough to believe that all other forms of life and all other cultures exist for our *sake! ❞*

Eva Moberg

Eva Moberg is a freelance journalist and writer in Sweden.

CULTURAL DIVERSITY
Serried ranks of young sugar beet stretch to the horizon in a British field (right). *Farming of this kind creates a bleak, monotonous landscape compared with the rich and varied vegetation of this agricultural scene in rural France* (above). *In ecological terms, too, there is a stark contrast between the poverty of intensive monocultural cropping and the richness of traditional mixed agriculture. Diversity of the landscape and diversity of species go hand in hand.*

feed people. But today these time-tested methods are breaking down, as severe population pressures force farmers to shorten the fallowing or regenerating phases of the cycles, preventing the soil from recovering its full fertility.

Over the last four decades, worldwide demand for food has nearly tripled, spurred by both population growth and rising affluence. This rising demand for food has forced farmers on to mountainous and often heavily forested terrain. Lacking the time that is necessary for building traditional terraces, farmers clear and plow steep land, knowing that it will have to be abandoned within only a decade or two due to erosion of the soil. Likewise, desperate farmers move into tropical forests like those of the Amazon basin, clearing land for agriculture, only to have to abandon it after three to five years of cropping, when the soil is exhausted.

MORE FROM LESS

From the beginning of agriculture until the middle of this century, expansion of the area of croplands in production accounted for nearly all the increases in food supplies. Increases in the productivity of the land, the output of a given area, were so slow throughout most of this period that their effects were scarcely perceptible within any one generation. Only since mid-century, as the expansion of croplands area has slowed dramatically, has growth in the output of crops depended on raising the productivity of the land.

Some 24 billion tons of topsoil are eroded worldwide each year. This is equivalent to all the topsoil on Australia's wheatlands, and represents the loss of 9 million tons of potential grain harvest.

Within the United States, the availability of cheap nitrogen fertilizer has led to impressive increases in grain production, as farmers abandoned the traditional rotations of soil-building grasses and legumes in favor of continuous planting of corn and other crops. But the price paid for continuous cropping of this kind has been an enormous loss of topsoil, which in itself is now setting limits on the productivity of the land.

TIME BOMB: FOOD FOR THE WORLD

We have become complacent about feeding the world. The increases in agricultural productivity of the 1960's and 1970's (through the introduction of so-called "miracle strains" of rice and other staples) have not been maintained in the 1980's. Opinions differ over whether this decline is a short-term problem or an indication of a more profound crisis. We are already paying some of the ecological costs (in terms of erosion, salinization, and pollution) of imposing Western-style intensive agriculture on countries where they are quite inappropriate.

Some scientists hope to boost crop yields through genetic engineering, but it is not certain that this approach will be successful. There is very little new land that can be brought into production, so the danger remains that the world's harvests will be unable to keep pace with the world's spiralling population.

VISION OF PLENTY
The Green Revolution has filled huge silos in Western Europe with surplus grain.

DURUM WHEAT

HOEING THE LAND
Given the limited resources of African farmers like these women in Mozambique, agriculture that relies on expensive machinery and chemical fertilizers is not the answer to their food shortages.

Western Europe
High-technology farming has produced astonishingly high yields, but two-thirds of the grain goes to feed livestock.

LESS THAN ENOUGH TO EAT
The graphs show the amount of grain produced each year per capita of the population in Western Europe, Africa, and the world as a whole. The world's population now consumes more than it produces. In 1987 world reserves of grain were sufficient for 101 days. By 1989 there were only enough for 54 days.

World Grain Production
Total world grain production has continued to increase over the last decade, but it no longer keeps pace with the rapid growth of the world's population. Per capita production of grain peaked around 1985; since then it has steadily declined.

Africa
Grain production, already below the basic subsistence level of 400 pounds (180 kilograms) per capita per year, is set to fall even further over the coming decade.

Pounds of grain produced per person per year

1200
1000
800
600
400
220

1960 | 1965 | 1970 | 1975 | 1980 | 1985 | 1990 | 1995

RICHARD SANDBROOK

Usually we think of unbridled economic growth as the only source of environmental problems. But poverty is just as bad for the environment, and much worse for people. For example, mortality among children under five in South Asia exceeds 170 deaths per thousand; in Sweden the figure is just under ten.

Consider one of the most publicized issues of environment in the Third World: forest destruction. It occurs primarily because of a hunger for land – not for timber, but for a cleared space in which to achieve a livelihood. So much so that worldwide as little as 10 percent of forest clearance can be laid directly at the feet of domestic or overseas logging companies. All the rest is down to immigration to forest lands by people in search of a livelihood. No matter how much we do in the North to ban, persuade or otherwise cajole the timber trade or the tropical forest countries to change, not much will happen until the people who live there have a secure way to grow food and make a living.

There are only two ways out of this Faustian bargain. Either we reduce the pollution of poverty by fair means while addressing our own excesses of affluence, or we just let the poor die. That is the challenge for our political leaders to face, and I know which path morality will lead them down.

Richard Sandbrook is Senior Executive Director at the London office of the International Institute for Environment and Development (IIED).

CARLOS PIMENTA

The agricultural policies of the developed world are damaging our environment. Paying to intensify agricultural production has led to the destruction of our soils, and the pollution of our environment with chemicals. Surplus production, particularly in the European Community, is sold at discount prices on the world market, ruining the agricultural economies of Third World countries. More public money is then spent trying to put right the damage done by intensive agriculture. Some sense needs to prevail; the developed world must rethink its agricultural policies. Farmers are the keepers of our environmental heritage, and should not be forced to be the opposite on economic grounds.

Carlos Pimenta is a Portuguese Member of the European Parliament.

Deforestation has also become a major problem. In addition to causing soil erosion, it indirectly affects the productivity of the land in some countries, including those of the Indian subcontinent. As firewood becomes scarce, villagers start burning crop residues and cow dung as cooking fuel. This deprives the soil of both the organic matter needed to maintain a healthy soil structure, and the nutrients needed to retain fertility.

COMPETITION FOR LAND

PULSES

As world population grows, not only is land degraded by erosion and loss of fertility, but croplands are increasingly being converted to nonfarm uses. Construction of towns and highways is beginning to chip away at the croplands base. In China, for example, a 12 percent rate of industrial growth during the 1980's led to the construction of thousands of factories, warehouses and roads. Not surprisingly, factories are built where the people live, and in China the people live where the croplands lie, primarily in a 1,000-mile (1,600-kilometer) strip along the eastern and southern coasts.

New-found affluence has also led to a housing boom in the Chinese countryside. Visitors in recent years have been impressed by the level of new construction in villages. Millions of families are either adding a room or building a new, larger house. The effect of this is the loss of more than 1 million acres (400,000 hectares) of croplands each year. Scarcity of land has led the government to encourage cremation of the dead rather than the traditional burial under a mound of earth. The dead are now competing with the living for land.

After the drought in the summer of 1988, grain harvests fell by 27 percent in the United States, 8 percent in the Soviet Union, and 2 percent in China, a loss of some 97 million tons in total.

Throughout the world, the city also vies with the farm for water. Because of population growth and increased urbanization, urban areas take water away from farms, reducing the amount that is available for irrigation. In some places, such as the arid southwest of the United States, loss of irrigation water means that the land reverts to desert. In other areas the farmers are forced to go back to less productive dryland farming.

The upshot of all this, on a world scale, is clear: any land added to the croplands base is now offset by croplands losses, from erosion of soil and conversion of land to nonfarm uses, as the world struggles to accommodate and feed an additional 93 million people per year.

HOLDING THE GROUND

However, some recent initiatives offer hope that croplands losses *can* be stemmed, or even reversed. In the United States in the early 1980's, public concern regarding the economic effects of topsoil loss converged with resentment over the soaring cost of farm subsidy schemes. Until that

FALSE PROMISES OF PLENTY
The use of chemicals increased greatly in the Third World in the 1980's. It is hard to envisage feeding the world without some controlled pesticide use, but the benefits of pesticides are often greatly exaggerated by the agrochemical companies. The Pesticides Action Network has estimated that up to 40,000 people die every year in the Third World of pesticide poisoning, often from chemicals that have been banned in the developed world.

THE ORGANIC OPTION

Consumers are becoming increasingly apprehensive about residues of pesticides in food and drinking water. The National Research Council in the USA has calculated that up to 20,000 North Americans may die prematurely each year from pesticide-related cancers.

Many of the chemicals used in farming are for purely cosmetic purposes, to make the produce look better. Consumers are now learning that quality is more about taste, texture, and nutrition than about appearance or standardized sizes.

"Alternative agriculture" is a term that embraces a wide range of different options, including low-input or extensive farming (reducing but not necessarily eliminating the use of fertilizers, chemicals, and concentrated feedstuffs), Integrated Pest Management (using a range of biological, chemical, and crop-rotation techniques to control pests), environment-friendly farming (laying greater stress on protecting natural features and local flora and fauna), and organic farming.

Organic farmers use no artificially produced fertilizers or pesticides, and rely on the good husbandry of crop rotation, different tillage systems, and diversification. In both Europe and the United States the number of organic farmers is growing all the time, with more farmers joining their efforts as consumer pressure and environmental awareness increase.

APPEARANCE VERSUS QUALITY
The unblemished, uniform appearance of the non-organic produce makes it initially more attractive than the organic produce, but the powerful chemicals that are used to achieve this cosmetic effect can remain both in the food and in the land.

ORGANIC CARROTS   NON-ORGANIC CARROTS

ORGANIC APPLE   NON-ORGANIC APPLE   ORGANIC GREEN PEPPER   NON-ORGANIC GREEN PEPPER

SELF-INTERESTED RESEARCH
Much of the agricultural research carried out in Third World countries, at field stations such as this one in the Philippines, is directly funded by Western multi-national companies. The primary goal of such research is to develop higher-yielding cash crops, so that the companies can increase their exports and profits. Funding for research centers working on indigenous food production is often lamentably low, yet it is on this kind of research that the fate of millions of poor people depends.

time, the croplands set aside from use (in order to control over-production) had been selected without regard to their erodibility.

A coalition of environmental groups and soil conservation professionals worked together to launch a new approach, the Conservation Reserve Program. The first stage of the plan, from 1986 to 1990, concentrated on converting the most highly erodible croplands to grasslands or woodlands before they became wastelands. Farmers who agreed to convert their highly erodible lands for ten years received annual payments from the government in exchange.

The second stage of the plan, which runs from 1990 to 1995, has been designed to control the erosion of topsoil on the remaining 118 million acres (48 million hectares) of highly erosion-prone land. Farmers who have such land are required to develop a soil management plan for approval by the Soil Conservation Service. Those who fail to do this will lose all their subsidy benefits, including price supports, low interest loans, and crop insurance.

MOSTAFA TOLBA

"Ever since my childhood in a rural area in the Nile Delta, I have been keenly aware of nature's wonders. I grew up mindful of the fragility of nature, of the thin margin separating the plentiful agricultural belt hugging the Nile from the harshness of the desert beyond.

In the face of unprecedented global problems, I am more confident today than at any time during my 15 years as head of the United Nations Environment Program that we are finally building global solutions. Individuals everywhere – in the rainforests of Brazil, the coast of the Mediterranean, the cities of Europe, the corn belt of the United States – are prepared to do their part to develop systems of ecological protection.

The onus now rests with political leaders everywhere to heed the cry of the people, to restore the balance of nature, and to build the kind of global partnership that will save our planet Earth."

Dr. Mostafa Tolba is the Executive Director of the United Nations Environment Program.

M.S. SWAMINATHAN

"The ecological prudence of the past is vanishing fast, along with the forests under whose canopies people acquired that prudence. There's an old North American Indian saying: 'The sky is held up by the trees. If the forest disappears, the sky-roof of the world collapses. Nature and man then perish together.' The forests I have seen in my childhood in the southern part of India have disappeared. Why?

Only a 'land-saving' system of agriculture can help save the remaining forests. For example, India produced 55 million tons of wheat in 1990 from about 57 million acres (23 million hectares). If we had continued to produce less than half a ton of wheat per acre (0.4 hectare), as was the case in 1968, we would have needed 136 million acres (55 million hectares) to produce the amount of wheat produced in 1990. In other words, 79 million acres (32 million hectares) of forest would have disappeared. The only way to meet the food needs of the future is to produce more and more food from less and less land. The growth of ecological economics is essential for overcoming hunger and poverty."

M. S. Swaminathan is the President of the World Conservation Union (IUCN), and the President of a research center based in Madras, India.

From 1986 to 1990, the Conservation Reserve Program reduced soil erosion by 600 billion tons. Agronomists estimate that by 1995, it will have saved another 500 billion tons of topsoil, reducing soil erosion in the USA by two-thirds in a decade. As available croplands shrink, protecting productivity becomes ever more important.

A gain in grain harvests of 28 million tons a year is needed to keep pace with projected population growth. The Worldwatch Institute estimates that just half this increase can be achieved in the next decade.

These results must be set against the fact that the world's croplands base did not grow at all in the 1980's, nor is it expected to in the 1990's. All growth in food output must therefore come from raising cropland productivity. Can farmers continue to increase yields fast enough to feed 93 million more mouths each year?

ON THE GREEN FRONT
MELAKU WOREDE

Melaku Worede is a geneticist from Ethiopia. Early in his career he was involved in planning the Plant Genetic Resources Center in Addis Ababa, of which he became Director in 1979, and for the work of which he received the Right Livelihood Award in 1989.

Ethiopia's genetic diversity is threatened by drought and modern farming methods. Worede has tried to preserve this diversity, while also building up "strategic seed reserves" of traditional varieties to be released to farmers in times of drought, when no other seeds are likely to thrive. His staff has already collected a considerable amount of genetic diversity, crucial to the agriculture of Ethiopia and its neighbors.

Worede is training a whole new generation of scientists in his home country. Moreover, he regards local farmers as crucial partners. Together they hope to increase yields by up to 5 percent each year.

Worede explains this partnership: "Plant genetic resources are the expression of the wisdom of farmers who have played a highly significant role in building up the world's genetic resource base. The world cannot therefore ignore or deny the intellectual contribution of farmers. As is already happening in my country, farmers and national genebanks in developing countries can work together to preserve and expand crop genetic diversity on behalf of all humanity."

AMISH HUSBANDRY
Amish farming is still practiced in small communities in the United States. Work is done either by hand or using old-fashioned implements. No heavy modern machinery or methods are used, and the land is not eroded or exhausted. The Amish way of life is also traditional. American poet, essayist, and farmer Wendell Berry said of them: "They alone, as a community, have carefully restricted their use of machine developed energy, and so have become the only true masters of technology. . . . They have escaped the mainstream American life of distraction, haste, aimlessness, violence, and disintegration."

BIODIVERSITY
THE RICHNESS OF LIFE
PETER RAVEN AND GHILLEAN PRANCE

We know more about the surface of the Moon than we do about many of the biological communities we are so rapidly destroying here on Earth.

HAZEL CATKINS
Corylus

THE IMPORTANCE OF DIVERSITY
PETER RAVEN

We are, whether we realize it or not, entirely dependent upon the plants, animals, fungi, and micro-organisms that share the world with us. Individually, they alone feed us; they provide many of the drugs and other products on which the quality of our lives increasingly depends; and they offer the promise of sustainable productivity – productivity that the Earth can support on a continuing basis, so our children and, in turn, their children will be able to live peaceful lives of relative serenity and prosperity.

We live in an age driven by the apparently insatiable desire of industrialized nations to go on getting richer. Though we are now willing to consider atmospheric changes as significant international problems, we have so far been unable to see biodiversity in the same way. The sad fact is that up to a quarter of the species on Earth may be lost in the course of the next three decades – within the lives of the majority of us alive today.

PARAKEET AND CRIMSON ROSELLA FEATHERS

ENDANGERED SPECIES (opposite) *In most parts of Africa the leopard is a highly endangered species. Yet there are still people who prefer to see them draped dead on their shoulders than alive in the wild.*

Peter Raven PhD is the Director of the Missouri Botanical Garden and a Professor of Botany at Washington University. He is also a member of the US National Science Board, and Chairman of the Report Review Committee of the National Research Council.

Ghillean Prance MA DPhil Fil Dr FLS is the Director of the Royal Botanic Gardens at Kew, in the United Kingdom. He spent 25 years with the New York Botanical Garden, where he became the Senior Vice President for Science.

FOSSILIZED AMMONITE

Each year, we are cutting and burning 1.5 to 2 percent of the world's remaining tropical rainforests; losing an estimated 24 billion tons of topsoil; and adding some 93 million people to a world that is already far too full, judging from the extent of human misery and starvation, let alone from the depletion of every conceivable resource. Every point on the Earth's surface, from the frozen wastes of Antarctica to the most remote stretches of the oceans, receives a steady shower of man-made chemicals. We are clearly "managing" the entire planet now, for better or for worse, whether we acknowledge this responsibility or not. In this sense, there is no longer any region that can be said to be truly "natural."

RESPONSIBLE STEWARDSHIP

Will we act as responsible stewards of the many organisms that share the Earth with us? We have certainly not given much evidence so far of our commitment; having given names to only 1.4 million of them, we don't know whether the total number may be 10 or 100 million. We understand even less – often nothing at all – about their individual properties, or the ways in which they interact with one another.

Moving beyond our growth-orientated mentality, which assumes that every productive system on the planet can be expanded indefinitely to meet our needs, regardless of its

RETURN FROM THE DEAD
After years of being hunted out in the wild, the Arabian oryx was in danger of extinction. Now the captive breeding program has gradually built up a large enough gene pool to allow the oryx to be reintroduced (and strictly protected) in its original habitat.

biological basis, is an essential ingredient of stewardship. Every nation must work to develop its own base of information on biodiversity, and strive to understand, to use, and to save it, both for its own purposes and for future generations.

For rich nations, this means understanding that we cannot continue to ravage our strictly limited home planet as if its productivity and stability were simply inexhaustible. For poorer nations, the challenge will be even greater, and will not be met without reversing the tragic flow of many millions of dollars from poor, starving countries to the rich industrialized North. Environmental stewardship and social justice go hand in hand.

LOVED TO DEATH

There are no more than 1,500 manatees (or seacows) left in the waters off the coast of Florida, and they are gradually slipping into extinction. Around 150 were killed in 1989. Most of these deaths were a result of collisions with tourist boats.

Ironically, the threat of extinction (and the increased publicity about the fate of the manatee) has only made things worse. Divers and photographers will visit marinas specifically to see and interact with the manatee. They are often to be found in even the busiest areas, because they have no fear of humans.

At the height of the tourist season there is approximately one diver for every 100 square feet (10 square meters) of open water, all intent on tracking down these huge, slow-moving mammals. The manatee is being literally "loved to death." With its low reproduction rate, and mortality and injury rates increasing by 25 percent every year, it could be extinct by the end of the decade.

END OF THE GENTLE GIANT
The manatee can grow up to 15 feet (4.5 meters) in length. Its size and placidity may be its downfall.

RESOURCES FOR THE FUTURE

If the world can attain true stability, we who are living now in the most rapid and destructive period of growth that may ever occur, will be seen as having great powers for good and for evil. Just as large areas of traditional cool-season pasture grasses in the central United States are currently being replaced with more productive warm-season grasses, from fragments of prairie that were spared from the plow, so the resources that the ravaged world of the late 21st century will need to heal its wounds and to feed, clothe, and shelter its people will come from those organisms that we had the foresight or the luck to save.

The Copaiba langsdorfii *tree, which grows in the Amazon basin, produces a sap so similar to diesel oil that it can be poured straight into a truck's fuel tank.*

The preservation of species around the world will result from a combination of different approaches: building up a system of parks and other protected areas, funded internationally, in which both the industrialized and the developing countries participate; setting up a series of botanical gardens, stock culture centers, and other facilities in which species can be preserved outside their natural habitats should preservation within those habitats become impractical; and expanding the management of this whole system in such a way that species can be reintroduced from cultivation into nature at the right time.

Individual plants, animals, and fungi, as well as micro-organisms, will be the sources of products that transcend anything we can imagine now, used for purposes that have not yet even been conceived. Genetic technology will widen the reach of our great-grandchildren, enabling them to put together altered kinds of organisms that will be productive indefinitely under the conditions in which they are grown.

For better or for worse, we find ourselves charged with responsibility for a gigantic, dispersed Noah's ark; what we do next will determine what can be saved. This challenge is equivalent to having been given a few years, in the middle of the age of the dinosaurs, 100 million years ago, during which we could devise ways to save for future generations some of the organisms that existed for our use, our enjoyment, our pleasure, or simply because we did not want to watch them being lost forever.

Several million species, each the product of billions of years of evolution, could be lost forever during our lifetimes. We simply must offer the commitment necessary to reverse the current trend of destruction as soon as possible. Whether we like it or not, it is all up to us.

DAVID SHEPHERD

THE WELCOME STORM

Elephants are the most gentle and benevolent of creatures; it is only man that is the dangerous, arrogant, and greedy animal. All of us who share this world have to live in harmony with nature, not in conflict with her. We ignore this at our peril.

David Shepherd OBE FRSA is a British painter.

SURVIVAL IN THE FOREST
The mountain gorilla is found mostly in the high rainforests of Rwanda and Burundi, the two most densely populated countries in Africa (350 people per square mile, or 135 people per square kilometer). The combination of habitat loss and hunting for trophies has reduced the gorilla population to a dangerously low level. Its survival owes much to Rwanda's Mountain Gorilla Project, which is a beacon of hope in such a politically volatile and densely populated country.

A WEALTH OF SPECIES

GHILLEAN PRANCE

The 250,000 species of flowering plants in the world provide us with a wealth of flowers, fruits, and vegetables. These plants affect every part of our lives. Yet while groups such as the Chácobo Indians, living in the species-diverse forests of Amazonian Bolivia, have a use for the majority of the plants that grow around them in the rainforest, only a small percentage of the world's flora is utilized by the industrialized societies. Never before has it been so vital to conserve our plant species and the genetic diversity that they represent.

OF FLOWERS, BIRDS, AND BEES

The variety of flowers that we enjoy today exists because of the methods that plants have evolved to enable the transfer of pollen from one plant to another. For example, the familiar catkins of an oak or a hazel tree are flowers which dangle on a delicate stem in order to be blown about by the wind. This shaking action releases the pollen, some of which is transported by the wind to other flowers. Birds are attracted by red and orange, so many tropical flowers are red or orange to attract hummingbirds, honey creepers, and other birds, which will transfer the pollen between plants.

Brazil nut trees cannot be grown in plantations, because the pollination of the trees is carried out only by the carpenter bee, which needs the mixed environment of a rainforest in order to thrive.

A familiar example of a bird-pollinated flower is the red-flowered *Hibiscus rosa-sinensis*. These bird flowers produce large quantities of nectar to feed their pollinators, but they are not scented since birds have a poor sense of smell. In contrast, bee-pollinated flowers, such as clover, often have a sweet scent, and fly-pollinated flowers, such as birthwort and the calico flower, smell of rotting meat.

A PROFUSION OF POLLEN (opposite) *Delicate rye grass flowers shed pollen, which is then blown away by the wind. Its evolutionary success can be the bane of hay fever sufferers.*

VISUAL DECEPTION (left) *The bee orchid (Ophrys speculum) has so realistically mimicked the outline of a bee, the insect on which it depends for pollination, that bees will try to mate with it. This ensures the successful transfer of pollen from the flower to the bee, and thus the survival of the plant.*

SCENT DECEPTION (above) *This veined Brazilian calico flower (Aristolochia) looks spectacular, but it actually smells of rotting meat – and for a good reason. The plant's pollination is carried out by different species of fly, which are attracted to the flower by the prospect of a juicy meal.*

HARD CASE (below) *The familiar Brazil nuts grow inside a fruit about the size of a tennis ball. The outer surface of this fruit is very tough, and does not break when the fruit falls from the tree.*

STRANGE SYMBIOSIS (right) *Seeds of the Galapagos tomato must pass through the gut of a giant Galapagos tortoise in order to germinate. This process may take several days, a timespan that makes even this slow-moving creature an effective dispersal agent.*

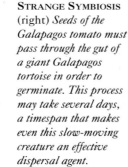

ESSENTIAL PARTNER (right) *Large, sharp-toothed rodents called agoutis can open the hard fruit encasing Brazil nuts, and bury hoards of the nuts.*

Moth-pollinated flowers open at night, are usually white, and possess copious nectar to satisfy the energy demands of their pollinators. In moth flowers, such as jasmine or gardenia, the nectar is often located at the bottom of a tube, out of reach of many insects. Moths, however, have long tongues that can extend to the end of the tube. Many cacti are night-blooming, such as the Amazon moonflower, which flowers only one night a year and yet is also visited by pollinator moths.

Early man began to discover the diversity of flowers, and used them to adorn the body. It is still possible today to find Amazonian Indians with flowers in their pierced ears or in their hair, and the traditional flower garlands or *leis* of Hawaii represent an ancient custom. More recently, people have experimented with flower species to produce countless new varieties.

SOWING THE SEEDS

Since plants are static organisms, they depend upon outside forces to transport their seeds from place to place. It is this need for fruit dispersal that has forced fruits to evolve with as much diversity

TIME BOMB: SPECIES LOSS

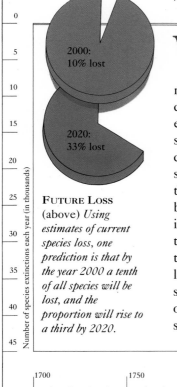

FUTURE LOSS (above) *Using estimates of current species loss, one prediction is that by the year 2000 a tenth of all species will be lost, and the proportion will rise to a third by 2020.*

2000: 10% lost

2020: 33% lost

Number of species extinctions each year (in thousands)

We still don't know exactly how many species there are on Earth, but the best estimate is around 30 million, 1.4 million of which have been officially recorded. If current patterns of deforestation and habitat loss continue, we shall soon be wiping out species faster than we can record their existence. Most at risk are species in the tropical rainforests, not only the more easily identifiable mammals and birds, but also many thousands of plants and insects. Loss of species here is about 1,000 to 10,000 times that before human intervention. There is no precedent for such major loss of genetic diversity, which may leave only half of all tropical species by 2050.

DEATH TOLL (right) *The rate of species loss has accelerated since 1950. Losses have a cumulative effect – the extinction of one plant species can cause 30 extinctions of other dependent organisms.*

ISLAND TRAP (left) *Island species have nowhere to go if their habitat is threatened. The flightless takahe (Notornis mantelli) is one of the endangered large birds on South Island, New Zealand.*

1700   1750   1800   1850   1950

as flowers have developed to attract their various pollinators. Sycamore and maple trees, for example, have their seeds wrapped in a propeller-like fruit that gyrates away from the parent tree as it is carried in the wind. Many members of the daisy family have light seeds with a parachute of hairs, which enables them to travel with the wind to even the most remote parts of the globe.

With seeds taken from the feathers of a single bird, Charles Darwin was able to grow 82 plants.

It is the seeds that have adapted to dispersal by animals that we generally recognize as fruits. These are usually fleshy and appetizing so that an animal will eat them. In the case of the wild strawberry, the tiny seeds can pass through a bird's gut and then be excreted some distance from where they began their journey. In winter, squirrels bury acorns in hoards, and the nuts that are forgotten by the squirrel are the ones that will go on to form the next generation of oak trees.

THE FIGHT AGAINST LEPROSY
Until recently, scientists knew of no species that contracted leprosy other than humans. This made it very hard to develop an anti-leprosy vaccine. Then it was discovered that the armadillo is a suitable "incubator" for the bacilli that cause the disease; after injection with diseased cells, tissues from its spleen and liver are now used in production of an anti-leprosy vaccine. While this is crucially important for leprosy sufferers, it raises difficult questions about how we measure the "value" of other species. Is the armadillo only considered to be of value because it is of use to us?

ROBERT MAY

❝ *It is remarkable that Linnaeus's pioneering codification of biotic diversity came a century after Newton, in the mid-18th century. This legacy lingers: today's catalogues of stars and galaxies are effectively more complete, and vastly better funded, than catalogues of the Earth's biota.*

I believe we need to understand the diversity of living things for the same reasons that compel us to reach out toward understanding the universe, or the elementary particles that it is built from. Unlike these other quests, understanding and conserving biological diversity is a task with a time limit. Future generations will, I believe, find it incomprehensible that Linnaeus still lags so far behind Newton, and that we continue to devote so little money and effort to understanding and conserving the other forms of life with which we share this planet. ❞

Robert May is a Royal Society Research Professor at the Universities of London and Oxford, England.

THOMAS LOVEJOY

❝ *Recently a friend asked me 'Is there really any reason to be concerned about the extinction of species?' I was sure he would appreciate the argument about species as the ultimate library for the development of the life sciences. But he cut me short, saying that was the same as wanting to keep the imperfect editions of Shakespeare, the ones with printers' errors. Not until then had I appreciated how widespread environmental illiteracy really is.*

It has been calculated that the information in one chromosome of a mouse is equivalent to all the editions of the Encyclopaedia Britannica *combined. From that perspective, current extinction rates are approaching the greatest act of folly in human history. Something is awry if people feel that it is all but sacrilegious to ask whether 104 Haydn symphonies may be too many, while being able to wonder 'if we really need all those species?'* ❞

Thomas E. Lovejoy is the Assistant Secretary for External Affairs of the Smithsonian Institution in Washington, D.C.

CINDY DE WIT

We live in a world where we know very little about the thousands of chemicals that we release into the environment. Personally, I also fear another type of pollution, which may be more insidious than anything invented in a chemicals laboratory – genetically engineered organisms (GEOs) released deliberately into the environment. GEOs are living organisms; they can reproduce and may spread uncontrolled. If they run amok, they cannot be recalled. At least chemicals that are discovered to be environmental toxins can be banned and withdrawn from sale.
We are being given the same types of assurances about the safety of GEOs as we once were given for chemicals. But we still know so very little about the complex webs that form ecosystems, and about the organisms that inhabit them, and cannot predict how GEOs will interact or function once they are released. My personal hope for the Earth's future is a new science that puts the environment first, and profits last.

Cindy de Wit

Cindy de Wit is a scientist working for the Swedish Environmental Protection Agency.

AMAZING SLIME
The rainforest is home to many different species of slime mold, a single-celled creature which continues to mystify scientists. In order to propagate itself, literally millions of individual creatures can merge at one point, making a small but visible column which then explodes out over a wider area. It remains unclear how such primitive creatures are able to "communicate" in order to achieve such a sophisticated dispersal system.

We have such a great variety of fruits and nuts in the world because of the variety of ways in which plants have adapted for fruit dispersal. The interactions of these plants with birds, bats, monkeys, and even fish are the reason for the cornucopia of fruit that we enjoy. As with flowers, fruit breeders have taken the basic model of the wild species and produced from it a plethora of new and better varieties of apples, oranges, bananas, pears, plums, and all the other fruits that are now cultivated.

SURVIVAL TACTICS

The plants of colder climates become dormant for the winter, so many species store nutrients in their roots or in other underground organs to survive the winter in a dormant state. These usually contain a good supply of carbohydrates in the form of starch, to boost growth the next spring. These underground storage organs form many of our vegetables: carrots, beets, parsnips, potatoes, and turnips, to name only a few. Underground storage organs also occur in various tropical plants such as sweet potatoes, yams, taro, and cassava; all have become staple crops somewhere in the world.

Beans, cucumbers, and tomatoes are examples of vegetables that are derived from fruits, greatly modified by plant breeders to form the now familiar varieties. The leaves of many species are also used as vegetables. In many of these cases the original wild species has been greatly modified to make it more palatable. Wild lettuce is full of a bitter white sap to protect it from predation by leaf eaters, so breeders have gradually removed this bitter compound to make lettuce more appetizing. Cabbage, cauliflower, broccoli, kohlrabi, and Brussels sprouts are all derived from a single wild species of *Brassica*. In the case of the cabbage, breeders have selected for large leaf clusters; for the cauliflower, large clusters of flower buds; and for sprouts, clusters of leaf buds. This illustrates the degree of change that we have brought about to transform a wild species into a crop.

PRESERVING DIVERSITY

The flowers we grow in our gardens and the fruit and vegetables that we eat were all originally derived from wild species. The process of breeding new cultivated varieties selected for a useful characteristic has often weakened the stock and made them susceptible to disease or attack by predators. Therefore, the wild relatives of the species we use are crucial genetic material for the long-term survival of our crops. From time to time, we need new genetic material from wild species for disease resistance and improvement of the crop. The annual profits of the tomato industry have increased hugely because of the recent discovery of a gene for sweetness in a wild species from Peru; maize is resistant to disease because of genetic material obtained from wild species from Mexico. Most of the crops that we use in the northern temperate regions are actually of tropical origin. Without that genetic diversity, life in the developed world would be very different.

Plants depend on a wide variety of animals for the pollination of their flowers and the dispersal of their seeds. Animals in turn depend on the plants for their sustenance. Therefore, the conservation of animals and plants go hand in hand.

In addition to these wild relatives of the crops we have already discovered, many other as yet unexploited plant resources occur in the wild. It is estimated that about 20,000 plants have edible parts, yet only 3,000 have so far been used widely by people. Our future crops are out there in the remaining rainforest, savanna, tundra, temperate forests, ponds, bogs, marshes, and other wilderness habitats of the world. If we want to discover new plant products in future, we must therefore protect these natural habitats.

The serendipity berry, found in West Africa, is 3,000 times sweeter than sugar, yet has a lower calorie content.

Biologists and conservationists are trying to ensure that their endeavors to study and utilize tropical biodiversity yield a proper return to the countries of origin. For example, contracts with pharmaceutical companies at the New York Botanical Garden and the Royal Botanic Gardens at Kew in London are only signed if there is a royalty agreement to benefit the country of origin should a new cure be found from the plants under study. It is essential either to share germ plasm and research results freely, or to ensure that the vast economic potential of the world's biodiversity is shared with the countries that most need it.

ON THE GREEN FRONT
ROYAL BOTANIC GARDENS

Every year, over 1 million people visit the Royal Botanic Gardens at Kew, London. They have one of the most important collections of seeds in the world, and are at the forefront of plant research.

There is a tendency to see such research as being somehow less "urgent" than environmental campaigning. But staff in many of the world's leading botanical gardens were involved in conservation and environmental issues long before they became fashionable: research at Kew began over 200 years ago. Today botanists advise governments on endangered species, and are searching for alternative crops as sources of food, fuel, and medicine. They are also now pioneering collaborative projects with tropical botanical gardens in several Third World countries.

The Prince of Wales praised this work in a lecture in 1990, saying: "The Royal Botanic Gardens at Kew have done much to point out the

RESCUE WORK
Kew scientists painstakingly raise rare orchids in sterile conditions.

astonishing diversity within the tropical forest. The evolutionary idiocy of eliminating that diversity, and replacing it with short-lived monocultures of cash crops or grassland, exemplifies the arrogance of the West in its dealings with the natural world. But how encouraging it is that botanists and biologists are now in the forefront of efforts to promote sustainable alternatives."

PREDICTING EVOLUTION
This beautiful orchid (Angraecum sesquipedale) is found only in Madagascar, and was initially discovered by Charles Darwin. Having measured the length of the flower's nectar spur at exactly 45 centimeters (nearly 18 inches), he predicted that one day a moth would be discovered with a tongue of the same length. Some 50 years later, he was proved right, and the new moth species was duly named Praedicta.

MOUNTAINS
LOSING THE HIGH GROUND

DAVID PITT AND DENIS LANDENBERGUE

ALPINE FLOWERS

There are very few mountain ranges high enough or remote enough to have escaped the bruising touch of man, and many now face a serious ecological crisis.

Most of the world takes its mountain ranges for granted. These rocks of ages and pure white snows seem remote from everyday life, apparently unaffected by the mess that modern industry and agriculture have made down on the plains. But appearances can be deceptive.

About 40 percent of the world's surface is mountainous, and one-tenth of the global population lives in these regions. Most of the rest of the world's population, those who live on the plains, depend on the mountains for water, energy, recreation, and inspiration. The mosaic of micro-habitats found in valleys and at different altitudes contain a bewildering array of rare fauna and flora. No less unique are the cultural variations brought about by people living in such remote and isolated places. Many of the world's 300 million tribal and indigenous people live in the mountains, often beyond the reach of powerful empires and the mass media.

The actual function of mountains in the planetary ecosystem, though only recently recognized, is highly significant. They are the key element in the cryosphere, the snowy regions of the Earth that reflect heat back into space; this "albedo effect" helps to regulate global

David Pitt MLitt DPhil is the secretary of Alp Action and a member of the Inter-Governmental Panel on Climate Change. A New Zealander resident in Switzerland, he has written or edited more than 20 books on development, health, the environment, and peace.

Denis Landenbergue has led many local conservation and ecosystems revitalization projects, in particular the Verbois biological reserve near Geneva. After gaining a degree at the Graduate Institute of International Studies of Geneva, he now works as projects manager of Alp Action.

warming. Sea levels depend on the melting of glacial ice, most of which is locked up in the most mountainous of all continents, Antarctica. The majority of the world's forests, so vital as absorbers of greenhouse gases in the atmosphere, are also in mountain regions. Mountains are a critical part of the world's hydrological system as well, acting as massive water-towers, gradually releasing water into the rivers which in turn provide the water we need for energy, sanitation, industry, and domestic uses.

Many of the world's great mountain ranges are severely threatened at the moment. In the industrialized countries, more than half the forests are dying prematurely from pollution and desiccation. In the Himalayas and the Andes, there is severe deforestation as a result of logging and population pressure. As has been vividly demonstrated on our television screens, the Ethiopian Highlands have been reduced to desert. Erosion and downstream flooding are just two of the consequences of such deforestation, and may assume catastrophic proportions as happened recently in Bangladesh when most of the country was underwater.

Climate change from the greenhouse effect is now creating additional pressures. For example, there are increasingly frequent monsoonal downpours which probably no forest could contain. Global warming may be the reason for the cracking of the West Antarctic ice sheet, which some experts say

MOUNTAIN
KIDNEY VETCH

SACRED PEAK (opposite) *Mount Fuji is revered as one of Japan's holiest places. Yet the mountain is often shrouded in smog.*

PRECARIOUS FOOTING (inset, above) *Rocky Mountain goats make their way across a ridge high on Mount Evans in Colorado.*

FREEMAN PATTERSON

ANDEAN DAWN

“ *I took this photograph one January morning as the sun rose over the Paine massif in Torres del Paine National Park in southern Chile. The Andes Mountains frequently generate their own weather systems and cloud formations, which in turn influence the whole spectrum of life in the region.* ”

Freeman Patterson

Freeman Patterson has won a gold
medal for photography from the National Film Board of Canada, and
in 1985 was awarded the Order of Canada.

may eventually raise sea levels. The melting of the permafrost in the Arctic will release huge amounts of methane (a greenhouse gas) into an already overloaded atmosphere, and will create conditions favoring avalanches and slides of mud and debris. Mountain lakes, formed naturally many thousands of years ago, may become unplugged, placing more pressure on hydro dams. In a number of regions, dams also face the constant threat of damage from earthquakes. A massive release of water could flood the plains and drown cities in a tidal wave.

ENDEMIC PROBLEMS

Poverty is a major problem in mountainous regions. Oppressive forms of land tenure, debt, high interest rates, inflation, chronic unemployment, restricted opportunities for cash earning, bad health, and poor education facilities: a combination of these has meant that countries like Nepal, Bhutan, Lesotho, and Ethiopia are listed by the United Nations as among the least developed in the world. Their infant mortality and illiteracy rates are much higher, and life expectancy much lower than average, even for a developing country. Nor are such conditions entirely confined to the Third World. In the Swiss Alps, there are still farming families without electricity, water and sanitation who live off the smell of a cheesecloth.

Poverty is accentuated by the frequency of war and political disturbances. Mountains are often frontier regions, or places that historically have provided refuges for dissidents. Since there are also many natural disasters, there are constant incursions of aid agencies, whose invading armies can often be highly disruptive.

VANISHING SKILLS

Population pressure in mountainous regions may not be as significant as is usually assumed. In fact, many areas suffer from depopulation when the able-bodied have migrated to the towns, leaving nobody to repair the terraces that hold back the erosion. The decline of many traditional communities has meant that old ways of living in harmony with nature are forgotten.

The most damaging kind of population pressure probably comes from tourism itself, which pours concrete over mountain meadows, cuts down trees for ski slopes and parking lots, and leaves only litter and a prostituted local culture. The tourist blight is now affecting even the remotest areas of the Himalayas and Andes, and the fact that many communities in these regions have few alternative sources of income poses a fearsome dilemma.

Not all is gloom and doom, however. A softer tourism is emerging, led by those who simply want to wander in the hills, enjoying the benefits such regions can bring to the human psyche. In ancient times, and for traditional peoples, mountains were held to be sacred. In many parts of the world, pilgrimage routes to mountain shrines, temples, and monasteries are being rediscovered.

CHANGING ATTITUDES

There are now many efforts being made to save the mountains, such as the famous Chipko Movement, where Himalayan women hugged the trees to prevent their exploitation. Agencies, too, are assisting at all levels. Environmental and development groups are cooperating to put the mountain case to the 1992 United Nations Conference on Environment and Development. The World Conservation Union is preparing a special mountain conservation strategy to preserve biodiversity, and the UN is coordinating programs of research, action, and education. Alpinists, community organizations, even tourists are organizing, with protected areas and mountain centers appearing around the globe. No longer does the flat Earth mentality of the plains people dominate. Let us hope that all this is neither too little nor too late.

MIRIAM ROTHSCHILD

66 *When I was 17 my mother took me to Italy to improve my mind and learn something about Italian painting. I was furious: I wanted to spend my vacation at home playing in tennis tournaments.*
We traveled by train and I was given the luxury of a sleeper.
I awoke in the early morning when the train stopped with a long sibilant sigh at the Italian frontier. The sunlight was seeping around the edges of the drawn blind, illuminating the dust particles which filled the air, and I leaned across my bunk and pulled it aside.
For the first time I saw snow-covered mountains against a clear blue sky. I was completely overwhelmed by their unearthly beauty. It was like a vision or a religious revelation, and remained with me all my life.
I let down the window and leaned out, discovering that mountain air involves a special experience of clarity and timelessness. Since then I have spent 30 winters at high altitude in the Alps. From my window, I could watch the first rays of the rising sun gild the saddle between two snow-covered peaks or the shadows in the glacier turn green when a warm wind threatened. High up the valley before it grew light you could hear the chimes of the snowfinches' dawn chorus.
I tinker with Byron's poem:

Art, Glory, Freedom fail,
But Mountains still are fair.

During the Second World War I did not sigh for petrol coupons or chocolate or sugar or a new dress – what I dreamed of was mountain air and the way sound travels across the valley. **99**

Miriam Rothschild is a British zoologist, a Fellow of the Royal Society, and one of the world's leading authorities on fleas.

RETAINING THE EARTH (right)
Millions of people around the world depend on complex systems of terracing for their food and livelihood. These terraced fields near San'a in the Yemen have been maintained in more or less the same way for the last 2,000 years.

THE WORK OF GENERATIONS DESTROYED (left)
These eroded slopes on Pemagatsel in Bhutan are a telling reminder of the fragility of cultivated terraces in mountains and hills. Many of the local population have been drawn to the towns in search of work, leaving too few able-bodied people to undertake essential maintenance and repair.

THE PLIGHT OF THE ALPS

Located in the heart of the European continent, the Alps are a link between regions and cultures extending over seven countries: France, Switzerland, Italy, Germany, Liechtenstein, Austria, and Yugoslavia. Long considered an oasis of wild nature and unspoiled landscapes in the center of industrial Europe, the forests and pastures of the Alps today still harbor an exceptional range of wild plants. Some 3,500 species have been identified in the French Alps alone, and nearly a third of the flora of the Alpine chain is endemic.

A varied fauna also survives, including such rarities as the golden eagle, the marmot, the Apollo butterfly, and the alpine salamander. The ibex, brought close to extinction by hunting in the 19th century, has since been reintroduced in many of its ancestral domains. Other species, including the bearded vulture, the otter, the lynx, the brown bear, and the wolf, have more or less vanished. Although young bearded vultures, born in captivity, now soar free over Alpine cliffs and valleys, the release program will not be counted a success until adult pairs breed freely once again.

Losing Stability

Overall, the Alpine ecosystem is under great threat. The forests have suffered widespread damage from air pollution, and are often decimated by acid rain. Their conservation is a vital priority. Apart from providing habitats for numerous animals and plants, forests protect human settlements against avalanches, rock falls, and landslides, and stabilize the banks of rivers.

Large dams have modified the hydrology of many valleys, altering landscapes and destroying the ecological balance of rivers and wetlands, both in the Alps and beyond. To restore this balance, a principle of minimum residual flow on dammed rivers should be legally established. Water pollution must also be controlled. In many Alpine rivers, fish are too contaminated for safe consumption. Last but not least, wide-scale climate change could have catastrophic consequences for the Alps' vital function as the "water-tower of Europe."

An integrated approach to all aspects of the Alpine ecosystem is under way. Several governments, in particular the Swiss, have promoted strong legislation to control the emission of pollutants and greenhouse gases, and the Alpine Convention project should lead to cross-border agreements on pollution control. In 1992, the UN Conference on Environment and Development will undoubtedly benefit from consideration of the "Alpine model" in its debates, and may find in it a prototype for the protection of other mountainous areas of the Earth.

FATAL SHROUD (opposite) *A sea of smog from northern Italy and other industrial centers creeps across the Alps.*

MATTERHORN DAWN (inset, above) *Scenes like this have inspired generations of Alpine climbers and visitors.*

RELIC OF THE ICE AGE (left) *Cotton grass is precious, being one of the typically "arctic" plants that clung on in the Alps, after the retreat of the ice that once covered most of Europe.*

BACK IN THE HUNT *The lynx* (below) *has been reintroduced in parts of Switzerland and Slovenia. Wilder, more remote areas of the Alps may also be selected for the eventual return of the brown bear and the wolf.*

ISOLATED POPULATIONS (left) *The ptarmigan,* Lagopus mutus, *is a bird of the Arctic tundra. Since the last Ice Age, it has survived in Europe, living above the tree line, in high mountains like the Alps.*

ON THE GREEN FRONT
ALP ACTION

The gravity of the Alps' problems has fortunately led to new and unexpected alliances. For example, in 1990, the Bellerive Foundation, under the presidency of Prince Sadruddin Aga Khan, established Alp Action, an alliance of environmentalists, scientists, industrialists, and businessmen.

Though there has been much hand-wringing about the environmental problems of the Alps, with many conservation organizations doing valuable work on specific problems, such as acid rain or the pressure of tourism, their lack of coordination has seriously hampered progress. The main thrust of Alp Action is to raise the necessary funds (largely from business) to support and coordinate practical grass-roots projects of this kind.

Alp Action has demonstrated what can be done on a relatively small budget: preserving unique habitats and endangered animal and plant species, reforestation, revitalizing rivers and alluvial zones, reviving traditional agriculture, and promoting soft tourism. The organization backs up its practical achievements with education initiatives and press awards designed to build up public awareness.

ANTARCTICA: WORLD PARK OR WASTELAND?

The continent of Antarctica accounts for 10 percent of the Earth's land surface, most of it covered with a massive icecap, in places almost 3 miles (5 kilometers) deep. Were this ice mass ever to melt completely, it would raise the levels of the world's oceans by more than 160 feet (50 meters).

As yet, Antarctica remains largely unspoiled, but if some of the world's most powerful industrial nations have their way, it will not remain so for much longer.

The seas around this frozen continent make it one of the most important biological reserves on Earth. Vast quantities of shrimp-like crustaceans called krill are the key element in a food chain that embraces whales, dolphins, seals, penguins, and many other bird species. There are now grave fears that the planned commercial harvesting of krill could entirely disrupt the complex relationships between these magnificent creatures.

Polarized Opinion

The continent itself has been protected by the Antarctic Treaty, which came into force in 1961. The Treaty guarantees freedom of access for all parties involved. There are now 39 signatories, many of which maintain permanent scientific establishments in Antarctica. Despite constant bickering, the Treaty has produced many specific agreements. But it is now under serious threat. The 1990 review of its operations revealed two schools of thought: one demanding that Antarctica be designated a World Park, totally protected from commercial exploitation, with strict controls over tourism and scientific research; the other, advocated by such countries as Great Britain and Japan, insisting that there should be no outright, irrevocable ban on mining or other economic development.

By the end of 1991, the issue should be resolved. Meanwhile, environmentalists will continue to campaign for a World Park. The Antarctic has become a symbol of our readiness to learn from past mistakes and to reassess our relationship with the living Earth.

THE ICE AND ITS EMPERORS
Each summer, gleaming new icebergs (above, right) break off from the ice sheet. During the long Antarctic winter, emperor penguins (right) are the only birds that remain ashore.

KNOWING OUR PLACE
As the moon rises over the Antarctic Peninsula, our tiny human presence is still dwarfed by the continent's elemental powers (opposite page). Nevertheless, research stations, like this British base at Signy on South Orkney (near right), must take care not to scar the virgin wilderness. Old building materials, empty oil drums, and food waste should be shipped out rather than left to accumulate on the land.

III

AIR

When we look into the sky it seems to us to be endless. . . . We think without consideration about the
boundless ocean of air, and then you sit aboard a spacecraft, you tear away from Earth, and within
ten minutes you have been carried straight through the layer of air, and beyond there is nothing!
Beyond the air there is only emptiness, coldness, darkness. The "boundless" blue sky, the ocean which
gives us breath and protects us from the endless black and death, is but an infinitesimally thin film.
How dangerous it is to threaten even the smallest part of this gossamer covering, this conserver of life.

Soviet space explorer Vladimir Shatalov, quoted in **The Home Planet** *edited by* KEVIN W. KELLEY

O ver the centuries, humankind has shown a marked disregard for the fragile atmosphere that makes life on this planet viable. Prior to the industrial revolution, such disregard was not unreasonable. Apart from the occasional irritation of woodsmoke in poorly ventilated buildings, people could take the air they breathed for granted. When the mills of the industrial revolution filled people's lungs with life-threatening

SPARKLING VIOLET-EARED HUMMINGBIRD

pestilence, air pollution was considered an acceptable price to pay for progress. Only in the 1940's and 1950's, when London's pea-souper smogs started to kill thousands of people, was any action taken.

Even then, the upper reaches of the atmosphere were still thought to be largely beyond the polluting influence of humankind. The occasional early warnings from scientists who could see that everything pumped out down here must end up somewhere up there were treated with utter contempt. As long ago as 1896, the Swedish scientist Svente Arrhenius had

SIGNS AND PORTENTS IN THE HEAVENS (opposite) *The ancients could look up and see a message of hope in the rainbow; modern man must read the skies for evidence of his folly.*

CALIFORNIA SUNSET (above) *Despite the strictest controls on vehicle emissions anywhere in the world, the streets of Los Angeles offer little hope of a cleaner, brighter future for our cities.*

expressed concern about the emission of large quantities of carbon dioxide into the atmosphere. The views of Sherwood Rowland and Mario Molina, the American researchers who, in the early 1970's, realized that the release of large quantities of CFC's and other chlorine-based chemicals would inevitably damage the ozone in the upper atmosphere, were dismissed as "bad science" or, even worse, "emotion."

AIR POLLUTION: OUR INDUSTRIAL CIVILIZATION REFLECTED IN A 19TH-CENTURY FRENCH PAINTING

For a brief, manic period, many eminent scientists even advised politicians that it was acceptable to fill the atmosphere with radioactive particles released in the testing of nuclear weapons. Between the first atmospheric tests of American nuclear weapons in the 1940's and 1950's, and the Test Ban Treaty in 1963 that eventually outlawed such tests, Britain, France, China, the Soviet Union, and the United States exploded dozens of devices in the atmosphere, guaranteeing the eventual fallout of detectable levels of radiation on to every patch of land and sea on Earth.

AIR POLLUTION: CONIFERS ATTACKED BY ACID RAIN – CAUSED BY THE BURNING OF FOSSIL FUELS – IN NORTH CAROLINA

PERHAPS ONLY HERE IN ANTARCTICA CAN TRULY CLEAN AIR NOW BE FOUND

Many people still find it hard to accept that on at least three counts, we have so comprehensively disrupted the natural balance of the atmosphere as to cause a profound threat to our future well-being: through the release of chemicals that contribute to the acidification of forests, lakes, and rivers; through the release of a variety of ozone-depleting substances, including CFC's and halons; and through the release of vast quantities of carbon dioxide from the use of fossil fuels and the burning of the rainforests.

AIR POLLUTION: RUSH-HOUR TRAFFIC FORMS A CHOKING HAZE ABOVE THE NEW YORK SKYLINE

It should be easy for all of us to be wise after these events. Sadly, we refuse to accept the end of an era that began more than 250 years ago as we first learned to draw on our fossil fuel reserves. With unrestrained enthusiasm, we have converted these natural deposits into man-made currencies, disregarding the full environmental costs of what we've been doing.

Politicians are only too happy to seize upon any residual uncertainty to excuse their own inaction. There are even a few scientists who still refute the overwhelming scientific consensus of the inevitability of a gradual warming of the atmosphere over the next century, and advise governments that they shouldn't be doing anything in anticipation of such a climate change, but should simply be prepared to adapt to it as and when it happens. There are even a few doubters still to be found on the issue of ozone depletion, despite the fact that the Montreal Protocol (signed in 1986 and renegotiated in June 1990) will ensure the phase-out of the vast majority of ozone-depleting chemicals by the year 2000.

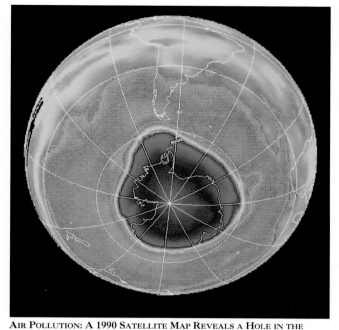

AIR POLLUTION: A 1990 SATELLITE MAP REVEALS A HOLE IN THE OZONE LAYER (PINK AND VIOLET AREAS), DUE TO DAMAGE BY CFC'S

The Montreal Protocol represents the most hopeful development in this whole area. It was a real triumph on the part of the UN Environment Program to bring about such an agreement; though the timetable is far slower than that sought by environmental organizations, the scope of the agreement and the fact that 30 countries are participating is highly significant.

GLOBAL WARMING: GROWING HERDS OF CATTLE ARE RELEASING MORE AND MORE METHANE – A GREENHOUSE GAS

Perhaps of greatest importance is the reluctant acknowledgement by the industrialized nations that they must help put up the cash to compensate Third World countries for having to forego the use (and financial benefits) of CFC's, which all the rest of us have already enjoyed. Since, through our use of CFC's, it is our countries that have caused most of the damage to the ozone layer, and it is our citizens that worry most about the threat to human health through ozone depletion, it is only right that we should fund Third World efforts to help protect that part of the global commons.

The atmosphere recognizes no boundaries, and can be protected only by international measures. Those countries that have caused or are causing the damage to the atmosphere should bear the brunt of implementing the measures now necessary to protect it.

GLOBAL WARMING: FLOODS, LIKE BANGLADESH'S 1988 DISASTER, COULD OCCUR MORE FREQUENTLY

VACLAV HAVEL

*As a boy, I lived for some time in the country
and I clearly remember an experience from those days:
I used to walk to school in a nearby village along a cart track
through the fields and, on the way, see on the horizon a huge smokestack
of some hurriedly built factory, in all likelihood in the service of war.
It spewed dense brown smoke and scattered it across the sky. Each time I
saw it, I had an intense sense of something profoundly wrong, of humans
soiling the heavens. I have no idea whether there was something like a
science of ecology in those days; if there was, I certainly knew nothing
of it. Still that 'soiling the heavens' offended me spontaneously.
It seemed to me that, in it, humans are guilty of something, that they
destroy something important, arbitrarily disrupting the natural order of
things, and that such things cannot go unpunished.
To be sure, my revulsion was largely aesthetic;
I knew nothing then of the noxious emissions which would one day
devastate our forests, exterminate game, and endanger
the health of people.*

Playwright Václav Havel is the President of Czechoslovakia.

R.S. THOMAS

*Cymru
(Wales)*

Whose beauty was responsible
for your prostitution. Mournful lady
weeping in your waterfalls and streams,
birch-brown hair on the wind,
body lissom as the young ash,
in your morning or evening
dance casting your veils of mist
to reveal the boniness of your structure.
You have put on industry
like a shroud; made your face up
with oil and coal-dust; announced
to the flourishers of checkbooks
you have your price. Forgive us
our failure to teach you the meaning
of true love, our readiness to watch
you soliciting, not for us to have
bread to eat, but for burying
under the excrement of factories
the clover that sprang where your foot fell.

R. S. Thomas is a Welsh poet.

WILLIAM REILLY

*To secure our environmental legacy for future generations,
we must find ways to reconcile humanity more satisfactorily with the
natural systems upon which all human life and civilization depend.
We must recognize that the natural systems of which we are a part have
an intrinsic worth transcending narrow utilitarian values.
They must be respected for their own sake.
No philosopher or religious thinker has been more sensitive
to this intimate relationship between humanity and nature than
St. Francis of Assisi. The powerful contemporary environmental
tradition of preservation, of reverence for wilderness and protection for
all living things – the ideal that sees, as John Muir said, 'in God's
wildness . . . the hope of the world' – virtually began with St. Francis.
My own religious and environmental thinking has been profoundly
inspired by the eloquent expression of love and respect for God's
Creation of St. Francis's life and work.*

William K. Reilly is the Administrator of the US Environmental
Protection Agency.

JEREMY RIFKIN

*The term 'biosphere' was coined
at the turn of the 20th century. It refers to the thin
chemical envelope extending from the ocean depths to
the stratosphere, that sustains life on the planet. A
'new way of thinking,' rooted in the politics of the
biosphere, is beginning to take shape, offering hope for
the first generation of the 21st century.
The new politics envisions the Earth as a living
organism and the human species as a partner and
participant, dependent on the proper functioning of
the biosphere and at the same time responsible for its well-being.
The transition into a biospheric culture will spell
the end of the nation state as the dominant political institution,
and the end of the multi-national corporation as the primary
economic institution. The biospheric era will spawn political and
economic arrangements more in keeping with our new ecological
understanding of the Earth as a living organism.*

Jeremy Rifkin is the Founder and President of two organizations
based in Washington, D.C.: the Foundation on Economic Trends and the
Greenhouse Crisis Foundation.

SURVIVING IN POLLUTED AIR

DON BINNEY

HAUTURU RATA

“ *Created in 1979 to convey the idea of sanctuary, this image shows the flowering rata vine on the sanctuary island of Hauturu. The birds, from top, are the kakariki or yellow-crowned parakeet* (Cynormaphus auriceps), *the popokatea or whitehead* (Mohua albicilla), *and the very rare but now increasing hihi or stitchbird* (Notiomystis cincta). ”

Don Binney is an artist working in Auckland, New Zealand.

TED TURNER

“ *I love and respect planet Earth and all living things thereon, especially my fellow species, mankind. I promise to treat all persons, everywhere, with dignity, respect, and friendliness. I promise I will add no more than two children to the Earth. I promise to use my best efforts to help save what is left of our natural world in its untouched state, and to restore areas where practical. I pledge to use as little non-renewable resources and as little toxic chemicals, pesticides, and other poisons as possible, and to work for their reduction by others. I promise to contribute to those less fortunate than myself, to help them to become self-sufficient and to enjoy the benefits of a decent life, including clean air and water, adequate food and health care, housing, education, and individual rights. I resent the use of force, in particular military force, and back United Nations arbitration of international disputes. I support the total elimination of all nuclear, chemical, and biological weapons, and the elimination of all weapons of mass destruction. I support the United Nation and its efforts to improve the conditions of the planet.* ”

Ted Turner is the Chairman of the Turner Broadcasting System, Inc., the parent company of Cable News Network.

PETER USTINOV

“ *It was in Osaka, Japan. I had just finished an address on the subject of refugees to a symposium. I prepared to listen to the next orator, a Japanese professor of natural sciences, holder of the Nobel Prize. He spoke with a considerable sense of self-effacement and hesitation. The English translation was as peculiar and truncated as the professor's own original. This is the true melancholy story he told: 'Born . . . to a mother and father of unusually advanced age . . . and being an only child . . . I was cherished by my father as a potential . . . participant in his lonely passion, the game . . . of golf . . . since he found it difficult . . . to find partners . . . he was especially impatient . . . for me to grow up . . . so that I could share his passion . . . it was a great deception . . . for both of us . . . that on my first attempt to play . . . I found myself less drawn to the ball . . . than to the grass which surrounded it . . .' A stillborn golfer won the Nobel Prize. One hopes the father recovered from his shock.* ”

MOTH, NATIVE TO MOROCCO
Syntomis mogadonensis

Sir Peter Ustinov's varied careers include those of playwright, actor, author, director, and opera and film producer.

GLOBAL WARMING
CLIMATE AT RISK

STEPHEN SCHNEIDER

Global warming is indisputably with us, but unavoidable uncertainties about the speed and consequences of climate change present a massive challenge to both politicians and scientists.

During the heat waves, floods, fires, and super-hurricane of 1988, the North American public discovered global warming. On 23 June that year, James Hansen, Director of the NASA Goddard Institute for Space Studies, told a US Senate hearing that the warmth of the 1980's was a record and that, in particular, 1987 had been the warmest year in recorded history. Hansen was "99 percent confident" that the warming trend is real, and said that we ought to stop "waffling around" and accept that the greenhouse effect is probably responsible for the warming. He

Stephen Schneider PhD is the Head of the Interdisciplinary Climate Systems Section at the National Center for Atmospheric Research in Boulder, Colorado. He is also a prolific writer and broadcaster on climate and other environmental issues.

never stated that he was 99 percent confident that the well-known, century-long build-up of greenhouse gases had caused the record warm years, but that implication was widely reported. With continuous media coverage of the record temperatures in the USA, floods in Bangladesh, and a super-hurricane in the Caribbean, it is not surprising that many people had the impression that the heat waves and drought of 1988 were primarily caused by the greenhouse effect. However, no responsible scientist ever made that assertion or even implied it.

Even though most scientists did not directly link the drought to global warming trends, an impression of cause and effect had been conveyed. So a backlash followed, in America and elsewhere, largely in the form of newspaper opinion pieces from disgruntled meteorologists

FIRE AS CREATOR OR DESTROYER
(opposite) *Fire is a natural part of many ecosystems. In areas like Yellowstone National Park in the USA (shown here), fires help to promote new growth and maintain the complex ecological balance. But fires sparked off by higher temperatures and loss of moisture, as a result of global warming, could cause massive habitat loss and threaten human settlements.*

TERRIFYING EXTREMES
In September 1988, the fertile agricultural land of America's Mid West was stricken by drought (left). In Bangladesh, exceptionally heavy rains resulted in hundreds of thousands of people being driven from their homes by floods (inset, above left). Scenes of this nature are symbolic reminders that the Earth's climate might indeed be undergoing catastrophic change.

WEATHER
PATTERNS (right)
*Hurricanes, like
Hurricane Dora in
1983, seen here from
above, could well
increase in intensity as
a direct consequence of
changes in climate.*

WEATHER
PATTERNS (right)
*Hurricanes, like
Hurricane Dora in
1983, seen here from
above, could well
increase in intensity as
a direct consequence of
changes in climate.*

CASTAWAYS (below)
*A Bangladeshi family
escapes the 1988 floods
on a makeshift raft. A
rise in sea levels in the
Bay of Bengal would
make such tragedies
even more frequent.*

or other critics. They argued that, given the substantial uncertainties that remained, action to slow down global warming was largely unnecessary.

A major policy debate has emerged, with environmentalists and a number of political leaders urging immediate action towards cuts in emissions of greenhouse gases, and some industrial interests and government officials claiming that such steps would be too costly given the lack of "cause and effect" evidence. The media like to portray this debate as an implacable dispute between those who assert that the evidence is conclusive and catastrophic, and those who claim it is equivocal and benign. This kind of phony polarization over a technically complicated issue like global warming tends to confuse public opinion and delay any decision on what action should be taken.

THE EMERGING CONSENSUS

Observations of the Earth have shown beyond doubt that atmospheric constituents such as water vapor, clouds, carbon dioxide (CO_2), methane (CH_4), nitrous oxide (N_2O), and chlorofluorocarbons (CFC's) trap a certain kind of heat (called infrared radiation) near the Earth's surface, causing the celebrated greenhouse effect. It is now virtually certain that an unprecedented 25 percent increase in CO_2 and 100 percent increase in CH_4 over the past 150 years have resulted from increased use of fossil fuels, more domesticated animals, the expansion of agriculture, and rapid deforestation.

It is also well accepted that the buildup of these atmospheric constituents has trapped two extra watts of radiative energy, the heat given off by one miniature Christmas tree bulb, for every 10 square feet (1 square meter) of the Earth's surface. For some idea of the total amount of heat involved, this would be equivalent to a grid of 500 trillion Christmas tree bulbs spread one foot (30 centimeters) apart over the entire Earth.

All this has been affirmed by at least a dozen scientific studies over the past ten years. Most recently, the UN-sponsored Inter-Governmental Panel on Climate Change (IPCC) prepared a report to the world's governments reconfirming, in more blatant terms than ever before, the international consensus on global warming. What, then, is the basis of the continuing, often polemical media debate over global climate changes?

First of all, the scientists' projections are based on not yet verified assumptions about how the Earth's clouds, soils, forests, ice caps, and oceans will respond to this heating. These factors could change in ways that influence the warming effect. They could either reduce it, as global warming critics like to point out, or increase it, as most present climate models seem to indicate. Such models predict that the greenhouse effect should have caused our atmosphere to become up to 1.8°F (1°C) warmer over the past 100 years, provided all other factors were constant, a dubious prospect.

Scientists have already confirmed that 0.9°F (0.5°C) of global warming *did* occur between 1890 and 1990. This is consistent with the lower to middle part of the projected warming range, but it is not clear whether other factors (such as natural climate fluctuations, changes in solar heat output, or dust generated from human or volcanic activities) have contributed to or have helped to offset global warming trends from greenhouse gas increases! The temperature fluctuations observed over the last century can thus neither prove nor disprove global warming predictions.

The five hottest years in the 20th century all occurred within the 1980's.

Only long-term, global temperature trends can confirm whether warming due to the buildup of greenhouse gases has been detected with 99 percent statistical certainty, the usual scientific criterion. This will take at least 10 to 20 years more to establish. Waiting that long would be a gamble. When the data confirmed our predictions, the Earth and its inhabitants would be forced to adapt to both a greater total amount and a faster rate of climate change than if we act now, to insure against such an eventuality. Of course, no one buys insurance with 99 percent certainty that she or he will get sick or hurt. By then it is too late to buy insurance, as no one will sell it.

IF NOTHING IS DONE

A dozen assessment bodies have suggested that if we continue to pollute the atmosphere with greenhouse gases, additional global warming of at least 1.8°F (1°C) and possibly as much as 9°F (5°C) can

GREENHOUSE GAS
Carbon dioxide (CO$_2$) is responsible for over half of the warming effect. The two primary sources of CO$_2$ are the burning of fossil fuels (above) and rainforest clearance (right). If China were to expand its energy consumption rate to match the US, global CO$_2$ levels would be tripled.

ON THE GREEN FRONT
UNEP
United Nations Environment Program

The UNEP was set up in 1972 as a direct consequence of the Stockholm Conference in that year on Environment and Development. Until the mid 1980's it was virtually unknown. Understaffed, underfunded, politically marginalized within the UN machine, UNEP was unable to get financial support for ambitious programs (such as controlling the spread of desertification).

In the mid 1980's the agency achieved a significant breakthrough with the Montreal Protocol to protect the ozone layer, the first international agreement of its kind. At the 1990 Review Conference of the Protocol in London, UNEP negotiated a special fund to assist Third World countries to adopt ozone-friendly alternatives to chlorofluorocarbons.

UNEP's current work on global warming and biodiversity also involves delicate negotiations between North and South. Third World countries are determined to win financial support from the rich North for any new environmental and conservation measures. The first priority of Dr. Mostafa Tolba, UNEP's Director General, is to encourage serious negotiations on how best to reduce carbon dioxide emissions and protect the rainforests.

TIME BOMB: GLOBAL WARMING

The global average temperature will be at least 1.8°F (1°C) warmer by the year 2030. That is the "best guess" of the Inter-Governmental Panel on Climate Change. It could become even warmer.

With different weather patterns developing, agriculture would be profoundly disrupted in many parts of the world. Climatic zones would shift towards the poles, and the polar ice-caps would start to melt. As a result, sea levels could rise from anywhere between 4 inches and 6 feet (10 centimeters and 2 meters). Low-lying coastal cities would be wiped off the map. A sea level rise of 3 feet (1 meter) would flood 770 square miles (2,000 square kilometers) of Bangladesh, a country already desperately impoverished and overpopulated.

AGENTS OF CHANGE (above) *Excess gas is burned off on a North Sea oil rig. The most significant greenhouse gas is the carbon dioxide released by the burning of fossil fuels: coal and oil. Other greenhouse gases include methane, CFC's, nitrous oxide, and ozone.*

COAL, ONE OF THE MAIN FOSSIL FUELS

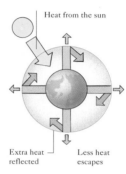

FUNCTIONING GREENHOUSE (right) *The greenhouse effect has always existed. Most of the sun's energy is absorbed by the Earth, but some heat radiates back into space. Certain gases in the atmosphere reflect part of this heat back to the Earth's surface.*

Heat from the sun
Atmosphere
Trapped heat reflected back to the Earth
Excess heat escapes into space

OUT OF BALANCE (left) *The Earth receives the same amount of energy from the sun, but as greenhouse gases build up in the atmosphere, they trap more of the heat radiating from the Earth's surface. The result is an overall rise in temperature.*

Heat from the sun
Extra heat reflected
Less heat escapes

LONG-TERM FLUCTUATIONS *The small graph (right) shows global average temperatures over the last 20,000 years. In all that time, temperatures have risen by only 9°F (5°C). Some scientists predict a temperature rise of the same magnitude in the next 100 years, an acceleration in the rate of warming that would have a disastrous effect on the world's climate.*

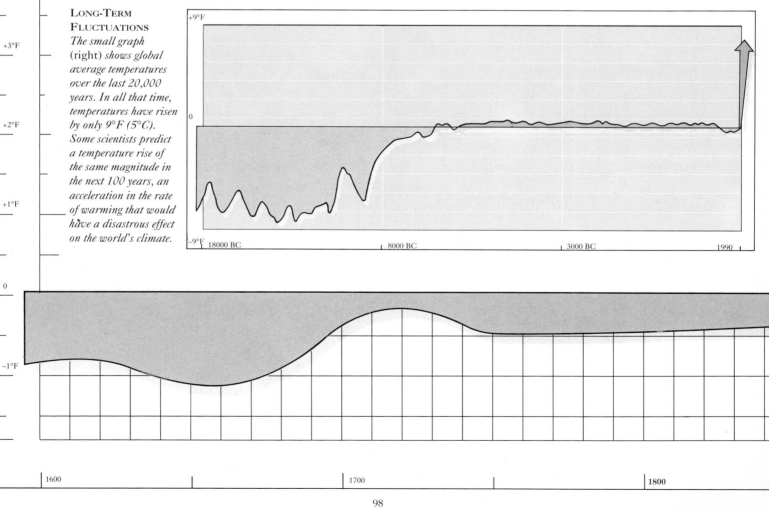

+9°F

0

−9°F   18000 BC   8000 BC   3000 BC   1990

+9°F
+8°F
+7°F
+6°F
+5°F
+4°F
+3°F
+2°F
+1°F
0
−1°F

1600   1700   1800

WORLDWIDE EFFECTS OF GLOBAL WARMING

The most dramatic result of higher temperatures would be the rise in sea level. Climate change would also have far-reaching consequences. Some parts of the world would receive more rain than before; others, including the productive croplands of the Northern Hemisphere, very much less.

USA *(left)*
A farmer in South Carolina shows the effect of the 1986 drought on his soybean crop, five times smaller than in a normal year. Agricultural land in the USA could suffer from greatly reduced rainfall.

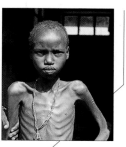

Sudan *(left)*
In the Sahara and sub-Saharan regions of Africa, scenes of drought and famine like this would become even more common than they are today.

Japan
Some parts of the world would benefit as a result of global warming. With changing patterns of rainfall, the area of land in Japan that could be used for rice-growing could double.

Brazil *(above)*
Coastal cities like Rio de Janeiro would experience severe flooding. The floods that swept through the slum district of Santa Teresa in 1988 were perhaps a taste of even greater destruction to come.

Caribbean
Tropical storms would become far more frequent, inflicting greater damage than ever on the islands' houses and vegetation.

Maldive Islands *(above)*
Rising sea levels would have catastrophic consequences for low-lying islands. If the sea level rises by 10 feet (3 meters), coral atolls like the Maldives will disappear completely beneath the waves.

HOW MUCH WARMER?

The graph at the foot of these two pages shows that the world's average temperature has risen by only 0.9°F (0.5°C) since 1600. If we continue to burn more and more fossil fuel each year, future warming will be at a much faster rate. The lower prediction shows the IPCC's "best guess" of how much average temperatures will rise over the next century. The steeper graph is their "upper estimate," or worst-case scenario, with temperatures rising by more than 9°F (5°C) by the year 2100.

+9°F
+8°F
+7°F
+6°F
+5°F
+4°F
+3°F
+2°F
+1°F
0
−1°F

1900
2000
2100

DOUGLAS ADAMS

The longest and most destructive party ever held is now into its fourth generation, and still no one shows any signs of leaving. The mess is extraordinary, and has to be seen to be believed.
One of the problems, and it's one that is obviously going to get worse, is that all the people at the party are either the children or the grandchildren or the great-grandchildren of the people who wouldn't leave in the first place, and because of all the business about selective breeding and regressive genes and so on, it means that all the people now at the party are either absolutely fanatical party-goers, or gibbering idiots, or, more and more frequently, both. Either way, it means that, genetically speaking, each succeeding generation is now less likely to leave than the preceding one.
So other factors come into operation, like when the drink is going to run out. The transition from full-time cocktail party to part-time raiding party came with ease, and did much to add that extra bit of zest and swing to the whole affair. They looted, they raided, they held whole cities to ransom for fresh supplies of cheese crackers, avocado dip, spare ribs and wine and spirits, which would now get piped aboard from floating tankers.
The problem of when the drink is going to run out is, however, going to have to be faced one day.
The planet over which they are floating is no longer the same planet as when they first started floating over it.
It is in bad shape.

British author Douglas Adams is best known for his comic fantasies such as *Life, the Universe and Everything*, from which the above extract is taken.

SICCO MANSHOLT

Before we can begin 'saving the Earth,' we must accept the fact that we, the rich inhabitants of the industrialized nations, are the greatest danger to the future of the world. We produce 3.5 tons of CO_2 per capita every year – ten times as much as people in developing countries. To avoid serious changes in the climate worldwide, we must rigorously limit CO_2 emissions in the next century. If we accept that poorer countries have a basic right to increase their use of energy, that means that the rich will have to reduce per capita energy consumption to one-fifth of current levels in one generation. Even with vigorous efforts to increase energy efficiency, that leaves little room for any increase in consumption or economic growth in the rich North.
Are we prepared for that future?

Dutch economist Dr. S. L. Mansholt has served as the European Economic Community Commissioner for Agriculture.

be expected in the 21st century. This rate of change would be unprecedented in the era of human civilization and some ten times greater than the longterm rate of natural global climate changes. For instance, the last ice age ended between 15,000 and 5,000 years ago. During that period the Earth has warmed by only 9°F (5°C), a rate of around 1.8°F (1°C) per 1,000 years at most.

Current forecasts are as likely to be too conservative as too radical, so the changes in the 21st century could well occur near the high end of the 1.8 to 9°F (1 to 5°C) range. In such circumstances, ecological systems would be catastrophically disrupted. I'm not a planetary gambler. I'd prefer to do something now to slow down the rapid buildup of greenhouse gases.

THE COST OF INSURANCE

The glib response of some industrialists and US government officials that CO_2 emissions controls would bankrupt the American economy simply doesn't hold water. Even the Yale economist William Nordhaus, a tough critic of severe cuts in CO_2 emissions, has argued that modest cuts of 10 to 47 percent in CO_2 emissions in the USA would, at present, yield economic benefits in excess of the costs. And his calculations did not even include the extra benefits of efficient energy use and emissions controls: less acid rain, less damage to health and ecosystems from local air pollution, better energy security, and a reduced balance of payments deficit due to importing less foreign oil.

Studies in Europe, Australia, and other countries all suggest it would be possible to stabilize CO_2 emissions at current levels and actually make money doing it. Some even predict that if "best practice" were initiated in power production, manufacturing, transportation, and housing, cuts in present emission rates of CO_2 of up to 25 percent could be achieved at no cost, or even with significant savings, thereby increasing profits.

We also need to eliminate government subsidies to inefficient fossil fuel uses and deforestation practices in order to move toward lower real costs. If we want the 21st century to be environmentally more stable than the present one, fuel prices must reflect total costs, including potential damage to the environment. It is then open to debate whether further cuts can be achieved without substantial investments, and whether investments of this nature can be justified as "insurance" against possible future climate change.

In the late 19th century, when Europe and the United States used cheap, dirty coal to foster industrial growth, there were fewer than 2 billion people in the entire world. Today, countries like India and China would like to use their abundant coal supplies as low-cost fuel for industrialization. But these two countries alone now have a population of 2 billion between them, so the global impact of their using coal would be far greater than that of coal burning in the past.

Alarmed at this prospect, the US and Europe urge them to adopt cleaner, more efficient, high-tech methods of power production. Developing countries naturally object that this is initially more expensive than the traditional options, a dilemma that highlights the need for a "new bargain."

Building just 1 mile (1.5 kilometers) of sea defenses to stem rising tides caused by projected global warming would cost about US $2 billion.

The simplest goal might be for all countries to agree to reduce their emissions of greenhouse gases by a fixed fraction, but this may not be the most globally cost-effective plan, nor the fairest. A better solution would be for developed countries to buy themselves out of some of their requirement to cut emissions by funding even larger reductions in energy-inefficient developing countries. This would not only eliminate Third World countries' opposition to emissions reductions, but could encourage them to compete with each other to be the venue for future limitations.

What determines fairness is not how much CO_2 emission each nation cuts at home, but who pays for all the cuts. Since the rich nations have been responsible for well over half of the CO_2 pollution to date, they should pay a disproportionate share of the costs. Investment by one country in emission cuts in another may be the most efficient system and the best opportunity for resource transfers needed for development.

Climate change "insurance" that pays other dividends is long overdue. Invoking uncertainty as an excuse to delay action merely commits future generations to greater environmental risks.

PERMAFROST MELTDOWN
Temperature rises caused by global warming will be greatest in polar regions. This could have a dramatic impact on the Arctic permafrost. Here, beneath the frozen soil of Alaska, are trapped vast quantities of methane, itself a potent greenhouse gas. Were this methane to be released as the permafrost melts, it would contribute further to the acceleration of global warming.

AIR POLLUTION
LIVING DANGEROUSLY

MICHAEL WALSH

The air is man's most precious resource. He can survive for weeks or even months without food, and for days without water. But even a few minutes without air threatens his hold on life.

Throughout most of our time on Earth, humankind has been blessed with an almost unlimited supply of pure air. The only events that seriously affected its purity were occasional forest fires or volcanic eruptions. Clean, healthy air was taken for granted. However, since the dawn of the industrial age, when human population began to climb steeply, air pollution has become a fact of life in all major cities. In many parts of the world, as pollution has increased and has been carried by the wind over long distances, it has now developed into a regional or even a continental problem.

In the early stages of the modern industrial era, the increasing numbers of factories and foundries were responsible for most of the world's man-made air pollution. Since that time, the blame has gradually shifted, first to power-plants, and more recently to motor vehicles, now the principal source of pollution in most of the areas badly affected.

Over the last few decades, several catastrophes – such as the London smogs of the 1940's and 1950's, when thousands of people were rushed to hospital and hundreds died in the course of a few days – have alerted the public to the dangers of severe air pollution. Fortunately, now that pollution controls have been introduced, and coal is no longer the primary fuel in most homes, these incidents are rare today. In most industrialized areas, the major health

Michael Walsh is an international air pollution consultant. He has managed programs in this field both for the city of New York and the US Environmental Protection Agency, and has advised the UN in many countries around the world.

SÃO PAULO SOUP (opposite) *This huge Brazilian city finds itself with roughly half a million new inhabitants to accommodate every year. The dramatic growth of São Paulo has brought with it air pollution on a phenomenal scale: a soup-like photochemical smog can hang over the city for days on end, causing grave damage to the health of young and old alike. As yet there are no plans to solve the problem, and little money to invest in transport alternatives.*

MEGALOPOLIS (left) *By the year 2000, Mexico City will be the largest city in the world, with a population of 25 million people. Sheer numbers of people and cars have already made it a pollution hell-hole. In the summer of 1990, the air in some parts of the city came so close to being unbreathable that a state of emergency was declared.*

YEW BRANCH
DYING FROM
ACID RAIN

HEALTHY YEW

ON THE GREEN FRONT
POLISH ECOLOGY CLUB

Founded in 1981, the Polish Ecology Club (PKE) has always had to campaign in the face of intense political pressure. It survived the period of martial law between 1982 and 1985 only by pointing to a clause in the Polish Constitution that read: "The citizens of the Polish People's Republic have the right to enjoy the full value of a natural environment, and a duty to protect it."

In 1986 PKE became the first Eastern European environmental group to join Friends of the Earth International. Since democratization, their major concern has been to refute the notion that Poland's economic woes are so serious that the country cannot afford to bother about the environment. They calculate that doing nothing about the damage caused by acid rain is costing Poland up to 10 percent of its GNP. Similarly, they have opposed plans for the rapid intensification of agriculture, advocating instead the use of low-input sustainable farming systems. Education plays a key role in PKE's campaigns: it will be up to the next generation of Poles to repair the environmental havoc wrought by their parents.

JERZY ZELNIK

❝ *To be deeply concerned about the environment: one could hardly be anything else here in Poland. We are poisoned by pollution much more than the West. But people in the West must confront our reality: poverty is the principal impediment to sorting things out. I only hope the life instincts of Europe will now inspire our Western neighbors to come to our aid – and help in saving the Earth, air, forests, and rivers of our beautiful land.* ❞

Jerzy Zelnik

Jerzy Zelnik is a Polish actor who works closely with the Mazowsze branch of the Polish Ecology Club.

CARL SAGAN

❝ *As scientists, many of us have had profound experiences of awe and reverence before the universe. We understand that what is regarded as sacred is more likely to be treated with care and respect. Our planetary home should be so regarded. Efforts to safeguard and cherish the environment need to be infused with a vision of the sacred. At the same time, a much wider and deeper understanding of science and technology is needed. If we do not understand the problem, it is unlikely we will be able to fix it.* ❞

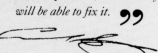

Carl Sagan, Professor of Radiophysics and Space Research at Cornell University, is at the forefront of the environmental movement in the United States.

concerns are the effects of air pollution on sick individuals, and the gradual damage caused by frequent exposure to lower levels of pollution.

The most conspicuous form of pollution is ozone or photochemical smog. In the upper atmosphere, ozone plays a beneficial role in protecting people from ultraviolet radiation but, at ground level, it is a serious pollutant. It is formed when the hydrocarbons in vehicle exhausts combine with nitrogen oxides in sunlight. Since the 1960's, ground-level ozone has increased by more than 60 percent in the United States and Europe. Around 100 million Americans live in areas where pollutants exceed the current "air quality standard" (the officially recognized level at which pollution begins to be harmful to health); many suffer eye irritation, coughs and chest discomfort, headaches, respiratory illness, increased asthma attacks, and reduced lung function as a result.

AIR UNFIT TO BREATHE

Smog is a problem worldwide. It became so bad in Mexico City recently that birds were dying in Chapultepec Park, in the center of the city. The authorities were forced to declare a state of emergency and to close schools. Similar problems have occurred frequently in Athens during late summer. Apart from these especially high peaks, ozone levels in much of Europe and Asia frequently exceed healthy levels.

In Athens, six times as many people die on smoggy days as on clear days.

New studies indicate that high ozone concentrations may reduce lung function, not only in people already suffering from respiratory disorders, but even in people enjoying good health. Joggers often experience chest pain and shortness of breath. Healthy young children can suffer adverse effects from exposure to ozone even at levels below the current air quality standard.

High levels of carbon monoxide from vehicle emissions have equally disturbing consequences. When carbon monoxide is inhaled, it replaces vital oxygen in the blood. Our hearts must therefore pump more blood to supply the oxygen needed by our tissues, and this puts a strain on those with weak hearts. Fetuses, sickle cell anemics, and young children may also be harmed by exposure to relatively low levels of carbon monoxide.

Other vehicle emissions, such as the oxides of nitrogen, cause direct lung damage. Exposure to nitrogen dioxide is linked with increased susceptibility to respiratory infection, increased airway resistance in asthmatics, and decreased lung function.

Most of the toxic trace metals, hydrocarbons, and acidic materials emitted in the exhaust fumes of cars and trucks also pose a serious health risk. A review by the Swedish National Institute of Environmental Medicine has identified an

ERNESTO SABATO

66 *It might be that the human race is incapable of withstanding the drastic changes that are taking place in today's world. For these changes have been so terrible, so far-reaching and, above all, so swift that they make those that caused the disappearance of the dinosaurs pale into insignificance. Man has not had time to adapt to the sudden and powerful changes that his technology and society have produced around him, and it might safely be said that many of today's illnesses are the means used by the cosmos to eliminate this proud human race.*
Man is the only animal to have created his own environment. Ironically, he is also the only one to have thus created his own means of self-destruction. 99

Ernesto Sabato is an Argentinian writer and human rights activist. This is an extract from his book *Hombres y Engranajes*.

ACID RAIN, ACID EARTH

Vast stretches of forest in Europe and the United States have been killed by acid rain. Of Sweden's 90,000 lakes, 40,000 are known to be seriously acidified, as are one in five of the lakes in the United States.

Acid rain is caused primarily by sulphur dioxide and nitrogen oxides from power stations, and by the same nitrogen oxides from vehicle exhausts. After years of arguing that there was not enough evidence, both the United States and all members of the European Economic Community (EEC) are now committed to reducing emissions of the main pollutants involved. EEC countries are bound by a Directive obliging them to reduce sulphur dioxide emissions from power stations by specified amounts by the year 2003. From 1993, all new cars sold in the EEC will have to be fitted with catalytic converters, but the USA and Japan are years ahead of Europe in their vehicle emission standards.

Economic damage caused by acid rain runs into billions of dollars a year. Those countries worst affected face a simple choice: either pay to clean up now, or pay a great deal more later on.

POISONED RAIN
Waldsterben *(literally "forest death") as a result of acid rain is a depressingly familiar sight in the Pyrenees* (left) *and in many other areas of Europe. Acid rain also affects lakes, rivers, crops, buildings, and human health. Swedish lakes* (below) *are often "limed" to counteract their acidity, but now scientists think that this intended remedy has serious side-effects on local flora and fauna.*

TIME BOMB: VEHICLE EMISSIONS

By the year 2025, there will be more than 1 billion cars competing for road space around the world. Apart from the grave damage this will cause to every local environment, the increase in carbon dioxide emissions will frustrate our efforts to slow down the rate of global warming. There will also be a correspondingly huge increase in the carbon monoxide, nitrogen oxides, and hydrocarbons that pollute the air we breathe with photochemical smog.

It is not just the emissions that cause concern; we must remember the steel, plastics, aluminum, rubber, and water consumed in the manufacturing process; about 8,000 gallons (30,000 liters) of water are used in the construction of each new car. Investment in efficient, clean, and safe public transport systems offers the only way out.

INHERITING THE EARTH *Population grows at 1.74 percent a year; the world's cars multiply by almost 5 percent.*

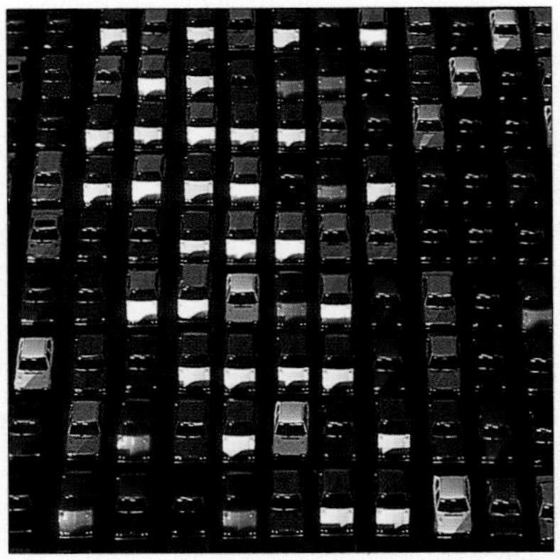

A RESISTIBLE RISE *The orange line shows the increase in the number of motor vehicles (in millions) in the world since 1980; the broken line traces the predicted continuation of this trend until 2025.*

Number of registered motor vehicles in the world (in millions)

100, 200, 300, 500, 600, 700, 800, 900, 1000, 1100, 1200

1980, 1990, 2000, 2010, 2020

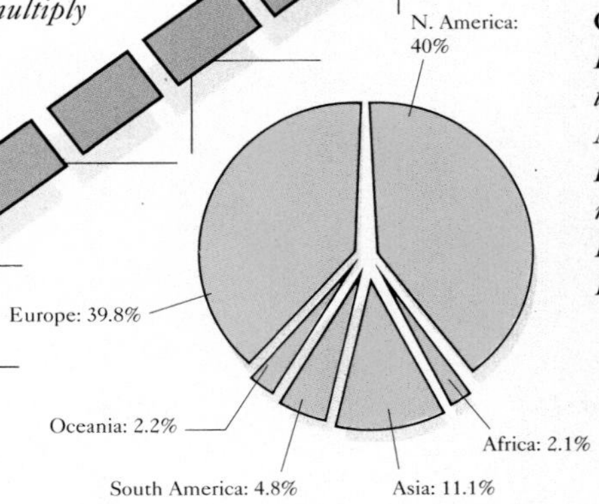

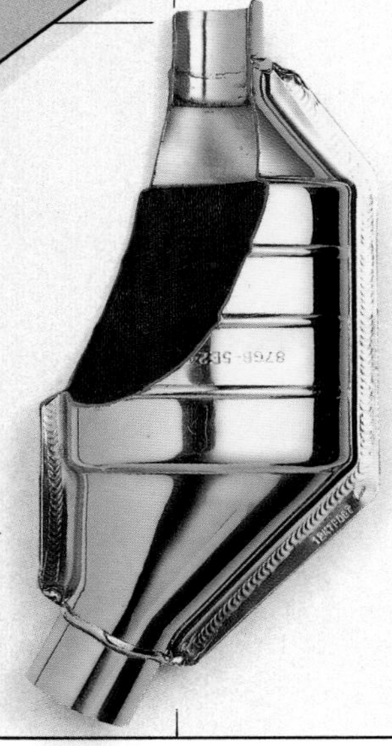

N. America: 40%
Europe: 39.8%
Oceania: 2.2%
South America: 4.8%
Asia: 11.1%
Africa: 2.1%

CARS BY CONTINENT (left) *In the late 1980's, four-fifths of the world's cars were in North America and Europe. Greater Los Angeles alone had twice as many cars as China, India, Indonesia, Pakistan, and Bangladesh combined.*

A CLEANER FUTURE? *The graph* (right) *shows estimated levels of hydrocarbons in the global atmosphere from 1980 to 2020. Thanks to legislation controlling car emissions and technological advances such as the catalytic converter* (left), *levels should fall until the end of the century. Then, however, the increasing numbers of cars will outweigh the benefits gained. Unless new controls are introduced, levels of hydrocarbons, along with nitrogen oxides and carbon monoxide, will start rising again.*

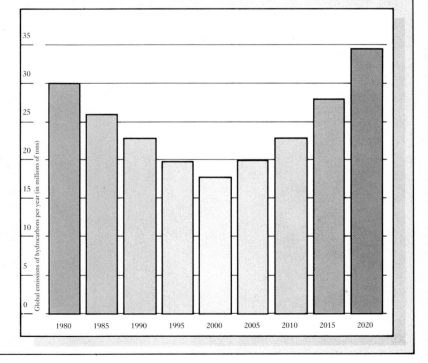

Global emissions of hydrocarbons per year (in millions of tons)
0
5
10
15
20
25
30
35
1980
1985
1990
1995
2000
2005
2010
2015
2020

association between exposure to diesel exhaust and lung cancer among forklift truck drivers.

Many studies have shown that photochemical pollutants damage forest ecosystems and seriously harm the growth of certain crops. Visible symptoms of *Waldsterben* (forest death) first appeared in Europe in 1979, and within four years the symptoms had spread over large areas of the continent. In many places, the forest damage is still increasing, both in intensity and in terms of the area affected. The specific causes of this widespread phenomenon (most often referred to as "acid rain") remain hard to pin down, but it is known that the chemical cocktail created by different forms of air pollution combines with other stress factors, such as insect infestations, needle and root fungi, and frost, wind, and snow damage.

Acid rain now affects nearly every tree species in Europe, including the four most important conifers (spruce, fir, pine, and larch) and six hardwoods (beech, birch, oak, ash, maple, and alder). According to one survey, the damage is worst in western Germany, where 55 percent of the trees are affected, followed by Switzerland and Britain.

In the United States, there are reliable reports of extensive damage to yellow pine, white pine, red spruce, Fraser fir, sugar and yellow maple, beech, birch, red maple, and a wide variety of other tree species. Experiments have shown that the levels of ozone commonly found throughout the eastern United States can cause significant reductions in plant growth and photosynthesis.

CALL FOR NEW TECHNOLOGY

In 1970, appalled at the country's pollution problems, the US Congress amended the Clean Air Act, setting up a new regulatory structure which has served as a blueprint for all subsequent progress in America. Recognizing that motor vehicles were responsible for an increasingly large share of air pollution, Congress demanded that all new cars be designed to emit far less carbon monoxide, hydrocarbons, and nitrogen oxides than the models then on the market. Such substantial improvements could not be achieved with the technology then in commercial use. In order to comply with the law, car manufacturers were therefore obliged to develop and commercialize technologies that existed only in research laboratories or on prototype models.

ARPAD GÖNCZ

"Many people believe that we are facing an ecological disaster. Every day we hear horrific statistics; the process seems unstoppable. And the destruction recognizes no national frontiers. I know all this, yet I cannot really comprehend it. I have the simple thought that my day starts differently if, in the morning, the sun is shining and I can gaze upon a tree bursting with strength. It smiles at me and all at once I feel like smiling back."

Arpád Göncz is the President of Hungary.

EDGAR MORIN

"The history of humanity is a history of interaction between the biosphere and mankind. This interaction intensified with the development of agriculture, which had a profound effect on the world's ecosystems. More and more it has become a dialogue (in a relationship at once complementary and antagonistic) between nature and mankind. Humanity must stop behaving like a Gengis Khan of the solar system, and think of itself not so much as the shepherd of the world, but as nature's co-pilot."

French sociologist, anthropologist, and author Edgar Morin is the director of the journal *Communications*.

ROADS OF FREEDOM? *Few people will deny the awesome beauty of this Los Angeles interchange, and for many, the car still represents freedom, security, and status. But the "American dream" of a car-owning democracy has become increasingly nightmarish as the huge social and environmental costs entailed in achieving it are added up.*

CRISIS MEASURES IN CALIFORNIA

The Los Angeles region of southern California is characterized by a unique combination of climate, topography, economy, and lifestyle that creates "ideal" conditions for air pollution. The region has a narrow coastal strip with lush coastal valleys in the west (where most of the population lives), foothills and high rugged mountain ranges to the north and south, and inland deserts to the east. Abundant sunshine and very light winds turn the whole area into a pollution trap.

There are 13 million people living in the area, and between them they own a total of 8 million cars. By the year 2010, there will be 21 million people with an estimated 13 million cars. Initially, the region's planning authorities wanted to "build their way out of the box," but they soon calculated that they would need to double the existing total of 600 miles (950 kilometers) of freeway just to keep that increased total of 13 million vehicles moving at today's snail-like average speed of 15 miles (24 kilometers) per hour.

One of the most important of the recent amendments to the US Clean Air Act has enabled the State of California to adopt more stringent standards for motor vehicles than those required by the national program. At the same time, a concerted effort is under way to reduce air pollution through alternative transportation policies. Measures include modified work hours; preferential parking for carpools; bicycle and pedestrian facilities; traffic signal synchronization; the purchase of low-emission, high fuel-economy vehicles by local government; and conversion to energy-efficient street lighting.

The South Coast Air Quality Management District (which covers the entire Los Angeles metropolitan area) has approved a 20-year, three-tier plan to achieve clean air. Tier I requires that all current emission control technology be put into operation by 1993. The goals of Tier II include converting 40 percent of the passenger fleet and 70 percent of the freight fleet to electric or alternative fuels, and reducing non-motor vehicle (aircraft, ship, and locomotive) emissions. Tier III aims to promote research and development of technologies that show promise for controlling emissions in the future.

CITY OF SMOG
Seen here from afar (above) *and close at hand* (right), *the Los Angeles smog problem makes life a misery for millions and constitutes a serious risk to public health. Most of it is caused by vehicle emissions. As the number of cars grows, the city's infrared air-monitoring devices* (inset, above) *are recording higher and higher levels of pollution, despite the fact that all new cars sold in California since 1980 have had catalytic converters.*

Although the manufacturers argued that the standards were impossible and would lead to economic catastrophe, the necessary technology, of which the catalytic converter is the most important component, was in fact developed so quickly that for over a decade all gasoline-fueled cars have been able to comply. Without exception, all new gasoline-fueled cars sold in the United States since 1980 have been equipped with catalytic converters and therefore require lead free fuel.

As a result, most areas of the country have cleaner air today than they did in 1970. Despite an additional 50 million cars on the nation's highways, there has been an 88 percent reduction in violations of the air quality standard. Unfortunately, most Western European countries have been slow to follow this lead, although the European Community has recently agreed that from 1993 all new cars will have to carry a catalytic converter.

MAKING UP LOST GROUND

Despite the introduction of the catalytic converter, any attempt to reduce air pollution must concentrate on changing the nature of transportation: there are already estimated to be some 500 million gasoline-driven vehicles in the world and, unless trends change, the figure will rise to 1 billion by the year 2030. Car manufacturers must also be required to find new ways of reducing vehicle emissions, if any real progress is to be achieved.

Once again, the US Congress has recognized that the clean air of the future must be safeguarded now; in 1990, it adopted sweeping amendments to the Clean Air Act. This new legislation not only requires significant advances in motor vehicle technology, but also dramatic changes in fuels. Apart from phasing out lead additives, the question of the actual composition of fuels was largely overlooked in the 1970 Act.

It is ironic that just as Europe and the United States are introducing radical measures to clean up past damage from air pollution, many Third World countries are investing in road transportation systems that will cause exactly the same problems in the future. In many Third World cities, air pollution problems are already desperate. Unwelcome as this message may be to motor manufacturers, the goals of a clean environment and of a permanent increase in the number of vehicles around the world are mutually exclusive.

YEHUDI MENUHIN

66 *This poem was written by an extraordinary ten-year-old Australian boy, who is perhaps one of the first of whole generations of human beings who will no longer be able to survive in our polluted atmosphere. Jonathan Wilson-Fuller can only survive under the strictest conditions; his room must be sealed off and supplied with the purest of air. Anything short of perfect purity will poison him. This poem is his* cri de coeur: 99

Why don't you smell our polluted air?
Why doesn't your nose tell of danger there?

Why don't you taste our polluted fare?
Why doesn't your tongue tell of danger there?

Why don't I notice my red hair?
I'm just used to it being there!

An eminent international violinist himself, Sir Yehudi Menuhin has also been involved for many years in teaching the violin to promising younger players.

RUSSELL PETERSON

DECLARATION OF INTERDEPENDENCE

66 *We the people of planet Earth*
With respect for the dignity of each human life,
With concern for future generations,
With growing appreciation of our relationship to our environment,
With recognition of limits to our resources,
And with need for adequate food, air, water, shelter, health, protection,
justice, and self-fulfillment,
Hereby declare our interdependence;
And resolve to work together in peace and in harmony with our environment
To enhance the quality of life everywhere. 99

President Emeritus of the National Audubon Society in the United States, Russell W. Peterson is also the President of the International Council for Bird Preservation and the co-founder of the Better World Society.

IV

FIRE

*I suggest that the foundations of peace cannot be laid by universal prosperity,
in the modern sense, because such prosperity, if attainable at all, is attainable only by cultivating
such drives of human nature as greed and envy, which destroy intelligence, happiness, serenity,
and thereby the peacefulness of man. . . . The cultivation and expansion of needs is the antithesis of
wisdom. . . . Only by a reduction of needs can one promote a genuine reduction in those tensions
which are the ultimate causes of strife and war.*
From **Small is Beautiful** *by* E. M. SCHUMACHER

MELPA HEAD-DRESS,
PAPUA NEW GUINEA

According to the ancient Greek myth, Prometheus stole fire from the gods and handed it over to humans on Earth. For his transgressions, he was punished by Zeus by being chained to a lonely rock in the Caucasus. Every day an eagle tore out his liver, which restored itself during the night. This was a grim punishment, but Zeus realized that with fire, humans might aspire to create and to destroy here on Earth as if they were gods themselves.

Zeus was right. Fire first liberated humans from cold and deprivation. Since then it has brought untold benefits, allowing land to be cleared, tools to be forged, machines to be built, new technologies to be developed, and great cities to be constructed and maintained through the burning of fossil fuels. We have not always used that creative energy to such benign ends. Many technologies have laid a heavy hand on the Earth and on those who thought they were technology's master and not its servants.

One of the greatest problems has been the different speeds at which technology has developed and the human mind has

OUT OF CONTROL (opposite)
*A Guyanese Indian girl tries in vain
to douse the flames, as a blazing
bushfire sweeps across the savanna.*

EASTER ISLAND STATUE (right)
*To erect these giant stone heads, the
islanders felled all their trees, reducing
a rich society to poverty and*

RURAL RESOURCES: BRINGING IN THE
SHEEP, SWITZERLAND

evolved to cope with it. If we accept, as we surely must, that plans to promote greater sustainability and justice can only succeed if new technologies are specifically harnessed to achieve such a goal, we must simultaneously acknowledge the vast challenge that this poses to our educational systems. It is simply not enough to transmit an ever-expanding body of apparently neutral scientific facts within the classroom; we must ensure that young people are given the tools to interpret that knowledge, and to develop a value system relevant to the world as it really is, rather than the world as most of today's rather confused politicians might like it to be.

In some ways, each of the four chapters in this section of *Save the Earth* is about just such a process of education. There is enormous ignorance in Europe and the United States about what is actually going on in Third World cities and rural areas. The only news that most of us ever see about these countries is overwhelmingly gloomy, focusing on disasters or intractable problems. The skills and experience of Third World people in creating sustainable alternatives go largely unrecognized.

RURAL RESOURCES:
AN INUIT HUNTER
RETRIEVING HIS KILL
IN GREENLAND

POPULATION: COLOMONCAGUA
REFUGEE CAMP IN HONDURAS

The truth is that many of these alternatives just don't fit in with the dominant model of economic success. All that matters to those who preside over today's economic world order is increased growth, shown in ever greater production and consumption. For instance, selling nuclear reactors to Third World countries (and even building them in earthquake zones in countries like the Philippines) carries a higher priority than promoting energy efficiency or helping to develop more sustainable, renewable energy sources. Nuclear power has proved an expensive liability in most industrialized countries; in the Third World, it has been an economic calamity.

When it comes to technology choices of this kind, both in the North and the South, far too many politicians espouse the point of view of those vested interests who will lose most as we turn to a more equitable and sustainable world order. It is tempting to take

TOWNS AND CITIES: BREAKING UP SHIPS FOR SCRAP IN CHITTAGONG
ON THE BAY OF BENGAL, BANGLADESH

TOWNS AND CITIES: THE BRIGHT LIGHTS
OF CHICAGO AT NIGHT

the line that the transition to such an order would leave everybody better off. But of course there will be losers. Some will be the innocent casualties of any transition from one kind of economy to another, including those who work in unsustainable or ecologically bankrupt industries. Others will be the people who own such industries, or those who depend on the profits made by them for their wealth. But at the same time, new jobs and new opportunities will be created, and new sources of sustainable wealth will be developed. It will be a different kind of economy, one which offers far greater prospects for future generations.

Today many of us have become victims of our own unthinking advocacy of economic growth as the only solution to all our problems. Confronted with the damage we are already doing to the natural world, the answer simply cannot be to persuade more people to produce and consume more things. Yet that is what we are all still urged to do. The argument for the most subtle varia-

TRIBAL PEOPLES: WOMEN OF THE
DINKA TRIBE, SOUTH SUDAN

tion on this theme goes something like this: "We're going to have to spend a lot of money cleaning up the terrible environmental mess we're in, and even more money on avoiding such a mess in the future. To find that money, we have to increase the level of economic activity across the world, to go on growing and getting richer quicker." Environmentalists have compared this self-perpetuating idiocy to trying to put out a fire by pouring gasoline on it, or hoping to pay off a debt by borrowing more money at an ever higher rate of interest.

There have always been some people active in the environmental movement who seek to depoliticize environmental concerns, to argue that they should be addressed as single issues, regardless of their political context. But there is no such thing as an environmental issue *per se*: what we are dealing with today is a series of overlapping economic and political failures that impact ever more powerfully on the natural world.

That analysis, and the prescriptions that arise logically from it, belong to no one political party. Indeed, it would be best if it were adopted by all political parties the world over.

TRIBAL PEOPLES: KAYAPO INDIANS WALK PROUDLY
IN CEREMONIAL DRESS, BRAZIL

GRO HARLEM BRUNDTLAND

66 *The future of our children depends on our ability to learn to live in harmony with nature and each other. Sustainable development means that we cannot continue to satisfy our own needs at the expense of those of future generations.*

All over the world, there is a growing sense of urgency that radical steps are needed to reverse present negative trends. People are more and more worried about the deterioration of their natural and social environment. We see rapidly increasing pressure on those who have political responsibility to act quickly and forcefully.

Developments in Europe illustrate reasons to be optimistic. The European nations have confirmed that security can no longer be defined in military terms alone. We must establish a concept of security that can deal with the threats from poverty and environmental degradation at the same level of attention and priority as has been given to the danger from war. 99

Gro Harlem Brundtland is the Prime Minister of Norway. She was the chairman of the UN World Commission on Environment and Development, which in 1987 published the Brundtland Report, *Our Common Future*.

THEO ANDERSON

66 *The attitude of most people in the developing world, especially in Africa, towards the recent preaching about global warming is that of 'he who is down needs fear no fall.' Be it increases in world temperatures, rises in sea level, drought, or whatever – all boil down to potential human suffering. To such people, suffering is not new. Already, Bangladesh has suffered flooding, drought is affecting food production in the Sahel region of Africa, the locusts are breeding in Somalia, and so on.*

We are happy that environmental issues have come to the forefront of the global agenda during our generation, but developing countries need to be equipped with the technology and the means to achieve the common goal of environmental sustainability. They need both human and financial resources to do so. I would urge environmental campaigners to explore how the various green options can be translated into concrete actions. 99

Theophilus Kwesi Anderson is the Director of Friends of the Earth, Ghana.

DAVID ATTENBOROUGH

66 *Since virtually nothing remains of our pristine wildernesses, perhaps we in Great Britain might be one of the first to develop a truly integrated land policy in which there will be a place for all: for the farmer growing food for our stomachs as well as the naturalist finding solace for the spirit; for the car owner using the motorway as well as the walker strolling along a bridle-path; and last, but surely by no means least, for the multitude of species of animals and plants, which were here long before we were.* 99

British broadcaster and author Sir David Attenborough has been making wildlife films since the 1950's.

NICOLAS URIBURU

OMBU: THE TREE OF LIFE

66 *The more developed nations are poisoning the Earth's land, water, and air, and destroying the resources of the Third World. I denounce the antagonism between nature and civilization, and look forward to the union of Latin Americans by the waters of their rivers – though not within the limits set by man. An entire continent united by nature.* 99

Nicolas Uriburu is an Argentinian artist.

DESMOND MORRIS

66 *If we are honest, there is only one root cause of the disaster facing the planet, and that is the appalling rate at which our human species has increased its population in recent centuries. Other animals employ a variety of natural control mechanisms that prevent their numbers from rising to dangerous levels. Their breeding efficiency declines rapidly when they become over-crowded, and disaster is avoided. With our ingenuity we have managed to overrule this essential control. If we fail to grasp this nettle, then all our efforts to clean up the environment will ultimately become futile. There is no way that we can hope to enjoy unpolluted air, land, and water if the human population, instead of gracing the planet, has become an infestation upon it. Who is to blame for the crisis we face? First and foremost, I accuse the religious leaders of the world. They have fed mankind with the dangerous myth that humanity is somehow above nature and that it is our god-given right to hold dominion over the Earth and subdue it. In many cases, they have actively encouraged over-population and have gone out of their way to prevent family planning schemes. They are a disgrace.*

Secondly, I accuse political leaders, almost all of whom follow a policy of national growth, regardless of the consequences. In their mania for power they foolishly believe that bigger is better. They constantly call for more housing, more schools, more hospitals, more industry, instead of insisting on an increase only in quality. But we are not designed as a high-quantity species. We are a high-quality species, and all our social thinking should be directed to this thought. 99

Desmond Morris

Desmond Morris, the Curator of Mammals at London Zoo from 1959 to 1967, writes on human and animal behavior.

SPIKE MILLIGAN

66 *There is only one subject to be addressed: depopulation. This done, all else will fall into place.* 99

Spike Milligan

Spike Milligan is a British broadcaster, actor, and writer.

LIVING ON THE STREET IN BOMBAY

PETRA KELLY

66 *Feminism and the power of non-violence are to me very essential concepts of green politics. Male-led revolutions have so often and so tragically been mere power exchanges in a basically unaltered structure, and have left behind dramatic accounts of their crises and heroism, such as the siege of the Winter Palace or the taking of the Bastille. These revolutions were often based on the concept of dying for a cause; feminist-conceived transformation is all the more about daring to live for a cause.*

'To think globally and act locally' is one of the mottoes of the Green Party and of the feminist movement in Europe. Feminism and non-violence are concepts that must belong together in struggling for a truly demilitarized society that preserves the ecological basis of life, guaranteeing social equality and justice, and respecting the needs of women and all those who have had no lobby – children, the sick, the old, the handicapped. As Norway's female Prime Minster Gro Harlem Brundtland has observed: 'We are one Earth, but far from One World!' 99

Petra K. Kelly

Petra Kelly is a former member of the German Bundestag for the Green Party.

RENÉ DUMONT

66 *Leaving Africa, a continent of ruined villages, of diplomats bereft of hope, of shanty towns without work or basic health care, and returning home to a civilization based on waste, I feel shame at the ever worsening disparity in wealth between Europe and Africa. Humankind is at the crossroads, and our future depends on the speed with which we wake up to the gravity of the crisis.* 99

USING A PUBLIC TAP IN KANO, NIGERIA

René Dumont is a French agronomist and author known for his interest in environmental and development issues.

POPULATION
CRUNCHING NUMBERS

JONATHON PORRITT

No other ecological challenge is quite as important as reducing population growth rates in developing countries, while reducing resource consumption levels in the rich North.

For the majority of politicians, population remains a taboo subject. Yet reducing the rate of growth in human numbers is the single most important goal to be found in this or any other book about the state of the Earth. Privately, many politicians acknowledge this;

HUMAN OVUM SURROUNDED BY SPERMATOZOA

in public, they keep their lips tightly buttoned. Why? Are they afraid of a pro-life backlash in their electorate? Do they suppose that even to mention population is to agree by inference to programs of compulsory sterilization or infanticide?

Fifteen years ago, I might have avoided such inflammatory language. In the intervening years, I have learned better, and so have the vast majority of serious environmentalists. For we still have a choice as to which way we go, but that "window of choice" will not last forever.

On average, every minute of every day, 274 people are born, and 97 people die. 177 extra people every minute means 93 million extra people every year. The vast majority of them are in Third World countries that are least equipped to manage such growth.

In ecological terms, it is not the simple population statistics that count, but the numbers of people multiplied by their average consumption of energy and resources. The average US citizen consumes at least

BIRTH RATES *This crowded street scene* (opposite) *demonstrates the acuteness of India's population problem. The country already has more than 1 billion people, with an annual growth rate of around 2 percent. Average growth rates in Africa are even higher. This mother and child* (right) *are from Rwanda, a country with one of the highest growth rates of all: 3.4 percent per year.*

50 times as much as the average Kenyan. It follows that preventing an unwanted pregnancy in the United States is 50 times as beneficial to the Earth as preventing one in Kenya. When environmental organizations talk about the need for every country to have a proper population policy, they are not just talking about providing patronizing advice and contraceptives for the Third World. Each developed country must aim first for zero population growth at home, and then for overall reductions.

CHOOSING SURVIVAL

Even so, the real challenge still has to be met in the Third World, where most of the new arrivals this decade will be born. The gap between the United Nations Family Planning Association's best and worst case scenarios for population stabilization is the gap between a sustainable future for humankind and ecological disaster caused by deforestation, inexorable soil erosion, and groundwater depletion.

The best case scenario would mean world population leveling off at between 7.5 and 8.5 billion. This would occur only if all developing countries were able to follow the example of those that have succeeded in reducing population growth rates most rapidly over the last two decades. If, on the other hand, many developing countries fail to get their population growth rates below 2 percent over the next 20 years, the population will rise to around 14 billion. The difference between the two scenarios, around 6 billion people, is greater than the total world population today.

ON THE GREEN FRONT
IPPF
International Planned Parenthood Federation

The International Planned Parenthood Federation (IPPF) is the world's largest voluntary family planning organization, working in 134 different countries. Set up in 1952, it is made up of autonomous associations in each country, run by local people for local people, implementing programs of their own making. Although it does important work through influencing public opinion at the national and international level (for instance, persuading governments to include population policies in their constitutions), it is this grass-roots approach that has allowed it to achieve such impressive results.

One of the best-known member associations is Pro Familia in Colombia, which won a special award from the United Nations in 1988. With little direct support from the government, Pro Familia operates 43 family planning centers, and over the course of 23 years has seen the population growth rate reduced from 3 to 1.7 percent. The key to their success has been the recruitment of local women to run community workshops and to make house-to-house visits, dealing not just with family planning, but with health care of all kinds. The main education tool is a health guide with diagrams and a calendar, directed principally at women with small children, to remind them of the dates for vaccinations, dental check-ups, and other medical appointments.

The instructors and health teams often have to operate in areas ravaged by guerrilla war, drug trafficking, and extreme poverty. In spite of this, the services they offer are wide-reaching and highly efficient: two in every three couples now plan their families responsibly, using contraceptive methods recommended by Pro Familia.

The real problem areas are Africa, South-East Asia, and South America. Much depends on whether countries like India and China are successful in continuing to bring down population growth rates. China's "one-child" policy has been effective in towns and cities, but has been largely disregarded in rural areas, not least because of the powerful cultural preference for boys rather than girls. Cases of female infanticide are widespread.

China's population policy, whether it succeeds or fails, has raised critical issues of human rights and the status of women which have yet to be resolved. But in other countries there is no shortage of encouraging success stories, in terms of reduced growth rates. South Korea, Taiwan, Sri Lanka, Thailand, Zimbabwe, Mexico, Cuba, the state of Kerala in India: all offer object lessons that can be built on in other countries. There are immense cultural and religious obstacles, not least from the hierarchy of the Catholic Church, which continues to uphold its edict against contraception despite overwhelming evidence of the terrible suffering caused to millions of human beings as a result. Even so, there is no insuperable reason why the examples of these countries should not inspire a decade of truly sustainable development in which family planning plays a key role.

If there is no reduction in Africa's population growth rate of 2.9 percent, the population of the continent will double in 24 years.

The United Nations' own estimates suggest that as many as one-third of pregnancies in Third World countries are either not wanted at the time or not wanted at all. In order to meet this huge demand for contraception and family planning around the world, the current annual expenditure of around US$3 billion would need only to be doubled to about $6 billion a year.

Poverty in the world's poorest countries is a dual scourge. Not only is it a powerful engine of environmental destruction in itself, particularly in rural areas, but high infant mortality provides an equally powerful

AT THE GRASS-ROOTS (above)
A family planning worker in Zimbabwe writes out prescriptions for contraceptives to farm workers. The government program is considered one of the best models for family planning in Africa. It has revealed the existence of a huge demand for contraception among women in rural areas.

THE CHINA SYNDROME (below)
At the latest count, in October 1990, the population of China had risen to 1,133,682,501. With more than 17 million additional people a year, the government has had to abandon its target of a total population of no more than 1.2 billion by the year 2000.

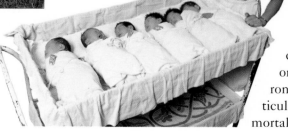

incentive to have large families as an "insurance policy" against the high risk of premature death.

The eccentric notion that population growth actually fosters economic development is now dismissed by almost all Third World countries. All the evidence supports the theory that fewer children means happier and healthier children. The ivory-tower scholars who persist in denying this must be unable to recognize human suffering and ecological degradation when it is staring them in the face.

LESSONS LEARNED

Two important facts have emerged from the many family planning programs in operation around the world. Firstly, countries in which income is more equitably shared between a larger number of people tend to reduce growth rates faster than countries where a relatively rich elite goes on getting richer at the expense of the poor.

Secondly, such programs are more effective if targeted on women, particularly on raising education and health care standards among women in the poorest communities. This is not just "feminist rhetoric," as has been argued by many of the development "experts" (almost all of whom are men) who preside over aid departments in the developed world. Throughout the Third World, women are food producers, household managers, and parents; 80 percent of the food for home consumption in Africa is grown by women. Yet such women are often undernourished, overworked, burdened with constant pregnancies, and culturally oppressed. Without the full participation of women in family planning programs, there will be no sustainable development in those countries with the highest population growth rates.

It is not always the case that such programs have to be funded by the developed world. China and India have had little help with their family planning from outside. But there are many Third World countries actively seeking financial assistance in this area today, and simply not getting it.

Our fate (and that of the Earth) is not predetermined; it is not too late to choose the way we want to go. The successful case studies are capable of replication in many other countries, and the reasons for acting now are crystal clear. Yet again, all that would seem to be lacking is political will and a resolute determination to give population and family planning issues the priority they deserve.

SHARING THE EARTH'S RESOURCES *Few shoppers in this Paris store may be aware that they too play a role in the world's population problems: each consumer in an industrialized country exerts the same pressure on Earth's life-support systems as dozens of people in developing countries. Correcting this imbalance is a vital part of solving the population equation.*

PAUL EHRLICH
ANNE EHRLICH

66 America and other rich nations have a clear choice today. They can continue to ignore the population problem and their own massive contributions to it. Then they will be trapped in a downward spiral that may well lead to the end of civilization in a few decades. More frequent droughts, more damaged crops and famine, more dying forests, more smog, more international conflicts, more epidemics, more gridlock, more drugs, more crime, more sewage swimming, and other extreme unpleasantness will mark our course. Or we can change our collective minds and take the measures necessary to lower global birthrates dramatically. People can learn to treat growth as the cancer-like disease it is and move toward a sustainable society. The rich can make helping the poor an urgent goal, instead of seeking more wealth and useless military advantage over one another. Then humanity might have a chance to manage all those other seemingly intractable problems. We shouldn't delude ourselves: the population explosion will come to an end before very long. The only remaining question is whether it will be halted through the humane method of birth control, or by nature wiping out the surplus. 99

Paul R. Ehrlich

Anne H. Ehrlich

Paul R. Ehrlich is Bing Professor of Population Studies and Professor of Biological Sciences at Stanford University, where Anne H. Ehrlich is Senior Research Associate in Biological Sciences.

TIME BOMB: OVERPOPULATION

Today the Earth's finite resources are unequally shared by 5.3 billion people, increasing by three people each second. The UN's *lowest* estimate of world population in the year 2100 is 7.5 billion. This figure is unrealistically optimistic; the true figure is more likely to be between 11 and 14.2 billion. The vast majority of these people would live in developing countries, facing crippling shortages of land, food, and water. There would also be a far greater number of older people for the working population to support. Our sole hope is to create a stable population by reducing the birth rate to equal the death rate. This can only be done by meeting the growing demand for education and family planning among women around the world.

TOO MANY PEOPLE, TOO LITTLE LAND (left) *Poor families in many parts of the world tend to have large families, believing that the extra hands will bring in food and income at little cost. But, as these Brazilian settlers have found, the result is often too large a population for the land available.*

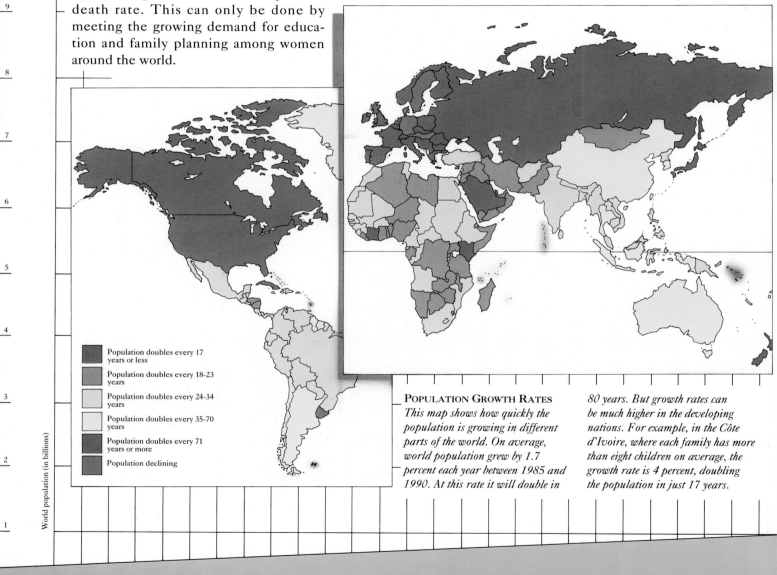

World population (in billions)

13
12
11
10
9
8
7
6
5
4
3
2
1

1600
1700

Population doubles every 17 years or less

Population doubles every 18-23 years

Population doubles every 24-34 years

Population doubles every 35-70 years

Population doubles every 71 years or more

Population declining

POPULATION GROWTH RATES
This map shows how quickly the population is growing in different parts of the world. On average, world population grew by 1.7 percent each year between 1985 and 1990. At this rate it will double in 80 years. But growth rates can be much higher in the developing nations. For example, in the Côte d'Ivoire, where each family has more than eight children on average, the growth rate is 4 percent, doubling the population in just 17 years.

NUCLEAR FAMILY

In industrialized nations, many women pursue careers and practice family planning. The preferred model is the nuclear family (left) with its two children, which results in a stable population. As the graph shows (right), only 10 percent of the world's population growth is taking place in industrialized nations.

2100

Developing nations

1950

Industrialized nations

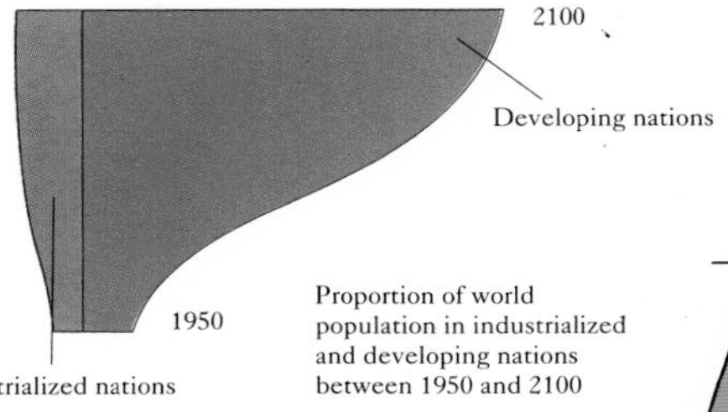

Proportion of world population in industrialized and developing nations between 1950 and 2100

AGE PROFILE (below)

Compared with industrialized nations, in the developing nations young people make up a very large proportion of the population. Women often start their families earlier (in India, the average marriage age for girls is 14) and have more children. People in industrialized nations usually have fewer children, and they live longer because of higher standards of living and better health care.

THE RIGHT BALANCE

(below) *In the industrialized world, the population is evenly spread across the age range; there are therefore more working people to support children and other dependents.*

Developing nations, 2025 — Industrialized nations, 2025

Males   Females

65+

15-64

0-15

Industrialized nations, 1985
Developing nations, 1985

300 200 100   0   100 200 300
Population in millions

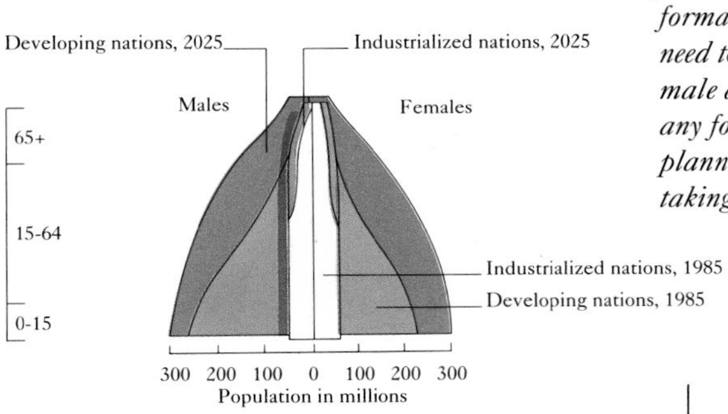

This graph shows the proportions of the male and female population in different age groups in industrialized and developing countries. The pink and white sections show the population in 1985 and the darker pink and grey areas show increases between 1985 and 2025.

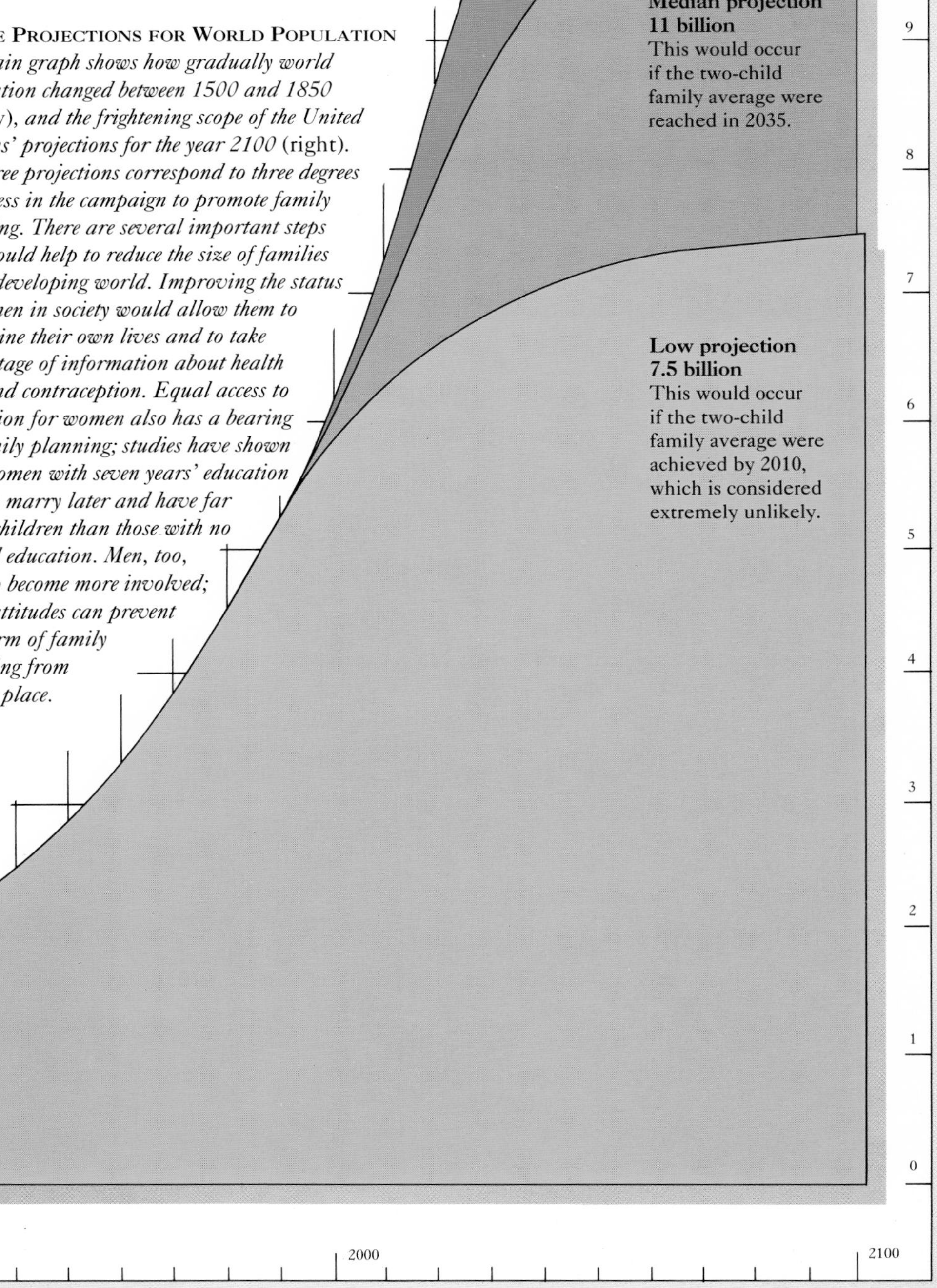

THREE PROJECTIONS FOR WORLD POPULATION

The main graph shows how gradually world population changed between 1500 and 1850 (below), and the frightening scope of the United Nations' projections for the year 2100 (right). The three projections correspond to three degrees of success in the campaign to promote family planning. There are several important steps that would help to reduce the size of families in the developing world. Improving the status of women in society would allow them to determine their own lives and to take advantage of information about health care and contraception. Equal access to education for women also has a bearing on family planning; studies have shown that women with seven years' education tend to marry later and have far fewer children than those with no formal education. Men, too, need to become more involved; male attitudes can prevent any form of family planning from taking place.

High projection 14.2 billion
This would occur if the two-child family average were not reached until 2065.

Median projection 11 billion
This would occur if the two-child family average were reached in 2035.

Low projection 7.5 billion
This would occur if the two-child family average were achieved by 2010, which is considered extremely unlikely.

13

12

11

10

9

8

7

6

5

4

3

2

1

0

1900   2000   2100

TOWNS AND CITIES
EMPOWERING PEOPLE
JORGE HARDOY AND DAVID SATTERTHWAITE

Without a major shift in urban policy, the 1990's, like the 1980's, will be a "lost decade" for most people living in large Third World cities.

Throughout the 1980's, average incomes declined in many Third World nations, especially in Latin America and in Africa south of the Sahara. Trends toward improved health slowed; in some areas, they even went into reverse, with increased incidence of disease, disablement, and premature death. The "material abundance" predicted in previous development decades failed to materialize.

We now find that the majority of people in the Third World did not benefit much (if at all) from economic change; many nations are now as badly off as they were 30 or 40 years ago. Uncertainty dominates the discussions among present Third World leaders, who will witness the beginning of a new century with no clear idea of what the future will bring for their impoverished nations.

Meanwhile, urban growth has continued relentlessly. The Third World's urban population is now larger than the total population of Europe, North America, and Japan combined: some 1.3 billion people. Poverty and destitution, more commonly associated with rural areas, are now a tragic part of urban life. Millions of people live in illegal housing structures on land sites for

SLUM DWELLINGS IN LA PAZ, BOLIVIA (opposite)
The poor, including their children (such as this rubbishpicker in Manila, above), are the planners of most Third World cities. It is they, rather than local authorities or large commercial concerns, who are responsible for financing and shaping much of the city. And it is they who undertake most of the housing construction, even as governments declare such housing illegal.

Jorge Hardoy MSc PhD is the President of the International Institute for Environment and Development America Latina in Buenos Aires. Twice a Guggenheim Fellow, he has written widely on both historical and contemporary urban issues.

David Satterthwaite is a researcher for IIED in London, and an advisor to the World Commission on Environment and Development. He and Jorge Hardoy edit the twice-yearly journal of the IIED, Environment and Urbanization.

which they have no legal title. Many other aspects of their lives are illegal: their work, sources of water, connections to the electricity grid, and even the health services and informal buses they use. Legal homes, jobs, and services are either not available or too expensive. Most poor people in the Third World die before the age of 40; in many countries, a third or more die before the age of five.

SCALE OF URBAN GROWTH

Most of the growth in the Third World's population in the next few decades will take place in urban centers. This is despite the fact that in most nations, the actual rate at which urban populations are growing is likely to slow compared with that of the 1950's, 1960's, and 1970's, usually because of stagnant economies. Many cities grew more slowly during the 1980's than during earlier decades. But most nations will continue to become more urbanized as economic, social, and political forces continue to concentrate new jobs, education opportunities, or just the chance of survival in urban centers. In countries where a small elite owns most of the agricultural land, rising agricultural production usually ends up destroying the livelihoods of poor rural households. Where land-owning structures are more equal, increased agricultural production and prosperity can still stimulate urban and industrial growth. And even where rural economies are stagnant, poor households often increase their chances of survival with a move to an urban center.

Cities also grow through the children born to those already living there. Even with slower

WRONG SIDE OF THE TRACKS (right)
Slums along the railway line into Jakarta are a symptom of Indonesia's growing population problems. The notorious Transmigration Program (partly funded by the World Bank) aims to remove millions of people from the Javan mainland to outlying territories. The real root of the problem, however, is not human numbers, but the concentration of fertile land on Java in the hands of a tiny minority.

SUBURBAN SPRAWL
With 20 million inhabitants, Mexico City is the world's largest urban agglomeration. For most of the population, housing is a pressing problem. The 3 million people who live in the gridplan streets of the Nizahua-Coyotl district (left), are only marginally better off than the inhabitants of the Valle de Chalco shanty town (below).

urban growth, no less than 60 cities in Africa, Asia, and Latin America are likely to grow by an average of 100,000 inhabitants or more every year during the 1990's. Some 150 other cities will grow by an average of 50,000 inhabitants a year.

While less than 3 percent of the Third World's population lives in what are now termed "mega-cities" with 10 million or more inhabitants, such mega-cities present unprecedented problems. They are already so large that a growth rate of 3 or 4 percent a year represents an enormous additional population. The Mexico City Metropolitan Area is expected to grow at an average of over 500,000 inhabitants every year during the 1990's, with São Paulo averaging over 400,000, and Karachi and Bombay (among others) 300,000 or more a year. By contrast, only two cities in Western Europe, Athens and Madrid, are expected to grow by even 25,000 new inhabitants a year.

> *An estimated 600 million people in Third World cities live in neighborhoods lacking clean water supplies, sanitation, and safe and secure homes.*

Though these numbers are daunting enough in themselves, the implications for the surrounding environment and natural resources are harder to envisage, especially in regions that were unsettled or only sparsely settled one generation ago. Much of the recent population growth has been within fragile ecosystems such as the moist tropical forests and dryland areas of Latin America, South-East Asia, and Africa.

The reasons for this are essentially political. In sub-Saharan Africa and South-East Asia, independence gave millions of people the freedom to move; under colonial rule, this right had been rigorously controlled. With these controls lifted, many moved to urban centers (both old and new), and others to the agricultural frontiers. In Latin America, there has been a similar development of new frontier areas, this time driven by the fact that a small elite already owned most of the good quality land under cultivation. People's search for new lands, combined with private and public initiatives to tap previously unexploited natural resources, was supported by the construction of new roads and communications systems in wilderness areas.

TIME BOMB: URBANIZATION

So far as many cities in the Third World are concerned, the population explosion has already happened. Cities like São Paulo and Mexico City have experienced a massive surge in numbers since the 1970's and are braced for more to come. The environmental fallout from this process of urbanization has been devastating, creating ever-widening circles of deforestation and soil erosion around each urban center, and adding chronic problems of air and water pollution to the already overburdened city infrastructures. In many urban communities, poverty, destitution, and poor health are now as prevalent as in the poorest rural areas.

Urban (Third World): 25%
Urban (industrialized nations): 17%
Rural (industrialized nations): 6%
Rural (Third World): 52%

1990 World Population

Urban (Third World): 46%
Urban (industrialized nations): 13%
Rural (industrialized nations): 4%
Rural (Third World): 37%

2025 World Population

URBAN/RURAL POPULATION PREDICTIONS (above) *As a result of migration to Third World cities, and growth within those cities, 59 percent of the world's population in the year 2025 will live in urban areas.*

LURE OF THE CITY (below) *Rural families driven from their homes by drought squat in tents on the outskirts of the Indian city of Ahmadabad.*

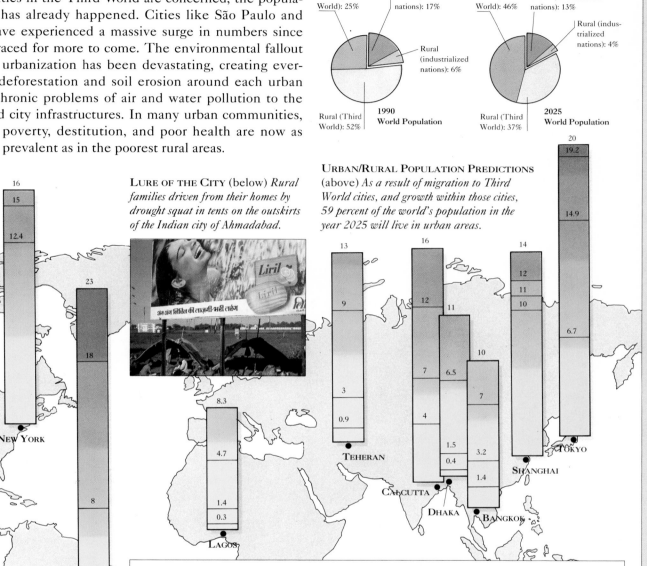

Key
The bar charts on the world map show the population (in millions) for the years below. (New York is an exception. Its peak population, 16 million, occurred in 1970. Since then, its population has declined to a stable 15 million.) All these figures are UN estimates.

2000
1990
1970
1950

The author holds reservations about the assumptions underlying the UN techniques for predicting urban populations.

MEXICO CITY (25, 20, 9, 3)
NEW YORK (16, 15, 12.4)
SÃO PAULO (23, 18, 8, 2.7)
LAGOS (8.3, 4.7, 1.4, 0.3)
TEHERAN (13, 9, 3, 0.9)
CALCUTTA (16, 12, 7, 4)
DHAKA (11, 6.5, 1.5, 0.4)
BANGKOK (10, 7, 3.2, 1.4)
SHANGHAI (14, 12, 11, 10)
TOKYO (20, 19.2, 14.9, 6.7)

BANGKOK

Cities all over the world suffer the same disastrous consequences of rapid urbanization: congested roads, polluted air, inadequate sewage systems and water supplies, poor public health. Yet every city must also face unique problems of its own.

For example, Bangkok stands on the rich alluvial delta of the Chao Phraya. The river and the city's many canals have played a vital part in Bangkok's recent economic success, but water is also at the heart of the city's most pressing ecological problems.

● Only 2 percent of Bangkok's population is connected to the sewage system.
● The water table has dropped 80 feet (25 meters) since the 1950's, causing land to subside at a rate of 5 inches (13 cm) a year.
● A third of the city's population has no access to public water supplies and must buy water from vendors.
● A quarter of the city's garbage is dumped on waste ground or into canals and rivers.
● The poor are often evicted from good building land into areas prone to flooding.

RUBBISHPICKERS
(above) *Outside Manila in the Philippines, scavenging among the rubbish on the huge dump known as the Smoky Mountains is a way of life for hundreds of people. Scavenging is a dangerously unhealthy way of earning a living, but it is now commonplace in most of the cities in the Third World.*

SMALL BUSINESS
Given half a chance, the poor in most Third World cities establish many small, informal enterprises – such as this watch repair stand in Nigeria (right, above), and a traveling shop in Lima, Peru (right, below). The cities' economies depend on small concerns of this kind.

This in turn has produced networks of cities, towns, and rural settlements where only a few decades earlier there was hardly any human habitation. Where towns already existed, the size usually multiplied in two or three decades. Others grew from nothing. The capital of Brazil, Brasilia, with some 2.4 million people in 1989 did not exist in 1960. Ciudad Juárez in northern Mexico grew from 262,000 inhabitants to over 1 million between 1960 and 1990. Modern atlases find it almost impossible to keep up with this demographic revolution. Places too small to mention in one edition may attract hundreds of thousands of inhabitants by the next.

As new urban centers emerge within some of the Earth's more fragile ecosystems, the environmental destruction they provoke is usually immense. The cost of it often outweighs the economic benefits. Each new settlement creates a circle of destruction around it, resulting in the deterioration of large areas of savanna and forest ecosystems. It is the settlers themselves who suffer most; the many diseases associated with impure water supplies, lack of sanitation, and overcrowded housing have spread rapidly in the cities of the new agricultural frontiers. Millions of people now live in the midst of the deforested and eroded lands, close to rivers and tropical sea coasts that are now polluted by oil spills and industrial and human wastes.

Somehow, it has to be possible to make the interchange between urban centers and their surrounding environments more sustainable. At the same time, we must ensure more adequate livelihoods for poorer urban households and provide city dwellers with the food, water, and other natural resources they need. These two policy goals are not mutually exclusive; innovative policies can seek solutions to both.

CREATIVE ANSWERS

For instance, resource conservation can generate many jobs and improve the quality of urban and rural environments – as in watershed afforestation, the use of waste water from cities for farmland irrigation, and the reduction of waste generation and the promotion of recycling, thus ensuring less waste has to be disposed of into rivers, lakes, seas, or landfill sites around the city.

Furthermore, it is usually far cheaper to meet increasing demand for any resource by increasing the efficiency with which existing supplies are used. For instance, reducing leaks in a city's piped water system is usually the cheapest way to meet rising water demands, while promoting greater energy efficiency is a cheaper and more manageable way of meeting increased demand than simply increasing supply.

Improved traffic management, together with measures that favor public over private transport on existing roads, can reduce congestion more cheaply than building new roads. This also helps to lower air pollution, which in many Third World cities has now reached extremely unhealthy levels. Such measures have to be accompanied by rigorous pollution controls, especially on industries, with public authorities charging businesses the full cost of the publicly provided roads, water supplies, drains, sewers, and other services from which they benefit.

The political future of most Third World nations will be influenced by their success or failure in managing their cities. We must begin by acknowledging four basic facts. First, trying to stop the process of urbanization does not serve the needs of

JACK MUNDEY

" *As a worker and trade unionist, I feel the environmental movement the world over, and especially in the rich countries, has failed to involve working people in the most important movement of our times. Equally, the international trade union movement must break with its narrow economism and accept socially responsible attitudes to the nature of work.*

The Green Ban movement in Australia in the 1970's successfully formed an historic alliance of middle class and working class people and won many environmental struggles based on the philosophy that work performed should be of a 'socially useful nature.'

Fashioning sustainable societies will require a thorough re-examination of the entire production and consumption process. Only if we can involve people of all social classes will it be possible to extricate ourselves from rampant and wasteful consumerism, and usher in an ethical revolution which can create social, economic, and political sanity. "

Jack Mundey

Jack Mundey is a national councillor of the Australian Conservation Foundation and President of the Urban Environment Coalition.

CHRIS ZYDEVELD

" *I have always lived in Schiedam, a town in a heavily polluted industrial area of Holland. Municipal workers spraying herbicides so lavishly that spray entered our home brought me to 'environmental awareness.' Getting only nonsensical answers when I questioned why spraying was necessary, I started campaigning against this pollution.*

Some years later, I was elected to the town council and was given a share in the responsibility for municipal decisions. We stopped spraying herbicides 16 years ago.

Then we banned the use of all pesticides in city parks. We planted huge quantities of trees. We improved public transport and put in separate bicycle lanes.

Then we asked architects to design energy-efficient housing, and were able to build homes that require only around half as much fuel for heating as the national average – without increasing the cost of construction.

In our town, with its 70,000 inhabitants, we make a small beginning. Keeping our Earth alive is a global task, but we can all make a beginning in our own surroundings. "

Chris Zydeveld campaigns on environmental issues in Holland.

WASH DAY IN THE SEWER
Where supplies of clean water are inadequate, the poorest citizens of cities in the developing world, like these women in Haiti, make do with what there is, even if it means doing the washing in an open drain.

poorer groups, nor does it improve the management of limited resources. Well-managed cities allow a cheaper provision of basic services (water, sanitation, health care, etc.), and can help to protect natural landscapes and sites of special ecological value by concentrating large numbers of people in a smaller area and reducing pressure on rural resources.

In the majority of large Third World cities, over 70 percent of all new housing is constructed "illegally" on unofficial settlement areas. In some cities the figure can be as high as 95 percent.

WEALTH FROM WASTE

Because it has no sewage-treatment works, most of Calcutta's human waste is channeled into a maze of shallow lakes on the edge of the city covering more than 6,200 acres (2,500 hectares). By a complex system of embankments, feeder channels and culverts, the sewage is divided into different ponds in a carefully organized way. If kept at the right level, it fertilizes the growth of algae and water plants, including water hyacinths and watercress which help to absorb some of the heavy metals in the sewage. The plants provide ample food for the carp, tilapia, giant shrimp, and other local fish which thrive in the ponds.

Sustainable System
The whole system is maintained by the local fishermen, who quite literally oversee the transformation of human waste into a valuable source of food.

It is the largest biological sewage treatment plant in the world, requiring very little maintenance, and costing the city of Calcutta nothing at all. It may offend the somewhat precious sensibilities of most people living in the rich North, but this is true sustainability in practice.

BIOLOGICAL WASTE TREATMENT
Calcutta fishermen display the day's catch, taken from the city's self-renewing system of sewage treatment.

Second, the economy and established environment of these cities will be shaped predominantly by people with low incomes: garbage collectors, shoemakers, peddlers, those making clothes, foods, and crafts in their homes, domestic servants, government clerks, factory workers.

Third, many households will be headed by women who face the triple responsibility of raising children, managing the household, and earning the main income. Finally, in most Third World cities, almost half the population will be under 15 years of age for the next decade or two.

The extent to which these children's needs and priorities are met will strongly influence their future attitudes and aspirations. Many children will have to begin work long before completing school. Although most of them will still live with their families, there will be millions whose home is the street, where they are constantly exposed to violence and exploitation.

A NEW PARTNERSHIP

The only way of dealing with these "problems" is to make a virtue of them. This means that politicians and civil servants must not only learn how to manage cities with very scarce resources, but do so by working with, not against, the low-income unskilled people who make up the majority of the population.

Individual ingenuity and community resilience among the poor cannot address such problems as the lack of paved roads, drains, sewers, piped water, or legal land sites on which they can build. Instead of ignoring or repressing them, often bulldozing their settlements, governments should recognize that working with low income groups can mean more efficient and democratic ways of developing cities. Governments could multiply the scale and quality of the poor's house-building by supporting their efforts: ensuring sufficient cheap land for housing close to their sources of income; providing loans on flexible affordable terms; providing technical advice on how to build cheap safe homes, and how to design the layout of sites. The costs of piped water, sanitation, roads, drains, and other essential infrastructures are enormously reduced by such a partnership.

There will be new leaders. The people who will build and manage the cities of the future will be different from the traditional politicians and technocrats. For example, women from all social groups will play increasingly important political, professional and economic roles in the development of the cities of the future.

LACK OF VISION

It may sound strange, but most governments and international agencies have no clear picture of what to do with their cities or with the urban poor. Cities are still regarded as voids into which apparently limitless amounts of money can be poured with little effect. In spite of all the information about what is happening, discussions on how to manage cities where the majority of the population is poor are very unrealistic. We cannot claim success simply by pointing to a few successful projects that have improved the chances of survival or living conditions for a tiny proportion of those in need.

SELF-DETERMINATION

It is obvious that if Third World nations are ever going to develop sustainably, the issues of basic human needs and urban development must be included at the top of the agenda of every nation and international agency. Governments and agency leaders have forgotten the immense resourcefulness of the people they regard as the problem and the strong sense of solidarity that exists among them. They do not see that these are the very people who can build and manage healthier, resource-conserving cities.

ON THE GREEN FRONT
ELA BHATT AND SEWA
Self-Employed Women's Association

Ela Bhatt set up the Self-Employed Women's Association in 1972. As a lawyer and social worker, she had become deeply concerned about the conditions suffered by poor, self-employed women in her city, Ahmadabad, in the Indian state of Gujarat.

The SEWA now exceeds 100,000 members in six states. These women include weavers, stitchers, vendors of fruit, fish, and vegetables, firewood and wastepaper pickers, and road construction workers. Most are subject to high rents for stalls or the tools of their trade and routine exploitation by money-lenders, employers, and officials.

To counter this poverty and oppression, they have set up cooperatives of various trade groups to share skills and expertise, to develop new tools, designs, and techniques, and for bulk buying and joint marketing. Most importantly, they have established their own bank. Today it has more than 22,000 accounts, and has rescued thousands of women from money-lenders and pawnbrokers, allowing them to accumulate land, small assets, and the means of production.

In Ela Bhatt's own words: "From a miserable passive acceptance of all the injustices, SEWA women, by organizing themselves, have attained the courage to stand up and fight, the ability to think, act, react, manage, and lead. There is no development without self-reliance."

HARLEM VISTA, NEW YORK
Urban deprivation is not restricted to Third World countries. Many millions of children still have to grow up in environments like these in some of the richest countries on Earth.

RURAL RESOURCES
RELEARNING CIVILIZATION
ANIL AGARWAL

Three billion people, in a million or so villages, use most of the world's land. "Educated people" consider them to be illiterate and ignorant; nothing could be further from the truth.

We live in a world cruelly divided between the desperately poor and the overly rich, the hungry and the overfed, the powerful and the powerless. It is in rural areas that the injustice and cruelty of this divide can be seen at its most vicious.

People have been living in many villages of Africa, Asia, and South America for thousands of years. They have a deeply rooted culture, and have experimented with their environment for centuries. They have found what sustains itself over time and what does not. Myriad environments have given rise to myriad cultures: on the slopes, people practice shifting cultivation; in the fragile desert, they take to gentle and seasonal use of the resources and, hence, adopt nomadism; in semi-arid areas, they practice a mix of animal care and agriculture; and, in the relatively robust environment of the humid tropics, they cut down the trees and bring vast tracts under paddy cultivation, supported by a web of "homegardens" with an extraordinary diversity of domesticated plants.

In global terms, the result is a huge range of sustainable livelihoods and cultures. The use of the land is usually gentle and non-violent, and lifestyles adjust to low levels of

Anil Agarwal, who started his career as a science journalist, is now the Director of the Centre for Science and Environment in New Delhi, an organization to promote public awareness of environmentally sound development issues.

productivity. Rural people have traditional ways of doing things that they cannot always explain. Over generations, sustainable practices were selected, while others that could not be sustained were abandoned. Culture coded these "dos and don'ts" into everyday life, forming a powerful body of traditional knowledge.

What has happened in colonial and post-colonial India provides a depressing example of how such knowledge has been disregarded. Farmers living in semi-arid lands have always had to adopt practices that are ecologically sustainable and relatively risk-free. The monsoon brings copious rain but only in three months of the year, and the actual amount of rain varies enormously from one year to another. As a result, village people have developed a complex system of recycling. Farming produces grains to feed the people and crop residues to feed the animals. Animal care not only gives milk, but also manure and labor. Forests and woodlands provide a sustained supply of green fodder and firewood. Thus, the land around each Indian village has been transformed into a complex ecosystem of croplands, grasslands, and forests. It is an interactive, "multi-purpose" biological system which responds to the seasonal rhythms of the area, and keeps the social and economic impact of rainfall variation down to a minimum.

Because the land is parched for most of the year, people have developed water storage devices to meet their needs year-round. They had no need to build huge dams; they simply caught the huge amount of water that fell in their own village before it disappeared into the river. When the British

REPAIRING THE DAMAGE WROUGHT BY MAN
Nepal has suffered terrible erosion as a result of its hills and mountains being stripped of their trees. Major reforestation programs are now under way, but it will be many years before the trees planted by this young

Nepalese woman (opposite) can help to restore the status quo. On the Indian subcontinent the most valuable work is often done by women, whether it is tea-picking on a commercial plantation (inset, above) or domestic chores such as the drying of rice in Bangladesh (right).

ON THE MOVE
Pastoralists, like these Yemeni camel-drivers, have adapted their lives to some of the world's most fragile ecosystems. Some 50 million people in the world depend on rearing cattle, goats, camels, donkeys, and sheep, but modern agriculture and development have begun to erode both their way of life and the few precious resources on which they depend.

SATISH KUMAR

66 *If we go on using the Earth uncaringly and without replenishing it, then we are just greedy consumers. We should take from the Earth only what are our absolute and basic necessities: things without which we cannot survive. The Earth has an abundance of everything, but our share in it is only what we really need.*

There is a story to illustrate this. Mahatma Gandhi was staying with the first Indian Prime Minister, Mr. Nehru, in the city of Allahabad. In the morning Gandhi was washing his face and hands. Mr. Nehru was pouring water from the jug as they talked about the problems of India. As they were deeply engaged in serious discussion, Gandhi forgot that he was washing; before he had finished washing his face, the jug became empty.

So Mr. Nehru said, 'Wait a minute and I will fetch another jug of water for you.' Gandhi said, 'What! You mean I have used all that jugful of water without finishing washing my face? How wasteful of me! I use only one jug of water every morning.'

He stopped talking; tears flowed from his eyes. Mr. Nehru was shocked. 'Why are you crying, what has happened, why are you worried about the water? In my city of Allahabad there are three great rivers, the Ganges, the Jumnar, and the Saraswati, you don't need to worry about water here!' Gandhi said, 'Nehru, you are right, you have three great rivers in your town, but my share in those rivers is only one jug of water a morning and no more.' 99

Satish Kumar

Satish Kumar, a former Jain monk, is the editor of *Resurgence* magazine and the Director of Schumacher College in Dartington, Devon, England.

started to colonize India in the early 19th century, there were hundreds of thousands of catchment ponds across the country.

This technology was supported by an elaborate system of property rights and religious practices. Croplands were private property, but grasslands, forests, and ponds were community property and rules were set by the villagers for their use. Not only the cow, but also the grazing lands were sacred. Parts of many forests were set aside as sacred groves, while the ponds themselves and their catchments acquired religious significance and could not be polluted.

A SYSTEM THAT WORKED

The wealth generated in such villages supported a range of skilled artisans, producing a great variety of world famous goods. Huge cities sprang up along the Ganges and elsewhere in the country. Before the British came, India was nearly 100 percent literate, and probably more urbanized than any other country in the world. The entire system would fail only during acute droughts and floods, largely because of lack of communications, which made it difficult to transport goods quickly from one area to another. Kings and kingdoms might fight with each other for their wealth, but life in the villages would go on, built around self-reliance and self-management.

But colonialism disrupted and destroyed all this. Europeans were very eager to share in the riches of India, but failed to understand the Third World concept of community property. Since the community owned lands yielded no revenue, the British considered them wastelands. They were turned into state property managed by a bureaucracy, which undertook a process of systematic plunder. Throughout the country they took over vast tracts of communally owned forests, without offering any compensation to the local villagers.

The entire economic-ecological system was turned around to produce goods not to meet local people's needs, but for the metropolitan markets of the colonizing power. The impact of this change was enormous. Old Indian cities, dependent on organic urban-rural links, were pauperized; India as a whole was de-urbanized; artisans went bankrupt and were pushed out into the countryside; widespread illiteracy set in. Even today, most of the old Indian cities remain extremely poor.

Indian society imploded under this colossal impact. The locals, having lost control of their environment, became increasingly alienated and finally joined in the plunder. What had once been "community managed commons" were turned into "free access resources."

CYCLES OF DEVASTATION

With the forests disappearing, firewood became scarce; so people began to burn cow dung, leaving little manure for crops. With less fodder available, grasslands were severely overstocked. The number of goats increased and, along with cattle, they began to roam on former forest lands. No regeneration was possible and, year after year, the rain god began to wash away the soil. Soon, half the land was wasteland, in the true sense of the word. The scarcity of biomass became an acute human crisis. Women suffered the most, as grass, leaves, wood, and water disappeared. Children, especially girls, who acted as assistants to their mothers, no longer found it possible to attend school.

A WOMAN'S WORLD
Nepalese women (above) carry bundles of rice straw back to the village after the harvest. In rural communities of the Third World, women, as well as looking after the household and raising the children, do much of the agricultural work. Western development projects are invariably dreamed up by men, so it is hardly surprising that so much aid money is so scandalously misused. The essence of genuinely sustainable development is self-determination. In some countries, such as Niger (left), women's cooperatives are proving highly successful in regaining control over local land and the systems of production used to cultivate it.

ON THE GREEN FRONT
THE SIX S ASSOCIATION

The primary role of the Six S Association is to provide the technical know-how to face the unprecedented challenges of drought and desertification in the Sahel, and to assist villagers in their negotiations with officials from governments and aid agencies. A federation of peasant organizations from Burkina Faso, Senegal, Benin, Mali, Togo, Niger, Mauritania, Guinea Bissau, and the Gambia, the Association's full title is *Se Servir de la Saison Seche en Savane et au Sahel* (Making Use of the Dry Season in the Savanna and the Sahel). Among its founders was Bernard Ouedraogo, a former teacher and civil servant from Burkina Faso.

When Ouedraogo realized that the assistance given to farmers by his own government was of little lasting use, because the recipients had no say in how it was allocated, he developed a network based on the villages' own traditional organization (called the *naam*). There are now 4,000 *naams* in Burkina Faso.

His next initiative was to set up the Six S. The Association keeps strict control of financial payments, but policy is decided by the farmers' groups themselves. Ouedraogo, winner of the Right Livelihood Award in 1990, has always stressed the need for solutions consistent with local culture and wisdom: "The danger for many Africans is that the erosion of our ways by the aggressive ways of others, our own values by foreign values, will destroy our sense of responsibility for solving our community's problems."

INDIGENOUS AND ALIEN TREES
The Chipko Movement (or "tree-huggers") has come to symbolize grass-roots action to protect community resources against so-called "development" (above). The movement started in 1974 in the village of Reni in the foothills of the Himalayas. When indigenous forests are cut down, they are too often replaced by monocultures, like this plantation of fast-growing eucalyptus in southern India (right).

But the British were not just looters. They came to rule. And in their bid to rule, they educated an entire class of Indians who no longer appreciated or understood India. This was the class that came to rule the country after independence. The result has been a headlong rush towards Westernization, now even more difficult to oppose, since it is being orchestrated by brown masters.

WESTERN GODS

With government loans becoming freely available to gear rural production to urban needs, those who could afford it have joined in the race. As new kinds of monoculture take over, the idea of bio-diversity has gone to the winds. The Green Revolution, a market-oriented strategy to meet growing food needs, has destroyed genetic diversity on the farms. And the White Revolution, a strategy to meet the milk needs of the urban population, is destroying genetic diversity in cattle and causing serious undernourishment among rural people. The 1980's saw the so-called "Program for Social and Community Forestry," a project sponsored by the World Bank, but all the trees have been private, exotic, and destined for the market-place, whereas the poor need the local varieties that have traditionally been planted on the commons. The urban system, abetted by Western aid and capital, has swallowed up every rural resource for its own gargantuan needs.

All this is being done in the name of science, technology, and progress. Traditional knowledge and culture, and the ecological rationality it possessed, have been pushed out; science-based lifestyles and modes of production are now in.

Rural people in India are now trying to reassert their rights over their environment. Through the Chipko Movement, it has been shown that rural people have a more important interest in the long-term management of their environment than private commercial interests or the government. This is the world famous "hug-the-tree" movement in the Garhwal Himalaya where the local people told the government that it would first have to axe them before it could get to the trees. "We must get our grasslands and forest lands back as community property," they have consistently argued. "Our future is inextricably tied up with our trees."

Faced by a mounting ecological crisis, rural communities have shown a growing desire to manage their local ecosystems, including the village commons. In villages where "free access" commons have been turned back into traditional community managed property, environmental regeneration has led to economic growth.

The experience of these villages shows that it is not the people's response to their environmental crisis that is lagging behind, but the archaic system of law and government. Most laws governing India's land, water, and forests were formulated by the British. This gives India the unique distinction of trying to deal with 21st-century problems of environmental management with out dated 19th-century laws and bureaucracy of a colonial ruler.

What can today's Westerners learn from all this? First, the West may indeed have developed systems of representative democracy to manage the nation-state with the help of bureaucracies, but in the process it has often destroyed or stifled the growth of participatory, rural democracy. The common property resources, from wetlands to tropical forests, can only be managed through a system of participatory, grass-roots democracy.

Secondly, the Third World does not need aid and charity, but a proper price for its products. Biomass products like tea, timber, bananas, coffee, chocolate, pineapples, and peanuts are grown on the land of the developing world, but largely consumed by rich countries and the elite of poor countries. The terms of trade for these crops have steadily deteriorated as rich consumers are not prepared to pay the true cost of production.

GLOBAL TAX

Barbara Ward, one of the founders of the Western environmental movement, suggested an international system of income tax for countries so that wealth can be automatically transferred as a matter of right and not just as aid and charity. The funds so raised could then be used to finance an international "Right to Survival" so that anyone, anywhere in the world, would be assured a minimum subsistence wage. Instead of being forced to scrape the soil, the poor could be mobilized to restore the productivity of the Earth, giving them the financial space to wait for returns that will come five to ten years later. Together with the establishment of basic grass-roots democracy, so vital for good environmental management, we would have moved a little way towards a just and sustainable world.

DESMOND TUTU

The injustice and exploitation of apartheid have horrible ecological consequences. In our rural areas, pylons carry electric power all over the country, but not to the farms where Africans live. So they have to cut down trees for firewood, and that has encouraged soil erosion. Justice and ecology are linked indissolubly.

The Most Reverend Desmond M. Tutu
is the Anglican Archbishop of Cape Town, South Africa.

RAVI BHAGWAT

One hundred and fifty years of colonial rule left us a legacy not only of denuded forests and dammed rivers, but also of a belief that this was progress. In the half century since independence, we ourselves have not only done precious little to challenge this belief, but have on the contrary pursued that same model of so-called 'development' with a vengeance. The irony is that while in many Western countries today ecologists are coming round to believe in the truth of Mahatma Gandhi's world view, in his own country, as in many other Third World countries, he seems to have been forgotten. There are, however, signs that we may be on the way to some genuine rethinking about development in the days to come.

Ravi Bhagwat is the Honorary Secretary of Parisar, a non-governmental environmental organization based in Pune, India.

FOR THE EARTH OR THE HEARTH? *A woman sells cakes of dried cow dung in an Indian street. As village firewood becomes scarce or more expensive, local people often turn to cow dung as an alternative fuel for cooking and heating. This deprives the soil of its most important source of nutrients, progressively reducing yields of grass and crops.*

TRIBAL PEOPLES
HONORING WISDOM
ROBIN HANBURY-TENISON

BEAD AMULET
FROM NORTH INDIA

AFRICAN MASK

Whereas industrial nations exploit and destroy,
tribal peoples nurture and manage their varied habitats in subtle
and efficient ways that have stood the test of millennia.

Throughout the world there are tribal peoples who have developed extraordinarily close and harmonious relationships with their environments, making use of a wide variety of ecological niches without destroying them in the process. Only now, almost at the very last moment, are we beginning to realize that these people provide a living expression of what sustainability is all about. Yet, in most cases, they are still regarded by the surrounding population and by governments as "obstacles to progress."

Many tribes have suffered terribly from the invasion of their lands. Some, like the Aché Indians of Paraguay, have been hunted down, captured, and confined in camps to die. This was happening as recently as the 1970's and there are now no "free" Aché left at all. In other cases tribal peoples die from diseases unwittingly brought in by outsiders. Their culture and society are destroyed by many so-called "development projects." As the roads and dams, mines and ranches, devastate the land, they undermine tribal peoples' livelihoods and force them to the edges of the invading society which holds them in such low esteem.

A common characteristic of tribal peoples everywhere is a deep respect for the natural world. They also share a sense of horror at the ruthless abuse of it demonstrated by modern man. "We belong to the land, not the land to us," is a

Robin Hanbury-Tenison OBE MA FLS FRGS is an explorer, writer, and campaigner for tribal peoples. One of the founders of Survival International, he has been on more than 24 expeditions, many of them to the rainforests of the Amazon.

sentiment I have heard expressed in one way or another by members of tribes in the Americas, Africa, South-East Asia, and Australia.

In the rainforest we are learning the hard way that the real wealth lies in the inherent richness of its biomass, not in the short-term profit which can be extracted through logging or cattle ranching, let alone by the greedy search for the minerals that lie beneath it. Even the most imaginative Western scientists are still desperately short of ideas about how the rainforest's resources can be tapped efficiently, profitably, and above all sustainably. Only the tribal peoples who live there know this. Only they can identify not just the names and external characteristics of every plant and animal, but also their uses as food, medicine, clothing, building materials, and much more. They are able to find and select at the right times of year the best rattan for furniture-making – a material that is worth more per ton than timber. They know about literally hundreds of plants with potential as food crops, which could be grown in order to supplement the dangerously small number of crops upon which the vast majority of the

SAMBURU WOMAN
AND CHILD, KENYA

CULTURAL HERITAGE
In the interior of New Guinea, many tribes, like these Melpa, still live in great isolation. With a population of just 4 million people, Papua New Guinea boasts more than 1,000 languages and dialects. The island's forests are equally rich in terms of species diversity. Three-quarters of its original forest cover is still intact, though parts are now threatened by mining and agricultural development.

CAROLINE JONES

The Holy Spirit of the Great South Land

ABORIGINES OF THE ARANDA
TRIBE DECORATING THEIR BODIES

I saw it first as a child, in wild storms sweeping down on Murrurundi, nest in the hills, country of Kamilaroi.

I hid under the kitchen table while hail splintered the windows and shredded the violets.

I have heard it hum in lichen rocks. It chatters in clap-sticks, drones and grunts in didgeridoo, shrills in cicada, kaleidoscopes in opal, wheels in grey heron at dusk, pulses in dense black star-crusted night on the Nullarbor.

It explodes in mauve umbrellas of jacaranda, swells in Banksia's grotesque pods, swirls in cream and pink whorls painted on snow gum trunks, gleams in their fat strap leather leaves: the living spirit of the great south land.

It dreams in my Aboriginal countrymen and women, keepers of the Spirit, of the family, the land . . . they who have clung for eons in the threat of the savage westerly brandishing its scourge of sand, threatening eviction.

Their patient bodies tell of courage, suffering, forgiveness and awe of the sacred; they whose currency is knowledge of religion, that which binds; they who sing the birds on their migration paths.

Their frail survival lights the turnings of my own journey.

They lay a template of meaning upon mystery and remind me of what it is truly to be human.

Caroline Jones

Caroline Jones presents *The Search for Meaning* on ABC Radio in Australia.

world's population depends. And their intimate pharmaceutical knowledge holds clues to many new cures to diseases. For example, over 3,000 different plants are used as contraceptives. More than 1,400 species are thought to have anti-cancer properties. Yet both this lore, and the flora and fauna themselves, are rapidly becoming extinct before their potential can be tested. Without the help of tribal peoples we will be unable to benefit from this astonishing "natural laboratory."

FERTILE DESERTS

Modern man tends to regard deserts as disaster areas, and it is certainly true that their rapid expansion over regions recently green and fertile is one of the most visible symptoms of our misuse of the planet. For many tribal peoples, however, deserts, wisely used and efficiently managed, represent a home where rich and successful husbandry may still be practiced. Kalahari bushmen have one of the highest protein intakes of any people on Earth, exceeded only by residents of the American Mid West, while the nomadic pastoralism of people like the Tuareg of the Sahara makes the maximum use of another supposedly barren "wasteland." By moving constantly in pursuit of the grazing that is made possible by intermittent rains, they carefully extract nourishment over a wide area without any part of it being overexploited. Strictly controlled by patterns that have stood the test of time, such farming methods are by definition truly sustainable.

OBVIOUS TRUTH

The same is true of traditional fishing methods, whether practiced by the Inuit people in the rich Arctic waters from which they take no more than they need, or by the Cuna of Panama, whose communal net I once saw laden with the greatest catch of freshwater fish I have ever seen. This net is only used a few times a year. "Otherwise," they told me, as though it were the most obvious thing in the world, "we would soon remove all the fish in the river and we would go hungry."

Harvesting the fruits of the forest or culling wild animals carries the same restrictions. Even the most sophisticated models and projections created by modern science cannot compete with the practical experience of people who have tested their methods in their every-day lives for countless generations. This simple truth is at last coming to be recognized by global institutions like the World Bank. They are beginning, hesitatingly and with some trepidation, to consult the real experts, and to listen to their advice. Guidelines have been prepared by the Bank for investment in indigenous areas; in a few cases, funding has even been withdrawn from damaging projects opposed by the tribal peoples affected by them.

KELABIT TRIBESMAN
FROM SARAWAK

It is still not too late to recognize the moral lessons that industrialized man has forgotten. There are powerful prejudices and vested interests to overcome, but as a critical mass of outrage builds up, I believe there is a real chance that the pendulum may swing toward a respect for all life, and a recognition of the greater wisdom of those who have always practiced this philosophy.

JUSTICE AND SENSE

For two decades the abhorrence of the cumulative genocide we have witnessed has inspired many campaigns to support tribal peoples in their struggle to survive. This has only come about because of vigorous campaigning by ordinary people working through organizations such as Survival International, the worldwide movement to support tribal peoples. Displacing communities in the interests of development projects such as dams or new mines, or "for their own good", as it is sometimes argued, is always disastrous, an indefensible crime which flouts both tribal peoples' own rights and the best interests of their environment. Land rights and self-determination are the keys to their survival. In reaction to international pressure and to the increasingly vigorous case put forward by tribal peoples themselves, some land is now being returned to its original owners. This is the best way to protect it, better in the long run than creating national parks or wilderness areas.

All tribal peoples respect nature, worshiping the Earth as a mother. They revere the forces of life which control the seasons, fertility, and the enduring cycles upon which the health of the planet ultimately depends. We used to be like that. If we

ON THE GREEN FRONT
SURVIVAL INTERNATIONAL

Since its foundation in 1969, Survival International has become a world authority on tribal peoples, upholding their right to decide their own future and helping them to protect their lands and their way of life. It is now working on more than 50 cases all over the world, from the rainforest-dwelling Indians of Brazil to the nomadic herdsmen of the Kalahari Desert, from the tribal people of the Narmada Valley in India to the Aborigines of Australia.

They have assisted in preventing dam-building projects in India and Guyana; persuading Scott Paper to pull out of a project in Indonesia, thus preserving the forest homes of 15,000 people; maintaining constant pressure on the Malaysian government to stop logging in Sarawak. Their appeal on behalf of the Yanomami of Brazil brought in over $100,000, and provided urgent medical care for a people devastated by the effects of gold mining on their hunting lands.

Although the genocide of tribal peoples and the destruction of their lands remains a constant threat, real change is under way. Governments are beginning to take notice; the World Bank has an environmental impact studies department; school books no longer refer to tribal peoples as "primitive;" most missionaries are now respecting indigenous cultures; and many tribal peoples now have campaigning organizations of their own.

PENAN HUNTER
Armed with a blowpipe and poisoned arrows, a Penan tribesman stands beside a cascading stream in his forest homeland. The Penan have been in the forefront of the fight against the Malaysian government's destructive logging policies in Sarawak. In a desperate effort to maintain their traditional culture and territory, they have organized blockades to keep out the logging trucks. Many have been arrested and imprisoned as a result. As a Penan elder, Unga Paran, explains: "The forest has been our way of life for thousands of years. The government say they give us development. That is a lie. . . . Because of the logging, we now have hunger."

TIME BOMB: GENOCIDE

TURKANA NOMAD OF
NORTHERN KENYA

The scale of the assault conducted by European colonial nations against indigenous peoples is sometimes hard to grasp. Since 1500, the number of Indians in South America, for example, has fallen from at least 10 million to less than 1 million. Today the very existence of tribal peoples in many parts of the world is threatened by those who would exploit their lands for mining, logging, settlement, or ranching.

Christopher Columbus set the pattern for the explorers and colonialists who followed him when he initiated the extermination of the Taino people on the island of Hispaniola in the West Indies. In the 500 years since Columbus, we have made very little progress: many governments in South America and South-East Asia still see their remaining tribal peoples as "savages" and seek to assimilate them into mainstream society in such a way as to destroy their identity and culture.

But the tide is turning. We are coming to realize just how much we can learn about the true wealth and sustainable management of the rainforests, the deserts, and the Arctic snows from the peoples who have lived for millennia in these precious environments.

CURSE OF OIL (below)
Until recently, the Waorani of Equador were one of the world's most isolated peoples. Now their land is being ruined by oil exploration.

THE LURE OF GOLD
A Yanomami girl (below right) prepares for a tribal feast. Her people have suffered greatly from diseases introduced by the white man. The map (right) shows the traditional territory of the Yanomami in northern Brazil. In 1988, the government allocated them only 30 percent of their original land, and even that is invaded by hostile goldminers.

MILITARY INVASION (right)
The Innu once moved with the migrating herds of caribou. Now they have been forced into fixed communities near a NATO training base on the Labrador coast, where people and animals alike are terrorized by low-flying military aircraft.

TRIBES IN DANGER (below)
The map shows some of the world's most endangered peoples, and lists the main threats to their way of life: the destruction of their lands for mining, logging, dams, plantations, or ranching.

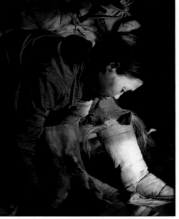

YANOMAMI
gold mining
(Brazil)

WAORANI
oil exploration
(Ecuador)

Area of northern Brazil which the Yanomami asked should be left untouched as a National Park in 1985.

Indian territory established by government decree of 1988.

Mining areas sanctioned by government in 1990.

INNU
military base
(Canada)

BHILS AND
TADAVIS
dam project
(India)

LUMAD
logging, and a planned power station
(Philippines)

BARABAIG
high-technology wheat farms
(Tanzania)

MENTAWAI
influx of settlers
(Indonesia)

DAYAKS
logging
(Malaysia)

ABORIGINES
(Australia)

RESETTLEMENT
(below) *Following the clearance of their forests for oil-palm plantations, the Mentawai people of Siberut Island are now threatened by the planned resettlement of 100,000 people from other parts of Indonesia.*

SACRIFICE TO PROGRESS (above)
Tribal musicians of western India keep alive the link with their forest homeland, which is at risk of being flooded by a huge dam project on the Narmada River. If the dam goes ahead, 60,000 tribal people, mainly Bhils and Tadavis, will see their lands submerged.

ANCESTRAL LANDS
(right) *An Aborigine stands in front of Ayer's Rock, a place of great spiritual significance to his people, now a tourist attraction. The land rights of Aborigines, once the sole occupants of Australia, have rarely been respected.*

NAVAJO ELDER
Many Americans are only now coming to terms with the way in which North American Indians have been persecuted and oppressed over the last 350 years.

can escape the hubbub and the stink of our civilization, and stand for a moment in the peace of a wilderness area or in the vibrant pullulation of a rainforest, we can remember how it was, and even gain some inkling of how it might be. But surrounded by the pressures and pounding of the modern world, whether it is the clatter and traffic roar of a modern city or, for many more, the stench, overcrowding, and hunger of the Third World, we forget the lessons of the natural world and look only to making good in the short term. This is dangerous, for it leads to chaos.

Tribal peoples themselves represent the solution to so many of the problems the world faces today. Their survival is the key to our own survival. They are the best friends the Earth still has, and we should listen to them with as much care and attention as we can muster.

AILTON KRENAK

66 *My people have lived in this place for a very long time, since the time when the world did not yet have this shape. The forest people hold the memory of the creation of the world, of the fundamental principles of life. We feel we have to keep civilization from offending nature. All of us still carry the memory of the day when the world supported all of its people – feeding us, taking care of us, putting us to sleep with the songs of the birds, rivers, waterfalls, and forests. Each season taught us that there is a right time for every activity. We want to show the people of the city that it is possible for the human race to achieve their adventure with nature still alive. We want to build in the hearts of the people of the city a beautiful forest, made of friendship, music, and celebration. Then we can pacify their spirit, so they can live with the people of the forest. This is our message.* 99

Ailton Krenak

Ailton Krenak is National Coordinator of the Union of Indian Nations and President of the Forest Peoples Alliance in Brazil.

CHIEF GARY POTTS

Mother Nature determined long ago
that we should live and die and be born
through the ages of ice, water, land, and snow.
In the echoes of our Mother's birth cry
we have continued to grow.

From the structure of our universal womb
we gaze out into the universe
through our window-pane of air.
And I wonder, will we become a universal tomb?

The languages of non-human and plant life
flow in concert with our Mother's soul.
The stone is our Mother's bone
the soil is our Mother's flesh
the lava is our Mother's marrow
the sun is our Mother's universal touchstone
the moon is our Mother's rhythm maker.

In 1990, as it left our solar system, Voyager II
sent back a picture of us, a dot of blue,
the color of peace in infinity.
It is not beyond the grasp of reality
to promise our Mother Nature life in perpetuity.

Chief Gary Potts

Since 1972, Gary Potts has been First Chief of the Teme-Augama Anishnabai in Canada. He has traveled internationally as an advocate of human rights.

V

WATER

Next day we were sailing in slack winds through an ocean where the clear water was full of drifting black lumps of asphalt, seemingly never-ending. . . . The Atlantic was no longer blue but grey-green and opaque, covered with clots of oil ranging from pin-head size to the dimensions of the average sandwich. Plastic bottles floated among the waste. We might have been in a squalid city port. . . . It became clear to all of us that mankind really was in the process of polluting its most vital well-spring, our planet's indispensable filtration plant, the ocean.

From **The Ra Expeditions** *by* THOR HEYERDAHL

In the waters of the St. Lawrence River in Canada, there lives the Beluga whale. The only freshwater whale in the world, it is white – and toxic. Industrial pollutants and dangerous chemicals that have been gradually building up in the river over the last 40 years are passed up the food chain to the Beluga whale. The tissues of the whales contain such concentrations of these chemicals that, under Canadian law, their bodies must be specially disposed of as toxic waste. Is this the high point of industrial civilization: that we are able to transform one of the world's most beautiful and astonishing creatures into a floating toxic tip? Some of the companies involved in this desecration continue to deny any liability, falling back on the industrialists' time-honored defense that their products are harmless until proven to be directly responsible for some environmental mishap. It has long been the argument of marine and aquatic experts that all new compounds introduced into our seas and rivers should be deemed potentially lethal until proven innocent.

MARBLE CONE (left) AND PRINCELY CONE

GLOBAL COMMONS (opposite) *South of New Zealand, the Antarctic Ocean stretches wild and remote. Yet it is part of a single body of water uniting the Earth as it washes the shores of every continent.*

FLAME SCALLOPS (above) *Shellfish that live by siphoning water through their bodies are especially sensitive to changes in the chemistry of the sea. Both their feeding and their reproduction can be affected.*

OCEANS AND SEAS: SOVIET FACTORY TRAWLER HARVESTING THE RICH FISHING GROUNDS OF ANTARCTICA

Before the Age of Reason and the advent of modern science, our ancestors invariably ascribed a special spiritual significance to their rivers and lakes, the oceans and the seas. It was sacrilege to defile a pure spring or beautiful river, not only as a source of great inspiration and aesthetic satisfaction, but as a source of natural, God-given wealth on which their lives depended. Pollution is just the contemporary way of describing the same process.

Some of that pollution is highly visible: foaming rivers, a sheen of oil on a lake's surface, streams filled with domestic rubbish. But much of it is invisible. Lakes affected by acid rain may still look stunningly beautiful, but beneath the surface they are devoid of life.

WETLANDS: WATER LILY IN THE FLORIDA EVERGLADES

Sadly, the abuse of our water environment does not end there. Our seas, lakes, and rivers teem with a vast diversity of different species, many of which have provided humankind with a steady flow of

SHORELINES: BRITTLESTAR (left) AND SPINY STARFISH (right)

nutritious food over many centuries. There was no threat to this sustainable food source until the 19th century, when bigger ships and more efficient fishing techniques first began to make serious inroads into the breeding stocks of key species. From the largest whale in the ocean through to the smallest freshwater crustacean, a range of edible species has suffered constant over-exploitation at the hands of industrial man. You would think we might learn from the errors of the past, but the same absurd cycle seems to be repeated in one fishery after another.

There are few clearer examples of what the American ecologist Garrett Hardin referred to as "the tragedy of the commons." For fear of losing out to competitors, no fisherman feels that he can afford to hold back; instead, he tries to take as much as possible. This gives rise to one ecological disaster after another, accompanied by great (and

OCEANS AND SEAS: A SKIPJACK TUNA, ONE OF THE SPECIES RELENTLESSLY PURSUED BY HIGH-SEAS FISHING FLEETS

THE GULF WAR

The war in the Persian Gulf in 1991 gave rise to one of the world's worst environmental disasters. Saddam Hussein's Iraqi troops not only released millions of barrels of oil into the Gulf itself, but in retreat set fire to around 570 of Kuwait's oil wells.

All wars damage the environment. In ancient Greece rivals destroyed each others' crops and poisoned water supplies, while as recently as the 1960's American troops destroyed forests in Vietnam. Going to war on an oilfield was guaranteed to lead to disaster.

Ecological Terrorism

Around 6 million barrels of oil a day were burning immediately after the war. A huge pall of smoke reduced the average temperatures by 18°F (10°C). Fortunately, the smoke stayed low in the atmosphere, reducing the risk of effects beyond the Gulf region. But the high-sulphur Kuwaiti oil has severely reduced agricultural productivity by increasing levels of acidification in the soil.

The loss of oil revenues to Kuwait runs into billions of dollars. The environmental damage is impossible to quantify, but it has at least galvanized many countries into seeking new international agreements to outlaw any further acts of "ecological terrorism."

INNOCENT VICTIM (above) *Turtles, rare sea cows, and thousands of birds were killed by oil slicks, which severely damaged reefs and the seabed. Because the waters of the Gulf are calm and shallow, the oil took longer to break down than it would have on an open sea.*

THE SPOILS OF WAR (right) *The sight of so many oil wells burning simultaneously was without precedent. Fire-fighting teams from America, led by Red Adair, were hampered by a lack of water and the danger from mines and booby traps left by the Iraqis.*

TIME BOMB: WATER SHORTAGES

More people demanding more water for agriculture, industry, and domestic use results in a massive increase in demand for fresh water each year. In theory, the 2,165 cubic miles (9,000 cubic kilometers) of water available for human use could easily satisfy this demand. But many parts of the world are experiencing severe water shortages, whether because of localized drought, or because groundwater, rivers, and lakes are polluted by industrial or sewage waste, or simply because abundant water supplies are used wastefully.

DAILY WATER USE
(left) There are grotesque disparities in average water consumption in different parts of the world. A large part of the vast quantity of water used by the average American household goes into sprinkling lawns and washing cars.

The world's population now uses nearly five times as much water each year as it did in 1950.

On average, each American uses up to 264 gallons (1000 liters) a day.

In rural Kenya, many people make do with just 1.3 gallons (5 liters) a day.

Nearly three-quarters of the world's population has access to only 13 gallons (50 liters) of water per day. The minimum needed for a reasonable quality of life is 21 gallons (80 liters).

IRRIGATING FARMLAND (above)
Crop irrigation accounts for three-quarters of the fresh water used in the world every year. Often much of this precious water is lost through evaporation or leakages.

GLOBAL WATER CONSUMPTION
The blue line stretching across this page shows the enormous increases in total fresh water consumption between 1940 and 1990. The figure for 1990 is an estimate.

VILLAGE TAP (above)
A tap provides drinking water for an entire village in Nigeria. Thousands of villages throughout Africa and Asia depend on communal taps or wells for their water.

United States
The vast groundwater supplies of eight Great Plains states have been reduced so much that the water table is falling by about 3 feet (1 meter) a year. In Southern California, drought and profligate consumption have caused severe water shortages. To satisfy the ever increasing demand, supplies of water are being diverted from lakes in the north of the state. There is even talk of building desalinization plants.

USSR
The Aral Sea was once a giant lake providing a vast area with fresh water. It has been poisoned and cut off from its river sources, leaving it less than half as big as it was 25 years ago.

Eastern Europe
Rivers here have been heavily polluted by industrial and municipal waste. The Vistula in Poland is too dirty even for industrial use.

China
China's population faces acute water shortages in 50 of its largest cities. For example, water tables beneath Beijing are falling by 3-6 feet (1-2 meters) a year, leaving one-third of the city's wells without water.

India
Thousands of Indian villages have no water and villagers must walk long distances to fetch it. The pumping of water for agriculture has caused the groundwater to fall dramatically, and government efforts to supply rural areas have not succeeded. Out of 2,700 wells provided in the north, 2,300 have simply dried up.

Total world water use per year, measured in cubic miles

50-100% have water

0-50% have water

data not available

WORLD VIEW
This map (right) shows the proportion of people who have access to safe drinking water. But "access" in some countries means merely that there is water within 15 minutes walking distance.

Egypt
Population growth and the anticipated low-levels of the Nile will leave Egypt with one-third less water by 2000.

Middle East
Water supplies in parts of the Middle East are vulnerable to strategic feuds. For example, Jordan and Israel, both with fast-growing populations, share the same rivers. Syria may suffer supply problems when Turkey's Ataturk Dam is finished in 1992.

largely unnecessary) human suffering as jobs are lost and livelihoods destroyed.

Looming larger even than these concerns are two issues that already affect the lives of millions of people: lack of access to drinkable water and outright water shortages. A staggering proportion of the illnesses and premature deaths in Third World countries are caused by infection-ridden drinking water. It is estimated that 25,000 people a day die from drinking polluted water. In 1980, the United Nations

WATER SHORTAGES: THROUGHOUT RURAL AFRICA, AS IN THIS NIGERIAN VILLAGE, EVERY DROP IS MADE TO COUNT

launched its International Drinking Water Supply and Sanitation Decade with the slogan "Clean water and adequate sanitation for all by the year 1990." Although millions were provided with safe drinking water, the increase in world population offset many of these gains. Roughly the same proportion of the world's population lacked clean water and sanitation at the end of the decade as at the start.

RIVERS: TAMBAQUI, SEED-EATING FISH OF THE AMAZON

In the Third World, the shortage is not of water itself, but of compassion, justice, and money from the rich North. In fact, it may well be the North that first feels the impact of real water shortages, as a result of its chronic wastefulness *(see opposite page)*. It is now reckoned that US$80 million would need to have been spent every day of the whole decade in order to have achieved the UN targets set in 1980. That sounds an enormous sum of money, but when you consider that the United Kingdom is currently contemplating spending up to £26 billion (US$5

GREAT POND SEDGE

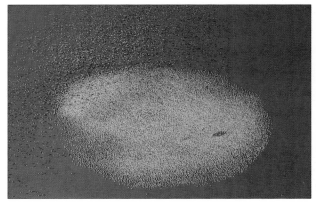

WETLANDS: BRILLIANT PINK LESSER FLAMINGOS RISING ABOVE ETOSHA NATIONAL PARK, NAMIBIA

billion) on improving its own water quality and environmental standards, it is clear that the money could have been found. Such disproportionate investments reinforce the widely held belief that talk about "protecting the environment" will only be translated into action in rich industrialized countries, thus widening the cruel divide between North and South.

PAUL MCCARTNEY

66 *Here is a story about a land with a hole in the sky. The rain that fell on this land was a poisonous acid that killed the trees. And only a few things grew in the soil because it had been spoiled by strange chemicals the farmers used. Sometimes the people would ask, 'Why is it so?' And the screen in the corner of every room would answer, calmly, 'It must be so.' The people didn't understand. They forgot their question, and went about their business.*

One day a young child woke to a grey morning. The rain was falling through the hole in the sky, on the soil where only a few things grew. And like a line of sad ants, the people went about their business. The child was listening when one of the people stopped and asked, 'Is this really the best way to be?' And the screen in every room said, 'If you want wealth, fine goods, and luxuries, you must pay a price. You must pollute the land. It must be so.' And everyone forgot the question, and began to wander off. But the child spoke up and said, 'There must be a better way to make the things we want, a way that doesn't spoil the sky, or the rain or the land.' And people listened, and switched off the screen, and went about finding a better way. The land began to blossom for the first time in a long time. The sky shone a beautiful blue, and the rain tasted sweet.

It's time that we became the young child to build a better kind of future. 99

PEARLSCALE BUTTERFLYFISH
Chaetodon chrysurus

Paul McCartney is an active campaigner on environmental issues. His 1989-90 World Tour "sponsored" Friends of the Earth groups around the world. This text was the introduction to the concert program, distributed free to almost 2 million fans.

PATRICK MOORE

66 *Fossil fuels are limited, and nuclear power has great problems. Why, then, are we not using the resources which the Earth gives us – the power of the waves or the wind? We must look ahead, and there is no time to waste. If we can split the atom, we can surely harness the tides!* 99

British astronomer, broadcaster, musician, and composer Patrick Moore is the author of more than 60 books, most of them on astronomy.

TIDAL-POWER BARRAGE, FRANCE

WILLIAM GOLDING

66 *It must be nearer 70 years ago than 60 that I first discovered and engaged myself to a magic place. This was on the west coast of our country, on the seashore among rocks. There was a particular phase of the moon at which the tide sank more than usually far down and revealed to me a small recess which I remember as a cavern. There was plenty of life of one sort or another around all the rocks and in the pools among them, but this last recess before the even more mysterious deep sea had strange inhabitants which I had found nowhere else. Only a hand's breadth away in the last few inches of still water they flowered, grey, green, and purple, palpably alive, a discovery, a meeting, more than an interest or pleasure. They were life; we together were delight itself, until the first ripples of returning water blurred and hid them. When the summer holidays were over, I carried with me like a private treasure the memory of that cave. . . .*

I have been back, since. The recess – for now it seems no more than that – is still there, and at low water springs you can still look inside. Nothing lives there any more. It is all very clean now, ironically so, clean sand, clean water, clean rock. Where the living creatures once clung, they have worn two holes like the orbits of eyes, so that you might well sentimentalize yourself into the fancy that you are looking at a skull. No life.

Was it a natural process? Was it fuel oil? Was it sewage or chemicals more deadly that killed my childhood's bit of magic and mystery? I cannot tell and it does not matter. What matters is that this is only one tiny example among millions of how we are impoverishing the only planet we have to live on. 99

SEAHORSE
Hippocampus

English novelist Sir William Golding, author of *Lord of the Flies* and the *Rites of Passage* trilogy, was awarded the Nobel Prize for Literature in 1983.

JOSEF VAVROUSEK

66 *Under our former totalitarian system, the attitude to the environment was loaded with arrogance, recklessness, and exploitation. As a result, our life-expectancy is five to seven years less than in more developed countries.* 99

Josef Vavrousek is the minister for Czechoslovakia's Federal Committee for the Environment.

ROSA FILIPPINI

❝ *I had the good luck to spend my vacation in a place where by night you can see the stars and, by day, the tuna playing among the waves. This isolated place, far from any town and without electric lights and cars, has made it possible for me to enjoy the performance that nature offers free to everyone, but which is now practically unknown to all those city dwellers who see the sky through smog and artificial lights and are surrounded by noise.*

Such a show has become a luxury but for the very few who are either so poor as to be 'condemned' to live far from our consumer society, or so rich as to be able to afford a 'wilderness vacation.' I was greatly astonished by such a long-forgotten spectacle, as old as the world itself. When I came back, I felt for the first time that the price we pay for the widespread affluence in our society is perhaps too high.

When we read ancient texts, we see that the dominance of man over nature is not an absolute concept, but a relative one. The purpose of creation is by no means limited to its use by man: even as man-made ships plow the sea, so too did God put Leviathan the whale in it, simply so that it could play in the waves. ❞

Rosa Filippini

Rosa Filippini is a Member of the Italian Parliament for the Green Party.

HAROUN TAZIEFF

❝ *Actually, the Earth, as a planet, is not in danger and we do not have to struggle for it. But millions of people are in danger, not because of fashionable problems like the ozone layer or global warming (which induce politicians to assign large sums of money to tilt at what are but windmills), but because of today's dreadful menace of pollution.*

Worst of all is the pollution of underground water-bearing strata: polluted underground waters may remain toxic for centuries. The pollution of surface waters comes next. And then the pollution of soils – by pesticides, chemical fertilizers, and all kinds of waste.

I only wish that the money and effort presently involved in preventing some of today's 'windmills' could be used, before the situation becomes irreversible, to combat the ever-increasing pollution of water, soil, and air. ❞

Haroun Tazieff

Haroun Tazieff is a Belgian vulcanologist, agronomist, and geological engineer.

HAWAIIAN TEARDROP
Chaetodon quadrimaculatus

CHARLES LYNN BRAGG

WATER'S EDGE

❝ *Evolution has shown us that nothing ever stays the same: continents drift across the oceans, jungles turn into deserts, and dinosaurs make way for silky anteaters. And where the wind and the sun once dictated the course of evolution, the near future of this planet resides in the mind and action of man. The balancing of and the struggle between greed, compassion, fear, and intelligence will now determine the destiny of all life on Earth.* ❞

Charles Lynn Bragg

Charles Lynn Bragg is an artist from Los Angeles. This image has been used in the campaign to reclaim Santa Monica Bay.

ALEJANDRO LERNER

❝ *We are all one. Birds, plants, animals, minerals – we are all different manifestations of the same essential energy. Our way ahead, our searches and dreams are the molecular expression of the life experience of everything that makes up our planet. By caring for it, we will help each other to grow.* ❞

Alejandro Lerner

Alejandro Lerner is an Argentinian writer and composer.

WIMPLEFISH
*Heniochus
acuminatus*

OCEANS AND SEAS
FAILING FISHERIES

JOHN BEDDINGTON

THREE-SPOT ANGELFISH
*Apolemichthys
trimaculatus*

The traditional freedom of the seas gave fishing fleets a license to trawl the oceans for as many fish as they could catch, with no thought for whether stocks could recover.

The oceans and seas are arguably the most vulnerable and certainly the most used of the global commons. The harvesting of fish and other sea creatures for food has a history as old as man, but only recently has this had any serious effect on the oceans and seas, and the life dependent on them.

The pervasiveness of marine litter from pole to pole emphasizes the need for international rather than national controls. In mid-ocean, ships still discharge oil and chemical pollutants into the water with impunity. But though deep-sea dumping and oil spills have important local effects, in general these waters are free of the worst effects of pollution. The main areas of

John Beddington BSc MSc PhD *is currently the director of the Renewable Resources Assessment Group at Imperial College, London. His earlier work and publications were chiefly in the fields of population biology and theoretical ecology.*

concern are those close to land and human habitation. It is here that pollution is concentrated and the majority of oil spills occur; it is also exactly where most marine life is to be found, on the continental shelves.

The major impact on living marine resources by man has occurred only in the last 100 years or so. Early and easy targets were marine mammals, particularly seals in their large breeding colonies. Much of the destruction occurred before the start of the 20th century, with the fur seals and elephant seals of the Antarctic being reduced to tiny fractions of their original abundance. The history of whaling in the 20th century, which depleted most of the large whale

MIGHTY OCEAN
(opposite*) Oceans cover more than 70 percent of the Earth's surface. The power of the ocean provokes a wide range of feelings – from outright terror to the reverence that moved the 19th-century English poet Lord Byron to write: "Roll on, thou deep and dark blue Ocean – roll! Ten thousand fleets sweep over thee in vain; Man marks the earth with ruin – his control stops with the shore."*

WHALE ROCK (left)
This ancient petroglyph of a killer whale was carved by North American Indians. In their attitude to the sea, its dangers, and its bounty, tribal peoples display a respect for marine creatures that modern industrialized societies would do well to follow. The cause of whales and dolphins has been well-publicized; it is often harder to convince people that the plight of fish and crustaceans is as important as that of endearing marine mammals.

MEDITERRANEAN MESS

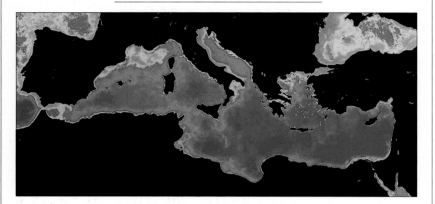

The Mediterranean accounts for only 1 percent of the globe's ocean surface, yet it is the dumping ground for nearly 50 percent of all marine pollution. The industrial chemicals that are allowed to flow into the sea are blended with terrifying quantities of human waste, especially in the summer when a flood of tourists more than doubles the resident population around the Mediterranean's shores.

In 1975, the United Nations Environment Program brought together 16 Mediterranean states to adopt the Mediterranean Action Plan, designed to prevent dumping by ships and to limit pollution from

SIGNS OF LIFE *This satellite image of the Mediterranean shows the distribution of surface phytoplankton, the microscopic plants on which the food chain of marine life depends. The red patches represent the densest concentrations, through orange, yellow, green, and on to blue (the least dense concentrations). Compared with the plankton-rich waters of the Atlantic (left) and the Black Sea (upper right), the Mediterranean is conspicuously barren.*

land-based sources. The success of the Action Plan has been limited: for such a measure to work, all the participating governments have to back it to the hilt and this universal support has never materialized.

HUMBERTO DA CRUZ

66 The Mediterranean has seen the birth of some of the richest cultures in the history of humanity. These days, its beauty and temperate climate have attracted the highest levels of tourism anywhere on the planet. The prosperity this has created has been at the expense of the region's natural resources. Measures to diminish the damage done, mostly embodied in the Mediterranean Action Plan, have been thwarted by short-sightedness and a lack of political will. Only decisive and immediate action, based on the principles of sustainable development, will protect the future of the region. 99

Professor of Economics Humberto da Cruz is President of the *Federacion de Amigos de la Tierra (*Friends of the Earth, Spain).

species, is well known. Less well known is the depletion of many highly valued fish stocks.

It is reasonable to inquire how this has come about, for at first sight the destruction of such valuable natural resources is in nobody's interest. It all stems from the fact that there was never any recognized ownership of the marine resources concerned. Where there is no ownership, there is no mechanism to limit the access of potential participants to the fishery, just simple *laissez-faire* economics and cut-throat competition.

PLUNDER AND MOVE ON

Typically, where access to promising fishing grounds is not restricted, a fishery develops, high profits are made, further participants are attracted into the fishery, and exploitation quickly increases beyond a sustainable level. Since it is in no one's interest to cut back and harvest at a sustainable level, resources are progressively depleted until the participants are attracted elsewhere. With the build-up of high seas fishing fleets in the 20th century, the process became even more destructive. As soon as stocks were depleted, the fleets moved on to more profitable areas, leaving behind them devastated fishing grounds and shattered communities on shore.

Economic changes have made the problem even worse. High interest rates have meant that short-term considerations predominate; today's income is more attractive than future income.

The most dramatic case of over-exploitation is, of course, the depletion of the great whales. However, less glamorous species like the herring of the North Atlantic, haddock, and tuna, have all suffered a similar depletion.

Initially, the international community attempted to deal with the regulation of high seas fisheries by setting up International Commissions, but their ability to deal with the problems of conserving stocks has been very limited. In essence, they have a history of short-term decision making which has been in the interests of the participating states, but which has led to the long-term erosion of the resource base

COMMON SEAL PUPS
Phoca vitulina

upon which they exist. Such criticism applies not only to the early history of the International Whaling Commission, but also to today's Commissions dealing with the fish stocks of the developed world.

TOOTHLESS WATCHDOGS

The major problem is that they do not have the authority to impose effective sovereignty over the resources. Decisions that need to be taken either require consensus of all states present, or involve objection procedures so that decisions are not binding. This means that individual states are often free to defend their own selfish interests.

Arguably the only positive benefit that these Commissions have produced is the scientific apparatus that has grown up within their orbit. These scientific committees supervise data collection and provide a forum for the give-and-take of critical scientific debate. Unfortunately, all too often the scientific advice has been ignored. The assessment of fish stocks involves a high level of uncertainty, and Commissions have often taken the optimistic view, giving the benefit of the doubt to the fishing industry rather than to the scientists.

During the 1960's, the UN Conference on the Law of the Sea was convened with a view to working out a fair way of sharing the mineral wealth of the ocean bed. However, as it happens, its main achievement was to agree that sovereignty of coastal states should extend 200 nautical miles (370 kilometers) from their coastline. In most parts of the world these new Exclusive Economic Zones more or less coincide with the shallow waters that cover the continental shelves.

CHANGING THE RULES

The reason behind this was simple: the damage being done to the fishery resources of the oceans by the unrestricted operations of the high seas fleets. An immediate benefit, it was argued, would come from the extension of national sovereignty so that nation states would be able to husband their resources. But in practice, the worldwide problem of unrestricted fishing by fleets on the high seas has simply become a national problem.

In a number of developed countries, the restrictions on their traditional fishing grounds (which now became part of the sovereign territory of other

HEATHCOTE WILLIAMS

In the water, whales have become the dominant species,
Without killing their own kind.

In the water, whales have become the dominant species,
Though they allow the resources they use to renew themselves.

In the water, whales have become the dominant species,
Though they use language to communicate, rather than to eliminate rivals.

In the water, whales have become the dominant species,
Though they do not broodily guard their patch with bristling security.

In the water, whales have become the dominant species,
Without trading innocence for the pretension of possessions.

In the water, whales have become the dominant species,
Though they acknowledge minds other than their own.

In the water, whales have become the dominant species,
Without allowing their population to reach plague proportions.

In the water, whales have become the dominant species,
An extra-terrestrial, who has already landed . . .
A marine intelligentsia, with a knowledge of the deep.

From space, the planet is blue.
From space, the planet is the territory
Not of humans, but of the whale.

Heathcote Williams

Heathcote Williams is a British poet. These are the closing lines of his *Whale Nation*.

ARCTIC BLUE (left) *Despite the inhospitable nature of much of the Arctic Ocean (shown here near Ellesmere Island in Canada's Northwest Territories), its fragile environment is threatened by the kind of large-scale development that has gradually supplanted the traditional, low-impact lifestyle of the Inuit people. Oil is eagerly sought after, as Canada and the United States make efforts to become less dependent on oil from the Gulf.*

TIME BOMB: OVERFISHING

The depletion of one major fishery after another is a telling indictment of our attitude to the Earth's natural wealth. The FAO estimates that the sustainable level of global fishing is 100 million tons per year. Yet in 1987, the commercial catch was 91 million tons and a further estimated 24 million tons was caught by local fishermen, whose catches go unrecorded.

TOTAL COLLAPSE

The Peruvian anchovy fishery (right) was once the largest fishery in the world, landing an annual catch of some 13 million tons. But in 1972, dramatic overfishing (combined with a change in direction of the warm El Niño current) sent catches plummeting (graph below).

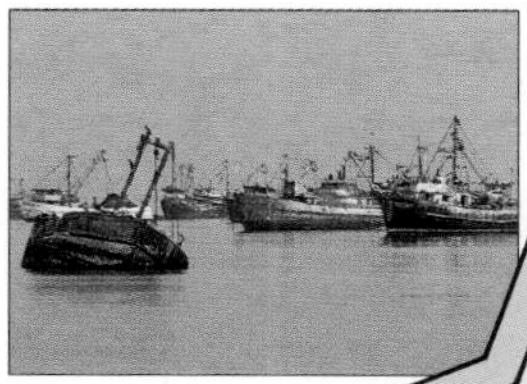

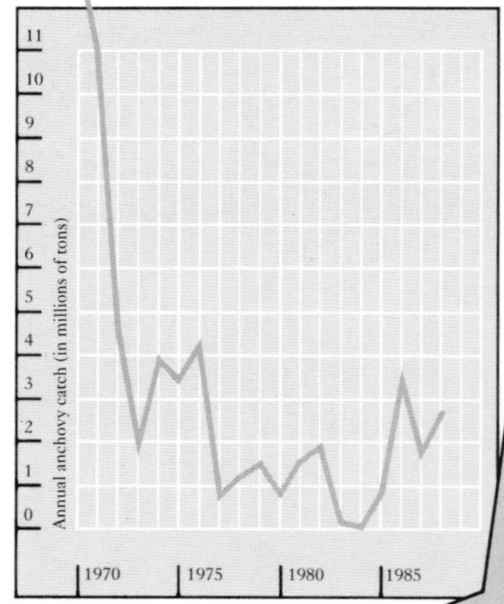

OVERFISHING

The graphs show catches in thousands of tons for the years shown below. The discovery of valuable fishing grounds leads almost inevitably to the depletion of stocks. Fish populations are very difficult to estimate, so scientists and fishermen alike must rely on the numbers caught from year to year. The speed at which fish stocks are depleted and recover depends partly on the species' migratory habits and breeding cycles.

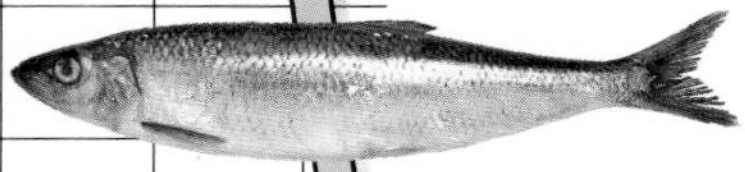

Herring

(Clupea harengus)
Industrialized fishing in the 1960's and 1970's decimated herring stocks throughout Northeast Atlantic waters. The figures used for this graph are for the North Sea herring fishery, which was completely closed between 1977 and 1982, to allow stocks to recover. But, although there is legislation forbidding the landing of fish less than 8 inches (20 centimeters) long in the North Sea, stocks are still threatened because of the taking of juvenile fish outside the North Sea's officially agreed boundaries.

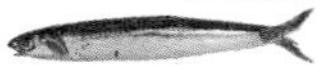

HERRING
Clupea harengus

ANCHOVY
Engraulis ringens

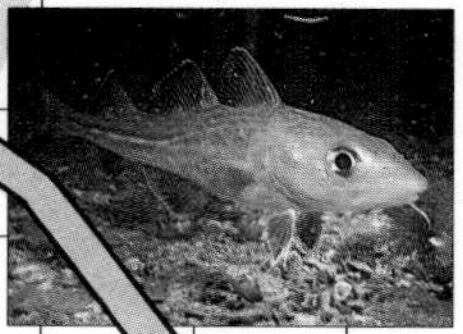

Cod *(Gadus morhua)*
Catches in all the traditional cod fishing grounds in the North Atlantic are at an all-time low. The figures given here are for cod caught in the North Sea.

Haddock

(Melanogrammus aeglefinus)
North Sea catches improved in the early 1980's, but the last few years have seen record low levels.

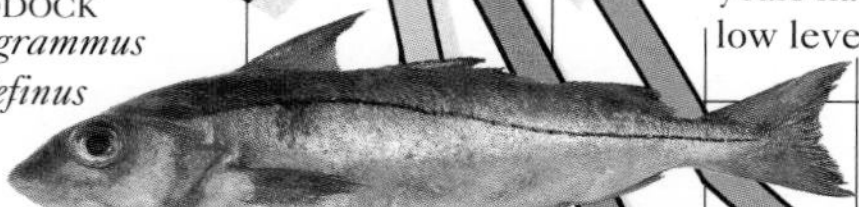

HADDOCK
Melanogrammus aeglefinus

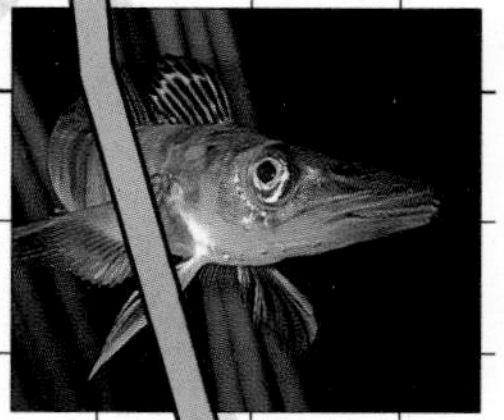

Cod Icefish

(Notothenia rossii)
Antarctic fishing fleets have seriously depleted stocks of this slow-growing species. To allow a recovery, scientists recommend that no catches be taken at all.

Pollack *(Pollachius virens)*
Fished extensively in the North Atlantic, pollack ("coley" or "saithe") has now been overfished, as shown by these figures for the North Sea and Baltic. Commercial fishermen often maximize catches, regardless of the long-term consequences.

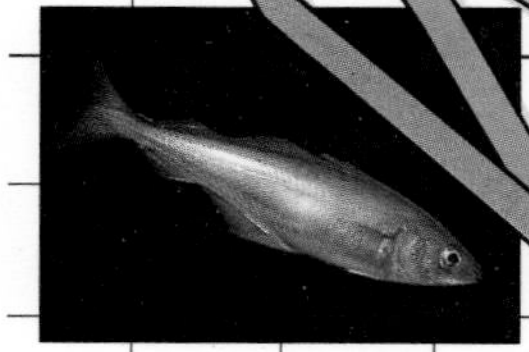

Annual anchovy catch (in millions of tons)

Annual catch of fish (in thousands of tons)

coastal states) meant that they were forced to return to their exhausted home fisheries. Compromises had to be negotiated between the interests of conservation and industry. Reductions in fishing were needed to permit recovery of the stock, while industry sought to ensure that their capital still gave a reasonable return. Many governments faced with the prospect of a depressed fishing industry took the worst possible action, simply subsidizing the fleets in order to buy peace. These subsidies kept uneconomic vessels in business, so fishing activity continued at unnaturally high levels. Instead of recovering, stocks declined. It is only in recent times that there are grounds for optimism, as some countries now have programs to buy out fishermen in order to reduce the level of fishing to sustainable levels.

SUBSIDIZED MADNESS

In the developing world, the new 200 nautical mile (370 kilometer) zone presented countries that had few natural resources with an apparent bonanza of potential wealth. This led to speculative investment in which development agencies and banks played a large part. In several countries, cheap loans and direct subsidies fueled such a boom in the building of fishing vessels that fish stocks were soon seriously depleted.

This often reduced the catches of traditional, shore-based communities, which had been exploiting local resources at low, but sustainable, levels. The operation of mechanized industrial fishing vessels, exploiting off-shore resources at the expense of coastal fisheries, has provoked political controversy and occasional violence.

It is not just at the level of industrial and commercial fishing that over-exploitation has occurred. In coastal communities themselves, population growth, along with more advanced technology (usually furnished by well-meaning development agencies) has led to an increase in fishing power and to over-exploitation of the local resources. Traditional ownership rights have been eroded as fishermen have moved further afield in order to make a living. The result is a decay in the living standards of the communities, as more and better-equipped fishermen pursue decreasing fish stocks. Despite these problems, the extension of national sovereignty over the world's fish resources must be viewed as an improvement. A recognition of the

NET LOSSES *This porpoise is one of many killed by drift nets every year. Narrow mesh, like the gill net on this page, also traps immature fish and so reduces the breeding population. International outcry has led to a ban on drift netting from June 1992.*

POLLUTION DILUTION (left) *As a result of pressure from environmentalists and from other European governments, Britain will have to stop dumping sewage sludge in the North Sea by 1998. There are alternative disposal methods, such as incineration and landfill, but these do not address the fundamental problem: the sludge is contaminated with heavy metals and other industrial pollutants. If these could be kept out of the human waste stream, sewage would no longer be something that had to be disposed of, but could be converted to fertilizer and become a source of real wealth.*

FARMING THE OCEAN (right) *In Japan, kelp-farming is already a multi-million dollar industry, providing a valuable source of protein-rich food. In many ways, we have not yet learned how best to make full use of the ocean's astonishing variety of potential foodstuffs. Surprisingly, these provide us with only a small percentage of the world's overall protein requirement.*

need for control is there and the mechanisms for control via sovereignty are in place.

But other kinds of fishing take place beyond the jurisdiction of national zones. Perhaps the most important and lucrative is high-seas fishing for tuna, carried out in all the major oceans except the Arctic and Antarctic. Tuna are highly migratory, moving between the zones of different states and between these zones and the high seas. This makes any regulation extremely difficult. The fleets may employ sophisticated purse seine vessels, in which tuna are caught for cannery markets, or vessels using long line or gill nets for the higher-value tuna eaten raw in the oriental markets.

The purse seine fleets of the Eastern Pacific have had a particularly unfortunate effect on the marine ecosystems, as they work most efficiently when catching tuna in the vicinity of schools of dolphins. Purse seines are large nets that are set around a school of fish by two ships. When the two ends are drawn together, the net can be closed beneath the catch. Although the ecological association between tuna and dolphins is not understood, the setting of a purse seine around a dolphin school often results in a substantial catch of tuna. Despite recent improvements in technology, purse seines still kill large numbers of dolphins.

WALLS OF DEATH

The most worrying recent development is the increase in drift netting, using large gill nets, often 30 miles (50 kilometers) long, primarily by the fleets of Japan, Taiwan, and Korea. Gill nets kill a great many species that are of no value to the fishermen, including marine mammals and turtles. The scale of these operations is quite daunting. It is estimated that 4,350 miles (7,000 kilometers) of nets are operated every year within the Pacific.

In December 1989, the UN General Assembly adopted a resolution which called for the banning of ocean-going drift netting from 1 July 1991. There are thus significant grounds for hope, even though Taiwan, a major fishing nation, is not a member of the UN, and what actually happens on the high seas remains all too often beyond the reach of any legislation.

DOLPHIN DELIGHT (opposite) *Common dolphins play in the Pacific near the Galapagos Islands. Resolute campaigning must surely outlaw the many "dolphin prisons" around the world, where people pay to see a sick travesty of these joyful acrobatics.*

SHORELINES AND ESTUARIES
TURNING THE TIDE

ROBERT EARLL

TOPSHELLS
Monodonta lineata

SHORE CRAB
Carcinus maenas

DOGWHELK
Nucella lapillus

The harsh boundaries between the land and the sea are immensely productive. But shorelines and estuaries the world over are now under intense pressure from expanding human activity.

Standing on a rocky headland, watching the stormy seas pound the coast, we often marvel at the sheer power of the sea. And as we wade through the gloopy mud of an estuary, the vast, mysterious expanse can provoke feelings in us of wonder and awe. It is here that many of our most cherished wildlife species occur in splendid profusion.

Since the dawn of civilization, people have colonized these coastal margins; the availability of food and the access to trade have continued to fuel this trend. Of the ten most populated cities on Earth, eight are situated on estuaries or the coast, and those cities alone contain over 100 million people. While scientists speculate over the wider consequences of the greenhouse

Robert Earll PhD is Head of Conservation at the Marine Conservation Society in England. He is the author of many papers on marine conservation, an active diver, and an expert in the marine ecology of both temperate and tropical waters.

effect and climate change, even small changes in sea level or the strength and frequency of storms will have a profound effect upon these coastal communities, putting millions at risk. The Maldive islanders in the Indian Ocean seem likely to be one of the first populations who will lose their homes due to sea-level rise.

The livelihood of coastal communities often depends on a very finely balanced network of interests. A new power station, or a new container terminal, can completely dominate the surrounding coastal zone, and can in turn have a devastating effect on local wildlife habitats and coastal communities alike.

The loss of our coastal wetlands to tidal barrages, reclamation, and a variety of forms of

BOUNDARY LINES
(opposite)
Tides have a way of bringing back to the shore what we have dumped and piped out into the sea. In many parts of the world it is rare to see a truly clean shoreline, such as this remote beach in New Zealand.

THE BALANCE OF LIFE (left)
Few birds display such aerial elegance and predatory efficiency as the gannet. Dependent on both land and sea, it is just one example of the spectacular wildlife that is to be found at the edge of the sea. Fortunately, gannets are still plentiful, but the past 20 years have shown that overfishing and marine pollution can decimate breeding colonies of sea birds by destroying the fish stocks on which the birds depend.

A FUTURE FOR DOGWHELKS?

In the mid 1980's stories started appearing in British newspapers about the sex life of the dogwhelk. Scientists had discovered not only that the dogwhelk was becoming much scarcer, but that the reason for this was that female dogwhelks were growing penises and sperm ducts, thus blocking normal reproduction.

Experiments had confirmed that this bizarre sex change was caused by the presence of small quantities of tributyltin (TBT) – no more than one part in a million was sufficient to set off the reaction. TBT is the active ingredient used in paints as an anti-fouling agent to ward off barnacles and mussels from the bottom of boats and nets of fish cages. It is highly popular with boat owners, precisely because it is so effective.

Evidence that TBT was deforming other marine life-forms brought increasing concern from the

DOGWHELKS *This shellfish species has suffered because of TBT in boat paint.*

shellfish industry: oyster fisheries were going out of business directly because of TBT. The British and French governments banned the use of TBT on small boats, but it is still being used on larger boats, and new research shows that TBT pollution extends far into the North Sea.

coastal "protection" are further examples of our arrogant assumption that we can predict in simple terms the outcome of altering our environment. Only now are we coming to realize that coastal "protection" is often an expensive illusion. It is far better, and much cheaper, to allow nature and erosional processes to take their natural course.

LIFE IN THE ESTUARIES

From the coastal wetlands of the Everglades, the great deltas of the Mississippi and Ganges, the complex lagoons of Chesapeake Bay and the Wadden Sea, to the bleak mud flats and marshes of the Thames, estuaries take many forms. The dynamic interactions between river, land, and sea form some of the greatest wetlands on Earth.

Estuaries are muddy. Rivers frequently carry burdens of silt, often increased by our destruction of forests and the resulting loss of top soil. When a river reaches the sea and the freshwater and seawater mix, the silt precipitates and settles out, leading to the formation of huge mud flats.

The mixing of the tides and currents ensures that the waters of estuaries are rich in nutrients,

HOLDING THE BALANCE
Throughout the tropics, mangrove trees form vast and rich inter-tidal forests at the edge of the sea. They have their roots in the seawater and are crucially important in protecting shorelines from erosion. Their forest-like canopy is inhabited by a huge array of terrestrial species, and they also provide vital shellfish and fish nursery areas. But the mangrove is being increasingly disturbed by reclamation projects, fish-farming development, and clumsy commercial exploitation. With the mangroves will go all their ecological benefits, and the delicate balance between sea and land will be destroyed.

and they are among the most productive habitats on Earth. Harsh and difficult conditions mean that estuarine habitats in general are much less diverse in species than the sea itself. But what the estuary lacks in diversity, it makes up for in the sheer numbers of each species present. Crabs, shrimps, worms, snails, oysters, mussels, and cockles occur in vast numbers. The most spectacular beneficiaries of this productivity are the birds – huge flocks of flamingos and geese and thousands of waders, which migrate the length of continents using the estuaries as feeding stations.

Estuaries and mangrove swamps can be up to 20 times richer in wildlife than the open oceans.

Because they're not exactly "pretty," muddy estuaries have attracted less attention than many other habitats. This must change. Groups like the Audubon Society in the United States, and the cooperative programs between Germany and Holland on the Wadden Sea, are trying to change the traditional attitudes by focusing on the importance of estuaries for migrating birds.

THE OPEN SHORELINE

There is stark contrast between the placid waters of the estuary and the battering waves of the open coast. The harder rocks of the headlands stand out as bastions against the enormous forces of the sea. It is the softer rocks that break down to provide the sand and gravel of the beaches and bays, and the long banks of pebbles behind which coastal lagoons develop with their rich wildlife. These coastal waters are often clearer than rivers, enabling light to penetrate to depths of 100 feet (30 meters) or more, so that beds of seaweed and seagrass can flourish.

Sea birds, turtles, and all the large marine mammals return to the shoreline to breed, and the great whales frequent the shallow water of coastal lagoons to reproduce. The uncontrolled commercial exploitation of these species has taken many of them to the verge of extinction. The strong traditional culture of coastal communities in northern latitudes can still exert a profound and destructive effect on wildlife, despite the best attempts of

SEA OF BLOOD (left) *Pictures like this of the annual slaughter of pilot whales by inhabitants of the Faroe Islands continue to shock the world. But the slaughter goes on.*

CAUGHT IN THE NET (above) *The loggerhead turtle now faces complete extinction. Many thousands are caught in fishing nets, and the death toll increases every year.*

ROEFIE HUETING

66 *Growth in production remains the highest goal of every country in the world. At the same time, an increase in national income is invariably accompanied by the destruction of the environment.*
A switch to behavior that protects the environment will certainly lead to a brake on growth, and most probably to a lower level of production. In terms of a nation's balance sheet, a bicycle ride, a sweater, an extra blanket, a serving of beans or a vacation by train represent a smaller volume of economic activity than respectively a journey by car, a high room-temperature, heating the whole house, a serving of meat or a vacation by plane.
The only way to save our environment is to adapt the nature of our activities (and the number of our species) to the carrying capacity of our planet. For this, what we need least is an increase in national income. 99

Roefie Hueting is a Dutch economist who works with the Central Bureau of Statistics.

SEWAGE POLLUTION
(right) *This sewage outfall off the coast of Britain is not exceptional: such practices have been only partly curbed through the European Community's Bathing Waters' Directive.*

OIL POLLUTION IN EGYPT (below) *Every year hundreds of beaches are seriously polluted by oil. It is not just the big spills, such as the Exxon Valdez, that affect the marine environment: there are many smaller incidents, as well as the "flushing" of tanks at sea.*

conservationists. The herding of pilot whales for the annual culls off the Faroe Islands, in the northeast Atlantic Ocean, is a particularly gory example.

GLOBAL GARBAGE DUMP

For far too long, we have thought that we could not damage such a boundless environment. We have treated the seas as garbage dumps, "out of sight, out of mind," thinking they have an infinite capacity to dilute and disperse our waste. Coastal industry spews forth a multi-colored variety of gross wastes from pipes on the beach or just offshore. Raw sewage and sanitary products go from your well-groomed toilet down the pipe and out to sea. Litter in all its forms, plastics that entangle wildlife and do not decay, medicinal wastes, toxic cargos "lost" at sea, and every form of humanity's junk gets washed up on the shore each day.

Every year, thousands of different chemicals that we cannot see enter the environment, the tiny "drops in the ocean" that build up insidiously: long-lived and toxic chemicals, heavy metals like mercury compounds, organic chemicals like pesticides. We do not know how to remove the mercury from the sediments of Liverpool Bay in England, or the pesticides from industrialized estuaries.

Between 1952 and 1960 in Japan, 40 people died and over 2,000 suffered gross mental and physical damage after eating mercury-contaminated shellfish from Minimata Bay.

Even the most beautiful areas are not exempt. Coral reefs, for example, are threatened by dynamite fishing, pesticides, silt, the exploitation of coral rock for building, and lime production for cement manufacture. All these factors work together resulting in wholesale destruction of a reef and accelerated erosion of the coastal margins.

Increasingly, the pollution and degradation of the coastal environment is a result of our activities inland, far away from the sea. Sewage sludge from large towns, and fertilizers on land, contribute to the enrichment of our coastal seas with nutrients at levels previously unknown. Just as applying fertilizer to the land induces more vigorous growth of garden plants and crops, a similar effect occurs in the sea. Evidence suggests that in addition to increased growth of plant plankton, the balance of algae species is altered. One species produces a frothy foam at the water's edge which is extremely unpleasant. When it decays, it forms a black slime smelling of rotten eggs. Some algae release substances that build up in shellfish and are toxic to humans. Other species release toxins that have caused mass deaths in European farmed salmon in Scottish lochs and Norwegian fjords.

FARMING THE SEAS

As John Beddington has described in his chapter, we depend upon the estuaries and the edges of the seas to provide us with food. However, we seem to have based our fisheries management techniques on those developed by the Walrus and the Carpenter to manage oysters.

> "I weep for you," the Walrus said:
> "I deeply sympathise."
> With sobs and tears he sorted out
> Those of the largest size,
> Holding a pocket-handkerchief
> Before his streaming eyes.
>
> "O Oysters," said the Carpenter,
> "You've had a pleasant run!
> Shall we be trotting home again?"
> But the answer came there none –
> And this was scarcely odd, because
> They'd eaten every one.

(Through the Looking-glass,
and What Alice found There, by Lewis Carroll)

Around the shorelines of many countries, fish-farming has become a major industry. Just as with farming on land, however, there are ecological restraints on the capacity of the sea, which must be respected. Whether it be scallops in Japan, or salmon in Scotland, fish farms produce a familiar range of problems: reduced growth rates caused by over-stocking, increased incidence of diseases, and serious pollution, resulting in toxic algal growths, and the production of poisonous gases such as hydrogen sulphide and methane from the sea bed. As with any intensive human activity, farming the sea will require care and suitable controls, to protect the farmers and the environment. More fundamentally, we should ask whether the intensive

ON THE GREEN FRONT
GREENPEACE

For more than 20 years, the very idea of Greenpeace has been synonymous with courageous, non-violent direct action in defense of the environment. From its origins in Canada (protesting at A-bomb tests by the United States government in the Aleutian Islands) to its current position as one of the world's leading environmental organizations, Greenpeace has made it its business to confront head-on many of today's worst polluters and exploiters of other creatures.

Constantly alert to the importance of good media coverage, Greenpeace campaigners have climbed chimneys, blocked factory outfalls, blockaded whalers and nuclear-armed warships in rubber dinghies, and put their own bodies between seals and the clubs of hunters. They have infuriated politicians and industrialists the world over, but have won immense respect and admiration for their uncompromising determination.

Greenpeace is currently active in more than 25 countries, including a number in Eastern Europe and Central and South America. Though their campaigning style now includes providing information to the public and research work, the organization remains true to these inspiring words from a book that greatly influenced some of the organization's earliest activities:

"Great are the tasks ahead, terrifying are the mountains of ignorance and hate and prejudice, but the Warriors of the Rainbow shall rise as on the wings of the eagle to surmount all difficulties. They will be happy to find that there are now millions of people all over the Earth ready and eager to rise and join them in conquering all barriers that bar the way to a new and glorious world. You've had enough now of talk. Let there be deeds." (From *Warriors of the Rainbow* by William Willoya and Vinson Brown)

GREENPEACE AT WORK
Greenpeace campaigners block the outflow pipe from the BASF works on the Schelde Estuary near Antwerp, Belgium (above), and the outflow pipe from Albright and Wilson's Marchon plant on the Cumbrian coast in England (right).

PEOPLE POLLUTION

The modern-day traveler enthusiastically seeks the coast. Our quest for recreation by the sea is almost insatiable. While tourism brings with it much needed revenue, the sheer volume of tourists is destroying the very thing that they have come to see.

Tourism will continue to be one of the main sources of income for coastal peoples in the 1990's. The increased numbers of tourists add significantly to the population of coastal resorts. For example, it has been estimated that the coastal population of the Mediterranean at least doubles during the summer months. United Nations' projections indicate that visitors could number 760 million by 2025 – with a resident population of around 150 million.

This influx of people means that vast quantities of sewage are discharged into the shallow seas, where it can kill seagrass beds by depriving them of oxygen, and lead to increased growth of poisonous algal blooms. The frequent threat of "algal slime" on beaches has lead the authorities in the Gulf of Genoa to build a 22 mile (35 kilometer) barrier just offshore to prevent the algae reaching the beach. This is a purely cosmetic exercise, for in the meantime there has been no treatment of the underlying sewage problem.

Our enthusiasm for the coast is also leading to the virtual extinction of species that require a habitat free from human disturbance, like turtles and the Mediterranean monk seal. For the turtles, the age-old threat has been their destruction on the breeding beaches and the removal of their eggs. To this has now been added the construction of tourist facilities.

The plight of the world's coral reefs is a particularly telling example of tourist damage. The nutrients in the sewage from tourist centers contribute to the growth of algae on the reef, where they ultimately replace the coral. The cumulative effects of careless divers trampling the coral, anchors destroying the reef as they are dragged, and the collection of coral for souvenirs, are all taking their toll.

COOKING AT COPACABANA (above) *Soaking up damaging ultra-violet radiation to get a tan remains one of the world's favorite pastimes. But the depletion of the protective ozone layer, and the ever-increasing incidence of skin cancer, are making people think again.*

SHELL COLLECTING *The over-collection of the Giant Triton shell* (below), *predator of the Crown of Thorns starfish* (right), *was thought to have led to a plague of the starfish, devastating areas of the Great Barrier Reef.*

industrial fishing methods used to produce the fishmeal for fish-farming are a wise or sustainable way to use the ocean's wild fish resources.

INTERNATIONAL ACTION

How is it that man has so comprehensively damaged the coastal margins that epitomize nature's unbridled power and vastness? Set against its power and size, many of our activities seem unconnected, trivial and insignificant. Yet, their cumulative effects can be devastating. They can, and do, lead to environmental catastrophes over which we suddenly discover we have no control. We can now observe large-scale effects of pollution in the Baltic, the Black Sea, and the North Sea.

In coping with problems of the marine environment, we always seem to be one step behind what is happening on land. But there are many encouraging initiatives underway. A major step forward will be the ratification of the Law of the Sea Convention. Many people regard this as the most important move ever made toward a rational use of the marine environment. Similar frameworks will have to be applied to the major regional seas, and these have begun to take shape through the UN Environment Program and cooperative initiatives with the North Sea and Baltic countries.

Much has also been achieved by environmental organizations taking a direct and confrontational approach, and no doubt this will continue to be a major tactic for effecting change. In the aftermath of that change, however, there will still be a major role for non-governmental organizations to play in helping to create new structures that better serve our environmental requirements.

Over the centuries, we have developed and exploited the fertile and spectacular margins where the seas meet the land. Despite their dynamic and seemingly boundless nature, these coastal margins are just as susceptible to our activities as other environments on land. We must therefore encourage a cooperative, holistic, and integrated view of our management of these margins.

With the dawn of a new world order in the 1990's, the seas, which are often common to many countries, will provide a major focus for cooperative efforts. It is only the actions of people with optimism and vision that will change attitudes and help to restore and maintain the splendors of our shorelines and estuaries.

GUY TAPLIN

GROUP OF TWENTY EGRETS

66 *My workshop sits on an isolated beach at the head of two tidal estuaries. In the winter, I collect the driftwood from which I make my birds. I like to use wood that has had a life before I find it, as to me this gives it a special quality and a life of its own. In this place of moving creeks and sand banks I am able to renew myself.* 99

Guy Taplin

Guy Taplin is a British sculptor.

LADY SCOTT

66 *The challenges that Peter first recognized so many years ago remain as great today as ever. But it is enormously encouraging to see how many more people are now prepared to take up these challenges, and it is good to know that Peter's work remains a beacon of inspiration to people throughout the world.* 99

Philippa Scott

Lady Scott, the widow of naturalist and painter Peter Scott, is Honorary Director of the Wildfowl and Wetlands Trust in England.

WHITE-FRONTED GEESE ON THE SEVERN ESTUARY
by Peter Scott

RIVERS AND LAKES
DAMMING THE FLOW
PHILIP WILLIAMS

BANDED
DEMOISELLE
Calopteryx splendens

GOLDEN-LINED FROG
Hylarana erythraea

The world's religions once taught people to show reverence for the waters of life. By contrast, our industrial "civilizations" have consistently abused and defiled our most precious resource.

At some point in life, who has not stood on a river bank and thought momentarily of the moving current as a living entity with a will of its own, angry in flood, subdued in drought, carving out its own channel, living in harmony with the woods, wetlands, and meadows of its valley?

Scientifically, we can treat such a river as a natural conveyor belt, carrying volumes of water downstream. We are also beginning to understand how streams, rivers, and lakes form an integral part of the global environment. Their capacity to erode the land through which they flow, and the sediment they deposit, have created the hill slopes, valleys, and floodplains that make up many of our terrestrial ecosystems. In

Philip Williams PhD
is the Founder and President of International Rivers Network, a Friends of the Earth affiliate organization based in San Francisco. He is a consulting hydrologist, and has lectured at the University of California.

turn, the river flow itself depends on the soils and vegetation formed by these ecosystems. In their natural state, rivers have evolved in balance with the runoff produced in their watersheds or collecting areas. This delicate and dynamic equilibrium has created its own ecosystems both within and along the river – whether for fish like salmon, which have evolved to take advantage of gravel naturally deposited on the river bed, or trees like the willow, which hug the banks of rivers and are regenerated by the shifting of river channels after floods.

Over the millennia, the silt spread by floodwaters has created extensive floodplains. Well-watered and nourished by river sediments, these floodplains sustain some of the world's

SERPENTINE GREEN
(opposite) *A river in Northern Australia provides a sinuous ribbon of life in an otherwise hostile desert environment. River flows in this part of Australia are seasonal and short-lived, and the breeding cycle of many creatures depends on their regularity.*

NEPALESE
FISHERMAN AT
DAWN, LAKE PHEWA
(left) *The importance of lakes and rivers to human culture has been reflected for thousands of years in our art, folklore, and language. Many people believe that we have an innate spiritual relationship with rivers and lakes; the 19th-century American author Henry Thoreau described still water as "Earth's eye, looking into which the beholder measures the depths of his own nature."*

ANITA RODDICK

This is what you should do: love the Earth and sun and the animals, despise riches, give alms to everyone that asks, stand up for the stupid and crazy, devote your income and labor to others, hate tyrants, argue not concerning God, have patience and indulgence towards the people, take off your hat to nothing known or unknown or to any man or number of men . . . re-examine all you have been told at school or church or in any book, dismiss what insults your own soul, and your very flesh shall be a great poem.

66 *With this quote, Walt Whitman has given us a 12-Point Plan for Self-Improvement. And self is the key word. Self-respect, self-confidence, self-control, self-questioning together will breed that ultimate selflessness that honors all life on Earth and truly creates the 'great poem' of which Whitman speaks.* 99

Anita Roddick

Anita Roddick is the Founder and Managing Director of The Body Shop, an international naturally based cosmetics company which is active on environmental and human rights issues.

most abundant and diverse terrestrial ecosystems for plants, insects, birds, and mammals.

These productive valley floors were the sites of the first human settlements. It was here that systematic agriculture first started. As each civilization developed, it became ever more reliant on its rivers' flows and floods for drinking water, transportation, and irrigation. At first, man learned how to adapt his settlements and his way of life to the river's constant changes. Then he learned how to manipulate these changes, and now, in this century, how to dominate them.

Deforestation, overgrazing, and plowing have caused a massive acceleration of erosion in many parts of the world. The resulting sediment chokes river channels and fills lakes and estuaries. With the loss of soil, streams and springs dry up and large flood flows occur. It is this inexorable process that led to the denuded landscapes of Greece, Lebanon, and Iran, and is now doing the same all over the world from Kenya to Colombia, from Madagascar to Thailand.

Man's progressive fouling of the flow of life-sustaining fresh water by sewage, toxic chemicals or agricultural pollution has been regarded as the

AGELESS IRRIGATION
Water buffalo drive an irrigation wheel on the banks of the Nile in Egypt. Such a scene has been re-enacted day in, day out for more than 2,000 years. There is a tendency for Western experts to dismiss such systems as "primitive." The truth is that many of the large-scale, high-tech irrigation schemes funded by agencies such as the World Bank have failed miserably, causing huge problems through soil saturation or salinization. To improve schemes such as these requires immense sensitivity to the connection between people and the land, to the timeless bonds that exist between culture and ecology.

regrettable but somehow unavoidable price to be paid for industrial development. For people in developed countries, the ever-increasing list of chemicals in rivers and drinking water is a serious concern. Massive programs of investment are required to carry out remedial work.

Across the tropics, contaminated drinking water is responsible for over 25 million deaths each year. Dirty water and poor sanitation account for at least 80 percent of all diseases afflicting the Third World.

This poses a ferocious ethical problem for the developed world. For example, £26 billion (US$50 billion) will be required to bring the United Kingdom up to standards set by the European Community's Drinking Water Directive. But such sums would be looked upon as a monstrous self-indulgence by millions of poor people in the Third World, for whom the quality of drinking water is a matter of life and death. When the only drinking water available to people living downstream from some of the large cities in India was tested, it was characterized as "thin raw sewage."

SYMBOLS OF AN AGE

While water pollution is often seen as a sad but inevitable byproduct of industrialization, the transformation of rivers by massive engineering works such as dams and dikes is usually seen as one of the most impressive and prestigious benefits of industrialization. These works are ostensibly carried out for straightforward economic reasons such as flood control, hydropower or irrigation, but they are also an expression of the ideology of our industrial age, powerful symbols of a philosophy that sees the domination of nature as the prerequisite for material progress.

Large dams are the world's most spectacular feats of civil engineering, creating reservoirs vaster than most natural lakes, turning mighty rivers into humble plumbing systems, and transforming the river and floodplain ecosystem. With such power on show, it is hardly surprising that large dams should be used by political leaders seeking to transform the societies of their countries, at seemingly any cost. Starting 50 years ago with Stalin's

A REMEDY CLOSE AT HAND

Bilharzia, or schistosomiasis, is a debilitating and eventually fatal water-borne illness which afflicts more than 200 million people in 74 countries. The methods currently employed to combat bilharzia are far too expensive for the communities that actually need them.

In 1964, a young Ethiopian doctor, Akililu Lemma, discovered that suds from the fruit of a common African plant, the soapberry, which African women have used as soap for centuries, are effective against the river snails that transmit the disease to humans via parasitic blood flukes.

Lemma established the Institute of Pathobiology at Addis Ababa University to test the effectiveness of the soapberry as a cheap, locally controllable means of eradicating this terrible disease. Yet progress has been desperately slow and only very recently has the international medical establishment swung behind this crucial initiative. As Lemma, who won the Right Livelihood Award in 1989, himself points out: "We have learned the hard way that

MALE AND FEMALE BLOOD FLUKES
These flukes are the cause of bilharzia in humans. They live in pairs in the small intestine, causing dysentery and diarrhea.

the root problems of scientific research in Africa are not only the lack of facilities and funds, but also the bias of individuals and organizations in industrialized countries. I believe the best future course for Africa is to invest in efforts to build on the capabilities of its own people by strengthening existing African scientists and research and training institutions."

A SEA RUN DRY
The Aral Sea was once the fourth biggest lake in the world. But over the past 25 years, more than half its 26,250 square miles (68,000 square kilometers) have been reduced to salt-flats and deserts. In places, the shore has receded by up to 35 miles

(60 kilometers). Over-irrigation using water from the Aral's feeder rivers, and the massive abuse of pesticides on cotton crops, have turned a once fertile ecosystem into a toxic wasteland. Infant mortality in the region is at least four times the Soviet average, and malnutrition is widespread.

THE BEAUTY OF BAIKAL

Lake Baikal is the world's oldest and most fascinating lake. It contains the largest volume of surface fresh water of all lakes, more than the five Great Lakes of North America put together. To the local people (many of whom are Buddhist), Baikal is the Holy Sea; to all Russians, it is venerated as is no other part of their vast country.

This has not given Baikal immunity from the kind of chronic pollution that has devastated so much of the Soviet Union's natural beauty since the Second World War. But one of the great benefits of *glasnost* within the Soviet Union has been the increased openness with which environmental organizations have been able to campaign on behalf of key areas such as Lake Baikal. The problems of the Soviet economy are, however, so great that environmentalists still face an incredibly difficult uphill task.

Environmental standards are far lower than in the West and corruption prevails. There are few government agencies willing or able to prosecute the polluters,

PRICE OF PROGRESS (above)
Dozens of factories (including the Baikalski paper mill shown here) pour out huge quantities of industrial effluent into Lake Baikal every day. Only in the last few years has any kind of remedial program been put into action.

and the effects on the environment are frequently discounted as irrelevant.

More than 1,500 species of animals and 1,000 plants have been recorded in Baikal, at least 1,300 of which are found nowhere else in the world. It is by far the most interesting ecosystem in the entire Soviet Union, with more than 300 rivers and streams heading into it, but with only one outlet, the Angara River.

This unique combination of flora and fauna has made Lake Baikal a mecca for scientists, from abroad as well as the Soviet Union. To raise additional funds for the crucial work that needs doing (there are, almost certainly, many species yet to be identified), the Soviet Union's Academy of Science has sought new collaborative agreements with bodies such as the Royal Society in Britain and the National Geographic Society in the United States. In 1991, scientists from the US Geological Survey joined Soviet researchers in collecting sediment cores from the floor of the lake, which, at more than 5,250 feet (1,600 meters), is the deepest in the world.

HOLY SEA (left)
Lake Baikal is revered by local people as a Holy Sea and has long played an important role in Russian literature and culture. Scientifically, it is of particular interest because of the 1,300 species that are found here but nowhere else. These include a freshwater shrimp, Acanthogammarus victori (top inset), *and a strange abyssal fish,* Comechorus baicalensis (bottom inset), *which lives at depths below 3,300 feet (1,000 meters). Most lakes are all but lifeless below 1,000 feet (300 meters) but the circulation in Baikal carries oxygenated water to three times this depth.*

hydroelectric schemes and Roosevelt's New Deal dams, big dam technology was then exported to the Third World. About 400 new big dams are now started every year. If all current plans reach fruition, few of the world's river systems will be left intact in a few decades. Even the mighty Amazon will be "tamed" by 20 huge hydro dams.

These projects' immense cost – as high as US$20 billion in some cases – has been a major factor in creating the Third World debt crisis. Once these projects are built, their benefits often prove illusory or short-lived, and their "unanticipated" long-term social and environmental costs overwhelming. Reservoirs like Lake Nasser are rapidly silting up, water-borne diseases are spreading at an alarming rate, new irrigation schemes are being abandoned due to salt build-up, coastal shorelines downstream are eroding, and millions of new "development" refugees are being created, evicted from their homelands as a consequence of reservoir flooding.

The human misery created by these projects inevitably leads to social conflict, which frequently escalates into civil war. In arid regions, dams and diversions have sparked international conflicts.

ROBBED OF THEIR BIRTHRIGHT

The construction of thousands of new dams and diversions in the last few decades has meant the expropriation by centralized governments of what was once a common resource, free-flowing rivers. When this happens, the ecosystems and traditional agricultural patterns that have fed millions of people for thousands of years are invariably destroyed, further contributing to the grim cycle of harmful development, environmental degradation, impoverishment, and debt.

Our destruction of rivers, lakes, and water resources is one of the most important elements of the global environmental crisis that threatens the basic resources on which all life depends. But if we can change direction in the next decade, the threat can be lifted. We know the steps that need to be taken:
● Stop the big dams. Although huge dam projects have been increasingly discredited by many water-resource experts, they are still being promoted as an economic panacea by the big international development banks. The first step must be to end the secrecy behind which these agencies operate.

ON THE GREEN FRONT

THE ECOLOGIST

For more than 20 years, *The Ecologist* magazine has consistently defended good ecological science and the rights of those people most severely affected by today's ecological insanity. It has a well-earned reputation for incisive analysis and for dealing with all those difficult and unfashionable issues that other publications refuse to touch. It is strong on the "doom and gloom" aspect of ecology, but, regrettably, most of the grim predictions it was making 20 years ago have been all too dramatically realized.

In 1984, its editors (headed by Edward Goldsmith, one of the pioneers of the modern green movement in the United Kingdom), produced the first volume of a study of the negative impact of large dams, particularly in Third World countries. It condemned the World Bank for its consistent failure to take account of environmental considerations.

RAISING AWARENESS IN GUJARAT
The message of this street play is how World Bank projects, like the Narmada Dam, transfer common assets into private hands.

Drowning Fertile Land
Together with environmentalists across the world, *The Ecologist* is currently campaigning against nightmarish plans for the Narmada River in India. A vast complex of dams has just been approved, costing US$20 billion, but even that huge sum is nothing when compared to its human, social, and ecological costs. The dams will drown vast stretches of highly fertile land, along with extensive forested areas teeming with wildlife. Much of the irrigated land will rapidly become waterlogged or salinized, and will eventually be abandoned. About a million tribal people will be driven from their traditional homelands. Most of them will end up in the slums of nearby cities.

Edward Goldsmith goes to the root of the problem: "Why then are such dams being built? The main answer, however cynical it may seem, is that a lot of powerful people stand to gain a lot by undertaking them. In the case of the Narmada, Western governments and corporations are pushing the project because they want to provide the engineering equipment. Local contractors are pushing it because it is their business to build dams. The World Bank is pushing it because it is easier to lend money on big projects (the World Bank has some US$25 billion a year to lend, and that's not easy). The governments of the states through which the Narmada flows are pushing it because it allows them to make a lot of friends among local businessmen, whose support they can then count on at the next election.

"That, in a nutshell, is the problem we face today: our society is hooked on so-called 'development,' and it is this kind of development that is making the planet increasingly uninhabitable for all of us. If we want to save our planet, then above all we must learn to 'dehook' ourselves very quickly from this development model."

VICTIM OF A
POLLUTED RIVER
*The white flag river
dolphin from China is
the rarest dolphin in the
world, and on the verge
of extinction. There are
no more than 100 of
them left at the mouth
of the Yangtze River.*

• Protect and restore our watersheds. The watershed functions of forests and grasslands are now much better understood, especially their dual capacity of halting soil erosion and controlling river flows by acting as a huge sponge, absorbing heavy rains and then gradually releasing them into the watershed rivers and streams. The growing public concern over rainforest destruction and desertification is leading to demands to protect and replant forested watersheds around the world, not just in rainforest countries.

• Combat pollution by taking effective action for control of pollutants at its source, before they are pumped out into our rivers and streams. Support for those environmental and consumer organizations campaigning for such reforms is essential.

• Provide safe drinking water. For many in the Third World, this is the most significant environmental problem. It cannot be dealt with by expensive, technocratic solutions imposed by distant bureaucrats in capital cities, but by supporting the initiatives of the people themselves, laying new pipes, drilling new boreholes, installing efficient and reliable pumps and standpipes, establishing safer sewage disposal and management systems. A key is to help improve the status of women, who typically are the principal providers of water for their families.

• Protect and restore common water rights. Throughout the world and throughout history, we have seen that people who live with and make use of a spring, river or lake have learned how to adapt their way of life so that it is both sustainable and naturally protective of the ecosystems on which they depend. When these traditional cultures are supplanted by centralized, technocratic planning, the invariable consequence is social, economic, and environmental degradation.

WATER POWER

The huge Ataturk Dam is just one of 22 dams that Turkey has built or proposes to build on the Euphrates, which flows from Turkey through Syria and Iraq into the Persian Gulf. In 1990, as the Ataturk Dam was being completed, the Euphrates was completely "turned off" for a whole month, despite strenuous objections from Syria and Iraq.

No lasting damage was done (Turkey increased the volume of water passing through to its neighbors before the closure), but it was a graphic reminder of the two countries' vulnerability. Syria is already desperately short of water, with daily water cuts in the capital, Damascus, while Iraq depends almost entirely on the Euphrates and the Tigris for its water. Yet Turkey intends to exploit the Euphrates to the full, turning an area one-third the size of Britain into "the bread basket of the Middle East." It has also signed a deal to sell water to the Israelis.

Experts on the Middle East predict that, unless there are mutually beneficial and binding agreements between all parties involved, water is just as likely to be the cause of regional conflict as oil.

THE ATATURK DAM
This huge dam is one of 22 the Turkish government has built or plans to build across the Euphrates. Syrians and Iraqis, whose lives depend on these waters, view it as a threat to their security. Other rivers provoke similar hostility between nations – for example, the Brahmaputra and Ganges, over which Bangladesh and India are in dispute; and the Colorado, which flows into Mexico from the United States.

MANAGEMENT BY THE PEOPLE

With modern communications, villagers in India or Indonesia are able to find out much more about the destruction of their water resources and are becoming increasingly vocal in protecting them. Giving such people the power to assert their common rights over their rivers will bring genuine and lasting benefits to those who need them most. We must build huge constituencies in each and every country for restoring watersheds, cleaning up pollution, stopping unwise dam projects, and protecting that uniquely elusive quality, a living river.

ANDY GOLDSWORTHY

Kinetic art (left):

**BRACKEN STALKS AND GARLIC LEAVES
PINNED WITH THORNS
LAID ON WATER**

*Scaur Glen, Dumfriesshire, Scotland
23 March 1990*

Andy Goldsworthy is a British artist.

BOB BROWN

66 *The flooding of Lake Pedder in 1972,
in the heart of Tasmania's western wilderness, sparked
Australia's first nationwide protest for the environment. In
the same year, the United Tasmania Group, precursor of
today's Greens, was set up. It was the world's first green
party, working for social justice, the environment,
peace, and democracy.*

*From the tragedy of Lake Pedder, we learned
that we had to meet the exploiters of nature head-on with
arguments on the economy and employment as well as on
the environment. That lesson was fundamental to our
success in saving the Franklin River from the
dam-builders in 1983.*

*While the Wilderness Society spearheaded
the Franklin campaign, it was people all over
Australia working together – fundraising, holding
meetings, showing films of the river, peacefully blockading
the bulldozers (1,400 people were arrested), changing their
vote to parties with a no-dams platform, and lobbying
politicians – who saved the river and its
magnificent, living wilderness.*

*The 1990's will repeatedly call every one of us to
nature's assistance. How we respond will determine
the fate of the Earth – the fate of ourselves, of our
fellow creatures, and of the rights of future generations
to inherit a planet with its wondrous,
living fabric intact.* 99

Bob Brown is a Green Independent Member of the Tasmanian
House of Assembly, and one of Australia's leading
environmentalists.

WETLANDS
DRAINING THE WORLD DRY

DAVID BELLAMY

The world's wetlands and peatlands are of vital importance to the future of millions of people. But it would seem that this simple message has still not reached the people in a position to protect them.

FERN FROND
Dryopteris carthusiana

The destruction of the world's remaining wetlands and peatlands is progressing at an alarming rate. In southern Africa, the great Okavango swamp is threatened with drainage, mining, and agricultural development. In the Sudan, one single development project could destroy more than 50 percent of the enormous floodplain grasslands of the Sudd, which are of key importance to wildlife and to sustainable nomadic lifestyles in the area. India and other countries are again thinking of using DDT on a massive scale in their wetlands and peatlands, to combat malaria. The Farraka Barrage in Pakistan is wreaking havoc on the wetland forests of the Ganges delta. In the United Kingdom, all but 2 percent of England's lowland bogs have already been destroyed; large tracts of Scotland's vitally important Flow Country,

Professor David Bellamy BSc PhD DUniv FLS FLBiol is a botanist, writer, and broadcaster, and the founder and Director of the Conservation Foundation. He is Honorary Professor for Adult and Continuing Education at Durham University in the UK.

bogland without equal, has been turned over to plantation forestry. The same sad process of destruction is also happening in Ireland.

Against such a backdrop, no one country can claim moral superiority when contemplating the environmental failures of any other country. We are all at fault. The destruction of wetlands and peatlands, for any reason, must be stopped, and wherever possible, whole systems must be rehabilitated and put back in working order.

THE SCIENCE OF PEAT

Peatlands have become my life-long love. I am as fascinated by the science of them as I am saddened by their

THREATENED SERENITY (opposite)
Lake Ichkeul in Tunisia is one of the great wetlands of the world, boasting a huge number of migrant birds as well as what is left of the north African buffalo population. But despite being designated a National Park, it is still threatened by a series of proposed dams on rivers flowing into Ichkeul.

MATING DAMSEL FLIES *Enallagma cyathigerum* (right)

BULRUSH
Typha latifolia

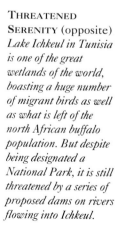

GIANT WATER LILY
(below) *Found in the Amazon region, this water lily (Victoria amazonica) can produce leaves up to 7 feet (2 meters) across.*

PEATLAND PLANTS
(left and right)
Peatlands are home to an amazing variety of plant life: some, like this pitcher plant (left), are insect-eating, while others contribute to the formation of peat. For example, sphagnum moss (right and cross-section, above right) manages to form peat despite the very low levels of nutrients and minerals in its habitat.

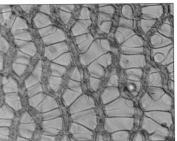

SUNDEW AND PREY
(right)
The insectivorous sundew plant, Drosera capensis, survives on exceptionally poor soils, supplementing its diet by the occasional insect. It attracts flies and spiders by secreting a sticky, honey-like fluid from the ends of its tentacles. Special glands on the leafy traps then secrete another fluid that gradually breaks down the body of its prey.

destruction. Their evolution begins when sweet water, in the form of rain, snow, and ice, irrigates the dry earth as it flows down toward the sea. The increasing water mass scours, erodes, and dissolves the face of the basin, releasing minerals and neutralizing acidity. Surface features will often reduce the water flow to a level where none of the eroded material (boulders, pebbles, sand, and silt) is carried away any longer. It's then that places are created in which wetlands can develop and peat may eventually form.

Where the conditions are favorable to the formation of peat, it can accumulate over a period of several centuries up to a depth of 65 feet (20 meters).

Peat is partially decayed organic matter, mainly of plant origin. It accumulates only in the stillest water, where there is not enough dissolved oxygen to speed up the natural process of decay. Peat comes in three basic varieties. Marshland peats are found all over the world, gradually displacing water from open lakes and setting in motion the whole process of peatland succession. The second sort, fen peats, are again widely distributed, but in hot, dry countries they are found only in the basins of major river systems, especially in deltas. There they gradually obstruct the river flow, inundating large areas of the flatland of the river valleys.

The last sort, bog peats, are found only in those regions of the world in which levels of precipitation are usually greater than levels of evaporation, allowing rainwater to accumulate. When that happens, the fen peats can grow up above the ground water level, carrying their own reservoir of water up with them, to form a dome or "cupola;" the expanding reservoir is replenished only by rain and melting snow falling directly on its surface. Such peatlands (which are best called bogs) are widespread in the colder, wetter regions of the world, but they are also important features of the coastline in the humid tropics, where they can form important sea defenses behind mangrove swamps and coral reefs.

While wetlands, areas characterized by standing water and/or a saturated soil or substrate, cover 6 percent of the Earth's land surface, the water is still enough to allow peat to form in only about

THE RAMSAR CONVENTION

The Ramsar Convention (named after the town in Iran where it was signed in the early 1970's) was one of the first international agreements that dealt with problems of the environment. It concerned itself with wetlands of international importance. The convention came into force in 1975; there are now more than 50 participating countries with around 470 listed wetlands.

That all sounds good in theory, but those sites amount to no more than 3 percent of the world's wetlands, and the World Wide Fund for Nature has calculated that at least 20 of these sites are seriously at risk. Moreover, many of the world's most important wetlands are still completely unprotected, either because they are in countries that have not signed the convention (such as Botswana, with its magnificent Okavango Basin), or because the wetlands have not been listed for protection.

Many Third World countries, understandably reluctant to commit themselves to new expenditure, have argued strongly that the developed world must provide appropriate financial assistance for them to guarantee the protection of wetland areas. At the Ramsar Convention meeting in 1990, a fund to assist in this process was set up, but the amount of money promised so far is measly.

It is also embarrassing to hear representatives of countries like Britain and the United States lecturing Third World countries on their environmental responsibilities, when they themselves have such a questionable record. Both the Scottish Flow Country and the Florida Everglades are at risk specifically because of defective environmental policies.

The Ramsar Convention could do much to help protect the world's remaining wetlands, but only with practical backing.

THE EVERGLADES *Florida's celebrated National Park is made up of many different habitats, including these cypress tree swamps. But tourism and a huge increase in population are threatening the entire ecosystem.*

THE FLOW COUNTRY *This area of northern Scotland contains some of the finest open bogland anywhere in the world, but the British government is slowly but surely destroying it by allowing it to be planted with conifers.*

FRAGILE SPLENDOR *The swamps of the Okavango Basin in Botswana are a crucial haven for African wildlife, but are now increasingly at risk from drainage and agricultural development projects.*

PEATLAND VANDALS (right) *Large-scale commercial exploitation of peat for horticultural use (such as here on the Somerset Levels) is destroying many of the important peatlands left in Britain and Ireland. Activity of this kind cannot be sustained; it takes many thousands of years for peatlands to replenish themselves.*

one-third of this area. Wherever they occur, peatlands are key elements of the water cycle, affecting both the evaporation of water from the land and the level of river flow. They are also home to a wide cross-section of the animal kingdom: leeches, worms, mollusks, arthropods, and, of course, fishes, amphibians, and wildfowl.

MAGICAL FLORA

The peatlands are only there thanks to a fantastic range of highly specialized plants, including the largest waterlily in the world, *Victoria amazonica*, and the smallest flowering plant, *Wolffia arhiza*. All wetland and peatland plants are specialists, pioneering the principles of "geodesics" (structures that combine maximum strength with minimum resource use) long before British inventor Barnes Wallace put similar principles to use in the construction of airships and airplanes.

Just listing wetland plants on paper, without even seeing them in the wild, has a magical ring to it: desmids, diatoms, stoneworts, mosses, ferns, reed grasses, crowfoots, milfoils, marestails, hornworts, pondweeds, sedges and rushes, horsetails and cattails, sundews and pitcher plants, bladderworts and butterworts, the last four being just some of the peatlands' insect-eating plants. Together these plants make up some of the most productive ecosystems anywhere in the world. Even the most ardent environmentalists seem to be unaware that peatland plants absorb almost as much carbon dioxide as do those of the tropical rainforests, sequestering it into long-term storage as peat when they die and partly decay.

ENVIRONMENT-FRIENDLY GARDENING *Peat producers claim that there are no alternatives to the peat used by many horticulturalists (left). But alternatives do exist, and are becoming increasingly popular in many countries (below).*

IRISH PEAT

FINNISH PEAT

SEAWEED AND STRAW MIXTURE

SLURRY AND STRAW MIXTURE

COCONUT FIBER (COIR)

MATING WATER-LILY FROGS *Hyperolius pusillus* (left)

The unique Pocosin forested bogs once covered 2.5 million acres (1 million hectares) of the southern USA. By 1980, over 75 percent had been cleared by commercial timber companies.

The best peat-formers are the bog mosses *(Sphagna)*. Scientists are now trying to understand just how these amazing ecosystems operate on the lowest levels of dissolved oxygen, very little mineral input, and the tightest of nutrient recycling regimes. This will provide vital information for the future rehabilitation and management of other ecosystems.

Peatlands contain detailed information about the partly decayed vegetation from which they have been formed. And thanks to the pollen falling on the plants' surfaces when they were alive, peatlands also contain a detailed record of the vegetation growing in their vicinity and therefore of climatic and landscape changes over time. Each peatland is in fact a gigantic history book, a record of the past. It is this record in the peat that is now allowing scientists gradually to piece together the scenario of change as the Earth's climate has warmed up and cooled down thanks to ice ages and greenhouse gases.

RACING AGAINST DESTRUCTION

Unfortunately, it is true to say that the destruction of the world's peatlands is proceeding faster than the research. Because of atmospheric pollution, which includes both acidification and mineral enrichment, no peatlands today are in absolutely pristine condition. More worrying still, throughout the main areas of population and agriculture, the vast majority of accessible peatlands have been or are being drained or burned for agricultural, forestry or catchment control purposes, or have been cut for peat. Traditional peat cutting has been practiced by rural communities for centuries without doing any real harm, and it could still be managed in a more sustainable way. By contrast, modern methods of peat mining destroy peatlands much faster than they can ever regenerate, and this type of commercial exploitation should be rapidly phased out.

Peatlands are of enormous importance as bird habitats. Scotland's Flow Country bogs are home to 70 percent of the greenshank in Great Britain, and the entire European population of black-throated divers.

The vital statistics of the world's peatland resource go something like this: there are 890 square miles (230 million hectares), covered with 330 billion tons of organic matter, which represent as much potential energy as some 12 trillion barrels of oil. For many people, that's all there is to be seen in the peatlands "resource." They forget that those same peatlands have tremendous aesthetic,

ROBERT RUNCIE

❝ *For centuries, far too many Christians have presumed that God's love is primarily directed at them, and that His natural order was created mainly for the use – and abuse – of humankind. Today such a man-centered attitude to our fragile and exhausted planet is at last beginning to look not only selfish and parochial, but also irresponsible and potentially disastrous. Hence all of us, especially Christians, must open our eyes and minds wider still. We must realize that the way to maintain the value and the preciousness of the human is by re-affirming the preciousness of the non-human also – of all that is. Indeed, the Christian God forbids the idea of a cheap creation, of a finite, dispensable universe. His universe is a work of non-expendable and ever-renewing love – and nothing that is fashioned in love must ever be regarded as cheap or secondary.* ❞

The Right Reverend Lord Runcie is a former Archbishop of Canterbury.

DERVLA MURPHY

❝ *The multiple threats to the Earth are so complex that in most cases they seem beyond the reach of an average citizen's influence. Yet we can all launch a personal campaign to reduce consumption – though perhaps only after a change of mind-set, to overcome the fear of seeming poor, parsimonious or eccentric. This does not mean being deprived or uncomfortable. It simply means stopping to think, before each purchase, 'Do I really need this?' For years a small minority has been living and thinking thus. If a large majority did likewise – if frugality and shabbiness could become trendy – then the Earth, though not saved, would be measurably less endangered.* ❞

Irish author Dervla Murphy has written numerous books about her travels around the world by bicycle.

ED ASNER

❝ *We all moan and groan about the loss of the quality of life through the destruction of our ecology, and yet each one of us, in our own little comfortable ways, contributes daily to that destruction. It's time now to awaken in each one of us the respect and attention our beloved mother deserves.* ❞

American actor Ed Asner is a supporter of many environmental causes, including the American Oceans Campaign.

BRENDAN PARSONS

" At the start of this century, over 2.5 million acres (1 million hectares) of Ireland was covered with bog. By the time this century closes, the most important part of this priceless resource will probably have all but disappeared, exploited for short-term gain.

The State, devoid of other resources like coal or oil, turned to the bogs as a source of fuel for its power stations, and for people to burn as briquettes. The development of special machinery for draining and harvesting the bogs then brought in private exploiters to accelerate the process.

Now, as the consequences begin to dawn at this eleventh hour, at least several small sections of raised bog have been preserved for conservation and more are being recommended by the State Wildlife Service. The government aims at preserving a total of 25,000 acres (10,000 hectares). Let's hope there may still be a little time left before Ireland's bogs are converted into forests of imported softwoods, or prairies churning out more agricultural produce than Europe needs or has a market for. **"**

Brendan Parsons, the Earl of Rosse, has taken part in the UN's work with nomadic tribes in Iran. He also maintains a botanical garden in Ireland with specimens of some of the world's rarer plants.

FIGHT FOR A WETLAND

The vast Coto Doñana National Park in the southwest of Spain is one of the world's most important wetlands. But defending the park's ecological integrity is proving immensely difficult.

In 1986, thirty thousand ducks were killed as a direct result of the application of pesticides by nearby rice-farmers in their efforts to wipe out competing shrimp-farmers.

In 1990, various acts of "ecological terrorism" (including two incidents of arson) were used to frighten conservationists and staff at the National Park. A bitter dispute is still raging over proposals to build a massive beachside tourist development a short distance from the park's boundary. The water consumption of this complex – 2.6 billion gallons (10 billion liters) a

COTO DOÑANA VICTIMS *Some 30,000 ducks were killed by pesticides in 1986.*

year – would severely deplete the Coto Doñana watertable, causing untold damage to the park's flora and fauna. A huge international protest (including the possibility of a tourist boycott) has caused the plans to be temporarily suspended.

biological, and educational value; that they are home to many endangered species; and that they hold 50 billion gallons (189 billion liters) of water passively on the catchment.

If opened up to oxidation by drainage for farming or by combustion, the world's peatlands are capable of producing 500 billion tons of carbon dioxide (200 times as much as the world's cars produce in a year), a huge additional contribution to the greenhouse effect.

Between 1950 and 1970, the United States was losing an average of 457,000 acres (185,000 hectares) of its remaining wetlands each year. By 1981, the state of Iowa had plowed up over 99 percent of its natural marshes; Nebraska had lost 91 percent by 1982.

Large areas of coastal peatland that have been drained for agriculture (including some of the arable and horticultural areas in Europe) are now oxidizing so fast that they are already below sea level, and have to be pump-drained and treated with vast amounts of fertilizer to keep them in production. If the greenhouse effect does bring about a rise in sea level, the cost of keeping what were some of our best lowland farms in production will become even more prohibitive.

What an ironic "feedback mechanism" that is: by "developing" the peatland, we contribute massively to global warming. Increased temperatures lead in time to increased sea levels, threatening the now "developed" peatland with flooding. Better to have left it alone in the first place.

CONSERVATION SUCCESSES

Non-governmental organizations and grass-roots movements the world over are not only stirring the reeds and rushes of concern, but are working to conserve and reinstate their wetlands.

The achievements of the Malayan Nature Society, which celebrated its 50th birthday in 1990, are to be especially commended. The Society's continuing work to ensure that conservation of wetlands is firmly on the country's agenda was marked in its jubilee year by the designation as a State Park of the Endau Rompin, which includes many important wetland ecosystems. This decision encourages hope that the forests and rivers of the Penan People in Sarawak state will soon become a World Biosphere Reserve.

Throughout South-East Asia and beyond, the work of the Asian Wetland Bureau has done much to identify key wetland areas and to put pressure on governments and international bodies to help to protect them.

In Britain, too, progress is being made: old gravel workings are being reinstated as wetland, even peatland reserves, rather than being turned back to agricultural use, and many schools are now turning part of their premises into wildlife areas which include ponds and mini-wetlands.

Thanks to all this pressure and positive action, the tide of public concern is at last beginning to turn. Attitudes are changing, even in those distant "high places" to which I referred!

American economists estimate that the sewage treatment, water purification, and other functions carried out for free by wetlands are worth some US$160,000 per acre (0.4 hectare) – cheaper than could be achieved by using man-made treatment plants.

I cut my wetland teeth and gained my webbed feet in the Broads of East Anglia. The Broads are nothing more than old peat cuttings, dug in the Middle Ages when the local people burned peat to keep them warm. This wetland wonderland became the focal center for a multi-million dollar tourist industry. Threatened by overuse (like so many of the world's beauty-spots), it was being literally loved to death, as well as grotesquely altered by excess nutrients from agriculture and sewage. The cry went up, "The Broads must be saved." In 1988, they became a National Park, and despite many problems that remain to be overcome, this was an immense step in the right direction.

But even when such breakthroughs are achieved, as in the Broads, or the Coto Doñana in Spain, we must still be constantly on our guard. Pressure for development or further exploitation is never far removed, and both scientists and environmental activists will have their work cut out just holding on to the wetlands and peatlands that we have managed to save so far.

ON THE GREEN FRONT
ASIAN WETLAND BUREAU

Many of the world's most important wetland areas are in Indonesia, the Philippines, Vietnam, Thailand, Malaysia, Japan, India, and China. The Asian Wetland Bureau was set up specifically to promote the protection of these sites. With the support of the World Bank, Western governments, and the World Wide Fund for Nature, the Bureau has been enormously successful in alerting governments throughout Asia to the crucial importance of their wetland areas.

Surveying Asia's Wetlands
One of the Bureau's key tasks is to establish the relative importance of different sites, and thus assess the priorities for conservation. The Asia Waterfowl Census Project is an ongoing concern across the region, involving hundreds of participants in more than 20 countries. Project spotters recorded the highly endangered milky stork in Malaysia in 1990, the first time it had been located for more than 50 years.

In Indonesia, the Asian Wetland Bureau is very active, and it has helped to coordinate resistance to large-scale logging proposals which would have devastated the mangroves of Bintuni Bay in West Irian Jaya, some of the most extensive and best-preserved mangroves in South-East Asia. The Bureau is pressing to have the whole area designated under the Ramsar Convention as a Wetland of International Importance.

It is the work of organizations like the Asian Wetland Bureau, often unsung and unrecognized beyond a small circle of experts, that supports so much essential environmental work across the world.

PROTECTING THE MILKY STORK
This graceful wetland species was spotted at Matang in Malaysia in 1990. It had been 50 years since the last sighting.

— VI —
HEALING

*Those who contemplate the beauty of the Earth find reserves of strength
that will endure as long as life lasts. There is symbolic as well as actual beauty in the
migration of birds, the ebb and flow of tides, the folded bud ready for spring.
There is something infinitely healing in the repeated refrains of nature –
the assurance that dawn comes after the night
and spring after the winter.*

From **Silent Spring** *by* RACHEL CARSON

**SUNSET OVER THE
WASH, ENGLAND**

The unifying theme of all the contributions to this book is a simple one: we're paying too high a price for what we call "progress." We have inflicted awful wounds on the Earth, and are now caught in the trap of trying to heal these wounds by prescribing more of the same Earth-defying remedies. In the process, the human spirit has also come under constant attack. Many of the intangible values (a sense of community, a pride in serving others, a love of the land and the rhythms of nature, spiritual enrichment) that once provided com-

fort, fulfillment, and meaning are increasingly denied to people, written off as so many wisps of nostalgic romanticism. It is not just the Earth that has paid the price of our obsessive pursuit of industrial progress, but that fragile part of us that responds to a higher reality than material wealth.

The healing of the Earth and the healing of the human spirit have become one and the same. As we struggle with the implications of pollution control, environmentally friendly technologies, green consumerism, or "sustainable

SPRING BUDS (opposite) *Life's rich potential,
and that of our own existence, can only be fulfilled
if we recognize and respect the sacred mystery
of the natural world.*

TRIBAL LORE (above) *To Westerners, the nomadic
life of Kalahari Bushmen may appear brutal and
harsh, yet theirs is a rich and ancient culture, a fact
reflected in this woman's elaborate body decoration.*

development," it is that overwhelmingly powerful convergence between our human needs and the needs of the rest of life on Earth that now begins to offer real hope for the future.

DOLPHIN AT PLAY

For much of the history of humankind, in all its different cultural manifestations, Mother Earth was held to be a living planet. But the Protestant Reformation and the intellectual revolution set in motion by 17th-century philosophers like Descartes and Bacon progressively turned nature into something inert, more like a machine than a living organism, stripped of its sacred values. A brave new world awaited, based on objective science and the power of reason. All meaning was to be derived from the conquering achievements of humankind alone. The Earth was ours for the taking.

MOTHER AND CHILD, MEMBERS OF THE HMONG HILL TRIBE, THAILAND

And take it we did, with hands outreached, clawing, chopping, smashing, overturning all that lay in our way. The diverse harmonies of the natural world were swept aside as impediments to progress, and with them went the equally subtle web of human societies and cultures that had co-evolved and co-existed with that natural world for hundreds if not thousands of years. "Fear not," people were told, "it's progress."

One of the more insidious impacts of this brave new world has been to persuade people that there is no metaphysical meaning or transcendent purpose to life on Earth. Most scientists still seem to believe that the universe "just happened," by accident, as it were.

If humankind is seen as merely a temporary biological phenomenon in a random process of evolution, then most people will find it hard to be concerned about anything other than their own material comfort. This secular attrition has not been nearly as marked in the Far East, where Buddhism emphasizes the oneness between humankind and the natural world, or in India, where Hinduism places great importance on the Earth's sacredness.

A WORLD FIT FOR CHILDREN TO LIVE IN: HAPPINESS AND A SENSE OF BELONGING WITHOUT GREAT MATERIAL WEALTH

But no country has been able to remain immune from the post-war economic order. Both the vanquished and the victors of the Second World War rapidly established up to a new political consensus: that peace depended on prosperity, that prosperity depended on producing and consuming more, and that increased well-being would automatically flow from this increased economic activity. There was an admirable simplicity about such a consensus. It has undoubtedly served the developed world well over the last 45 years, and is by now so deeply engrained in our culture and politics that to question it is to be considered deeply subversive. But it needs to be questioned. For many millions of human beings, it is simply not delivering the goods, and is never likely to, either. And as for the rest of life on Earth . . .

PLANTING THE CORN CROP, MADHYA PRADESH, INDIA

A YOUNG WOMAN PREPARES FOR THE FUTURE IN TIMBUKTU, MALI

Little wonder then that the questions are coming thick and fast: from economists, who can now see and even measure the damage wrought by adherence to economic growth as the be-all and end-all of progress; from politicians, who are confronted by a series of converging problems for which conventional solutions no longer seem adequate; from scientists, who not only provide us with the facts about ecological decline, but are beginning to challenge the mechanistic explanations of life on Earth; and from religious leaders, who at long last seem to be rediscovering the notion that the Earth is part of God's creative purpose, and should therefore be revered as part of that mystery.

Good science and informed spirituality lead to the same conclusion: that the destiny of humankind is inextricably linked with the well-being of the rest of life on Earth. In symbolic terms, the Earth is not just our home, to be kept clean and properly managed, but is indeed, as every ancient civilization recognized, our "Mother," a living planet, a sacred place.

A FLOCK OF BARNACLE GEESE CIRCLING OVER THE MOORLANDS OF ISLAY, OFF THE WEST COAST OF SCOTLAND

RALPH STEADMAN

" *If each of us was given a suitcase, a personal compartment, to fill with ten items we could choose to take with us over the border into the new, clean millennium, who would choose an oil slick or nuclear waste? Who would choose the blackened stumps of a burnt-out rainforest? Who would choose a dying river or a dead whale?*

The 1990's could well bring the most radical upheaval the world has ever known. But vested interests in fossil fuels and other finite resources deny us all the right to choose, and the massive stranglehold of the world banks over countries in debt forces them to deny their future with short-term measures. Nobody asks whether this is right, or even legal, because it is business, and in business, so it seems, everything is legal. If green issues make good business sense, then maybe we have a chance. But God help us when the Third World decides that it now wants to repeat the 20th century in the 21st because it's their turn — and let's be fair, their turn it is.

HOPEFUL CARTOONS NO. 1:
THE PLAGUE DEMON'S LAMENT

So there's a challenge. Ten years to clean up our habits and persuade the corporate giants to release us from industrial slavery. Ten years to persuade hungry moguls to love life more than profit. Ten years to restructure our economic ideas on how the precious harvests of this brow-beaten planet are to be used, and ten years to reassess our priorities in order that Mother Earth can catch her breath before we lose ours.

Seems pretty hopeful to me. No problem.

Once across the border into a new century, we can begin creating a world that really cares how the human spirit is used. Freed from the tyranny of mindless market invention and economic miracles, freed from endless growth spirals, we can pay attention to the mind, and grow there instead. We can make self-knowledge the most important part of a school curriculum, for that is where all reason starts, and if we do not realize that, all other knowledge is bankrupt stock. "

Ralph Steadman is a British artist, cartoonist, and writer.

ACCEPTING RESPONSIBILITY
ECOLOGY BEGINS AT HOME
JONATHON PORRITT

Nobody can make people "save the Earth" against their wishes.
We will eventually do what is necessary because we feel it is right,
albeit with varying degrees of enthusiasm.

Over the years, I have inevitably met people who have given up on the collective ability of the human race to do right by future generations, let alone by the rest of life on Earth. Such despair has encouraged a few people to speculate on the prospect of some "green world order" being imposed from on high. Not just "world government," but compulsory green living whether you like it or not: rationed lentils; obligatory tree-hugging on Sundays; one washing machine for every 20 people; lights out at 10 p.m. to save electricity, and so on. Such a totalitarian view can only be compared to Eastern Europe before 1989, but with a green flag flying, not a red one, and with knitting needles and a bowl of organic muesli instead of the hammer and sickle.

To me, it all sounds deeply improbable, indeed, fantastical. It wouldn't and couldn't work. The green dictators would be overthrown in the twinkling of a democratic eye, and millions of involuntarily restrained consumers would be unleashed anew (and even more ravenously) on a fragile Earth, much as is happening today in Eastern Europe. The upshot of this is a simple one: the Earth will be saved democratically, or it will not be saved at all.

This is precisely why the idea of personal responsibility looms so large in any green prescription for the future. A sizeable majority of people will have to enlist voluntarily in the business of rescuing the Earth and ourselves from our own worst tendencies. In the West, after a 40-year consensus that "progress" for humankind depends exclusively on an unrestricted increase in production and consumption, it is hardly likely that such a majority will be forthcoming either quickly or easily. And even when it does come forth, many people will have joined this new consensus more out of a feeling of obligation to their children than out of any conviction that they themselves will be better off.

Personal responsibility is therefore as much about our responsibility to our children and to future generations as it is

THE FACE OF THE FUTURE (opposite) *Doing right by future generations is a key principle of the international green movement. That means minimizing the environmental impact of our own lives: acting locally now while thinking in terms of a global future.*

STARTING YOUNG *Too much of today's waste* (inset, above left) *is left as an unwanted legacy for our children. But if enough people adopt greener lifestyles, practices like recycling* (left) *should become second nature. In many parts of the world, young and old alike are now beginning to reassess the true costs of our get-rich-quick, throw-away industrialized society.*

SIMON DREW

MAN IS THE ONLY ANIMAL THAT BLUSHES: OR NEEDS TO
(Mark Twain)

❝ *It's hard to celebrate the world when it vanishes piece by piece, but I'm still an optimist. I'm sure it doesn't pay to be too serious all the time, even about issues such as global warming.*
I used to spend hours trying to persuade my professor of zoology that biology could be regarded as an art subject as well as a science. He wasn't convinced, but nowadays people tend not to pigeonhole the world quite so rigidly. This has helped us all to understand the environment and enjoy ourselves at the same time. ❞

Simon Drew is a British artist, illustrator, and verse-maker.

EIJI FUJIWARA

❝ *I would like to confront the issue of the 300 minke whales that Japan is now killing for 'scientific purposes.' We often hear that because there are as many as 700,000 minke whales, killing just 300 of them every year will have no effect on the overall population. However, when we look beyond the numbers, and recognize, from a social science perspective, that these creatures have a deep relationship with human beings, this becomes an extremely dangerous way of thinking. Whale research is necessary, but it is not necessary to kill whales to carry it out. Scientific whaling should be stopped outright at once.* ❞

Eiji Fujiwara is President of the Institute for Environmental Science and Culture in Japan.

about our immediate obligations to those with whom we happen to share our own short tenancy on planet Earth. The beliefs of some cultures already embody such an outlook. The Hopi Indians believe that the interests of the seventh generation should feature as large in any decision as those of the people actually making the decision. This is not some left-over, unworldly romanticism. It is the hallmark of any vital and healthy culture, constantly enriched by what has gone before, constantly alert to what will come after.

I do not suppose that the developed world will ever recapture the innocent sophistication of such a civilization. In the absence of the voice of God, we are almost all corrupted by the voice of Mammon. Neither the suffering of the world's poor nor the progressive depletion of the Earth's genetic treasure chest will suddenly persuade us to change our ways. We have already lived with these tragedies for so long, yet it has never been quite the moment to break the habits of a lifetime. The human race has an astonishing capacity to deny the suffering of others and of the Earth.

All that stands between us and a slow slide into a brutal, survival-of-the-fittest decline is the umbilical link between us and our children. It is their presence, their expectations, their rights that most powerfully intrude on humankind's self-absorbed dance of destruction.

To me, that is what personal responsibility ultimately boils down to: a readiness to take up the cudgels on behalf of the Earth and of future generations. Not to prove how pious and green one might be, but just to tread a little more lightly on the Earth today so that others still have a rich and beautiful Earth to tread on in the future.

Or, as has been said a thousand times before: to live more simply, that others may simply live.

THE INDIVIDUAL, GOVERNMENT, AND BUSINESS

If personal responsibility is the cornerstone on which any transformation is to be built, it is by no means the whole edifice. There is only so much any one person can do in his or her own right. To accelerate the process of change, and to ensure its durability, there are many different levels at which progress must be made simultaneously:

● At the community level. Joining organizations, supporting community initiatives, sharing resources: umpteen Goliaths have been toppled by community-backed Davids. A sense of community can come from one's neighborhood or workplace, from recreational or charitable activities, from a shared religion or spiritual concern.

● **At the local level.** However restricted its powers may be, local government can be a tremendous force for the good in terms of environmental improvement. It is at the local level that people experience quality of life, and by the use of local bylaws, planning controls, and local finances, politicians and officials can powerfully reinforce individual efforts.

● **At the national level.** Ultimately, there is no substitute for direct government involvement in developing and enforcing policies to protect the environment. In the market-based economies of the Western world, it is up to government to set achievable standards for individuals and businesses, to create a "level playing field" so that best business practice becomes common practice, and to give regulatory bodies the appropriate powers and necessary resources.

● **At the international level.** More and more issues can only be resolved by international cooperation, not just in terms of the better management of the global commons (the atmosphere, oceans, shared rivers, mountain ranges, and so on), but in recognizing the commonality of all parts of this human family of ours. "Sustainable development" is a meaningless concept if it cannot be made to work for rich and poor alike.

With action at all these levels, as well as in our own lives, the "benign circle" of environmental transformation can be completed by a profound shift in the priorities and day-to-day practice of business itself.

It seems unfair to look to business to rescue humankind from its own failings. We (and our politicians) have built up an economic system that obliges businesses to go on producing more if they want to be "successful," which demands increased competitiveness at almost all costs, which penalizes companies that are concerned about more than their bottom line, and which entirely fails to reflect the genuine costs and benefits involved in creating our wealth in this way.

True enough, some companies have always taken advantage of such economic illiteracy to get "dirty rich" at our expense. More recently, others have been genuinely striving to get their own

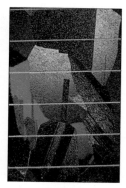

SOLAR SENSE *Silicon-based solar cells, photographed here in cross section* (near left), *are already used for a wide variety of purposes. This street light in Holland* (far left) *is powered by batteries recharged during the day by an array of solar cells.*

HOUSING FOR THE FUTURE (right) *The "Thermoplastic Concept House" was built in Massachusetts in 1988, and has caused quite a stir with its innovative use of building materials and increased energy efficiency.*

NATURAL HERITAGE *Today, nobody would dream of building on Hampstead Heath, one of London's most beautiful open spaces. But it is only there to be enjoyed today because earlier generations campaigned to protect it from housing development.*

green house in order, often against the grain of conventional business wisdom and despite the conflicting messages coming out of government.

It is a mistake to suppose that these vanguard companies will automatically pull the rest up by their bootstraps. Unless they are both cajoled by consumer pressure and regulated by government intervention into achieving higher environmental standards, there will always be a majority of companies that either don't care enough to go green, or claim that they can't afford to go green for fear of losing their competitive edge.

Companies like that do not deserve our support, either as consumers or as potential employees. And that brings us right back to where we started: shouldering responsibility for those aspects of our individual lives that we can control. It is not just charity that begins at home!

HARMONY (left) *Unlike this child playing on a swing in the Katmandu Valley in Nepal, millions of urban children all over the world have no contact with the Earth and its self-renewing cycles.*

TED HUGHES

First Things First (An Election Duet, performed in the Womb by fetal Twins)

FIRST TWIN:
If the cost of a mountain of butter is
    poisoned water in your tap and Cot-Death

If the cost of a mountain of grain is
    poisoned bread on your plate and for the
    farmer's child (and yours) Leukemia

If the cost of the Gross National Product is
    for trees no leaves
    for waters no fish
    and for you cortical plaques, neurofibrillary tangles
    Presenile Dementia

And if the cost of Annual Expansion of the World Chemical
    Industry taken as a whole over the last two decades is
    a 40% drop in the sperm count of all human males
    (nor can God alone help the ozone layer or the ovum)

Then let what can't be sold to your brother and sister be
    released on the 3rd World and let it return by air and
    sea to drip down the back of your own throat at night

Because

BOTH TWINS (singing):
Man's brain is such a toxin
    (O hear our fetal shout)
Nothing surer than man's brain
    Will wipe the menace out.

SECOND TWIN:
Man's riddle is: "Why aren't I right?"
    So to correct his error
He can only double it
    In exponential terror.

Snap your fingers at Death's frown.
    Eat, drink and be jolly.
The only folly of our fun
    Is to bewail our folly.

Who wants to last forever?
    Then take another sup
For everything pitched in the ditch
    Comes back into the cup.

BOTH TWINS (singing):
Then off to bed, for every head's
    In labor with the pains
Until the Monkey Mutant
    Can bear a brain with brains.

Ted Hughes

Ted Hughes is the British Poet Laureate.

MAKING THE DIFFERENCE

There are dozens of practical steps that people can take to help protect and improve the environment. Some are very small, like not leaving the lights on when you go out of the room, and some are rather larger, like having a full "energy audit" done on your house. But they all contribute to redressing today's environmental problems.

It is impossible to draw up a universal list of steps each of us can take, as the situation differs dramatically from country to country. In Japan, for instance, recycling policies are already highly effective: 95 percent of newspapers and 65 percent of bottles are recycled. Energy efficiency per unit of output is also high. But Japan's depletion of the world's rainforests, and the way it uses its "aid muscle" in developing countries, are staggeringly irresponsible. In Britain, by contrast, the Overseas Development Administration supports reasonably enlightened aid policies, geared more to promoting sustainable development, but the government's overall approach to recycling and energy efficiency remains antediluvian.

What Can Be Done

These things can be put right in any country with the appropriate combination of individual commitment and government pressure. The tropical timber trade (whether it be in Japan, Britain or anywhere else) will only be pressured into developing truly

CONSUMER ACTION
While international agreements are crucial to the long-term conservation of tropical rainforests, consumers can take immediate action to save trees simply by not buying imported hardwoods.

sustainable forestry management practices by a combination of consumers refusing to buy hardwoods unless they know they come from properly managed sources, and by governments insisting on proper labeling and binding codes of conduct.

In almost all countries there are practical guides and "green manuals" covering these issues, and there are many environmental organizations that offer lifestyle advice. It is getting easier to find out what needs to be done; a few of the most essential contacts and resources are listed on page 202.

Much of it comes down to common sense: saving energy and water; not throwing things away if they can be re-used, repaired or recycled; walking, cycling or using public transportation; buying fresh food and ensuring a balanced diet; avoiding environmentally-damaging goods or wasteful packaging.

Though insignificant when assessed as individual acts, these lifestyle choices can indeed make a difference collectively. For instance, consumer action and environmentalist pressure forced the aerosol industry in many countries to stop using ozone-depleting chemicals as propellants.

Good Business Practice

Businesses and large retailers are now far more exposed to consumer pressure than ever before. Many realize that improving their environmental credentials will give them an edge over their rivals. In contrast to the kind of green public relations and promotional gimmicks which we saw so much of in the mid 1980's, businesses are now genuinely working to clean up their act.

Lifestyle changes, consumer pressure, and the acceptance of personal responsibility over those issues where we have some direct control, will not of themselves bring about a sufficiently thorough transformation of our industrial society. But without them there will be no transformation whatsoever.

INTERNATIONAL EFFORTS
Good environmental policy takes many forms, and any one country may not be successful in all areas. These figures (from Environmental Indicators *published by the Organization for Economic Cooperation and Development) show where 20 of the OECD's 24 industrialized nations stand on six environmental policies. Some figures are encouragingly low, but averages (in the last column) still reveal a sorry picture of environmental dereliction.*

	AUSTRALIA	AUSTRIA	BELGIUM	CANADA	DENMARK	FINLAND	FRANCE	(W.) GERMANY	IRELAND	ITALY	JAPAN	NETHERLANDS	NEW ZEALAND	NORWAY	PORTUGAL	SPAIN	SWEDEN	SWITZERLAND	UK	USA	OECD AVERAGE
Population per square kilometer *(square mile)*	2.2	89.4	324	2.7	118	14.8	102	243	52.6	190	327	362	12.7	13	111	78	18.4	157	232	26.6	25.9
	5.6	*231*	*840*	*6.9*	*306*	*38.5*	*265*	*630*	*136*	*493*	*847*	*939*	*32.8*	*33.6*	*289*	*202*	*47.6*	*408*	*602*	*68.8*	*67*
Energy use per capita, in tons of oil	5	3.8	4.6	9.6	3.7	6	3.7	4.5	2.7	2.6	3.3	4.4	4.3	6.7	1.5	2.2	6.7	4.2	3.7	7.8	4.8
Motor vehicle ownership per 100 people	46	38	37	47	32	38	41	49	22	46	27	36	51	38	18	29	42	44	38	58	41
Carbon dioxide emissions per capita, in tons	4.3	2.2	3.2	4.8	3.4	3.7	1.8	3.2	2.2	1.9	2.2	3.4	2	2.1	1	1.5	2.5	1.9	2.9	5.8	3.4
Municipal waste per capita in kilograms *(pounds)*	681	228	313	632	469	608	304	331	311	301	394	467	662	475	231	322	317	427	353	864	513
	1501	*503*	*690*	*1393*	*1034*	*1340*	*670*	*730*	*686*	*663*	*869*	*1029*	*1459*	*1047*	*509*	*710*	*699*	*941*	*778*	*1905*	*1131*
Per capita imports of tropical wood/cork, in US$	6.1	2.6	8	1	2.7	1.7	6.2	4.8	8.7	6.2	21.6	15.2	2.4	1.5	11.1	5.8	1.3	1	5.5	0.7	6.1

AL GORE

❝ *My own religious tradition teaches me that we've been given dominion over the Earth, but that we must be good stewards of the Earth. We can't say, 'We didn't know.' In the parable of the unfaithful servant, who is asleep when the thief ransacks his master's house, it is not enough for the servant to say, 'I was asleep, master.' Our home, our planet is being ransacked. We cannot plead ignorance. We are responsible. We have an obligation to respect life itself, an obligation to understand and respond to the inextricable links between justice and environmental protection. The issue is not just the greenhouse effect or the depletion of the stratospheric ozone layer or the loss of living species. The deeper issue is a change in the relationship between humankind and the ecological system of our planet. Industrial civilization is on a collision course with the environmental system that supports life as we know it. The Earth's environment is crumbling in what seems like slow motion, in response to the onslaught of more and more people, and more and more technology, and more and more willful environmental vandalism. The solutions we seek will be found in a new faith in the future which justifies action in the present, a new moral courage to choose higher values in the conduct of human affairs, a new reverence for absolute principles that can serve as guiding stars for the future course of our species and our place within creation.* **❞**

Al Gore is a United States Senator from the State of Tennessee.

MARGARET ATWOOD

❝ *Concern for the environment is no longer the preserve of a small, eccentric minority. It cuts across the political spectrum from left to right. When politicians start posing beside lakes, pledging their undying love to nature, it's a sure sign they know which way the wind is blowing. It's blowing from the local dump, and it doesn't smell too good. Once, we were threatened with disaster in the time of our children, or our children's children; we shrugged and kept on polluting. But now, we're told, all these unpleasant things are going to happen to us. No wonder people are worried.* **❞**

Margaret Atwood is a Canadian poet and novelist. She has taught English literature at universities in the USA and Canada.

WETLAND OASIS IN FARMED FIELD, CANADA

ALEXEY YABLOKOV

❝ *Ecological troubles have no limits. In spite of ideological and spiritual differences, we are all citizens of the World Polluted States. Ignorance cannot serve as an excuse. The environmental threat to man's survival must become one of the fundamental elements of political thought. It is quite clear that the whole world cannot just copy the production and consumption patterns of our industrialized society. The world simply has neither enough resources, nor space for the wastes of such a 'civilization.' Developed countries should now devote a part of their expenditure to helping preserve the natural resources of the developing countries, and should share their environmentally friendly technologies with them. Environmental interdependence inevitably leads us to a new concept of global security, which includes not only military but environmental security. We must overcome the conflicts between policy makers, economists, and ecologists, which often reflect the different time-scales in their thinking: while the time-scale for politicians is five years, and for economists ten years, for most ecological processes it is 50 years. To achieve this, we need knowledge and political will. If we have the will, the resources can be found. We can start by reducing our tremendous military expenditures and by restricting the development of our consumer economy. Let us awaken ourselves – before it is too late.* **❞**

Professor Alexey Yablokov is the Deputy Chairman of the Committee of Ecology of the Supreme Soviet in the USSR.

ROBYN WILLIAMS

❝ *In Australia, we are guardians of a landscape of great age which has only recently been revealed to non-aboriginal eyes as an astounding treasure. Once, we saw it as a hostile 'Bright and Savage Land' that needed taming. Instead of thrilling complexity, we saw only 'bush' and 'outback' and creatures that seemed something of a biological joke. Now, science and thoughtfulness have opened our eyes and we are astonished, indeed chastened, by the task we face to protect and cherish what is left of this unique natural inheritance.* **❞**

Robyn Williams is the presenter of *The Science Show* on ABC Radio in Australia. He is also the Chair of the Commission for the Future.

JULOS BEAUCARNE

Hello, hello, do you know that you and I,
each and every one of us,
are members of the crew on the
spaceship "Earth."
It depends on no one else but us,
it depends on every one of us
that the planet "Earth" keeps turning,
that the water stays pure,
that the air gets cleaner
so that the human flower may continue to blossom
once we have turned the page of this century.
We have just eight years to the year 2000
to roll up our sleeves and clean up our house
to welcome the 21st century.
On the ninth day of the ninth month of the year 1999
the world will be in the cradle or the grave.
If all the televisions and all the radios of the world were ready
to make the effort,
with all the satellites that spin and relay the pictures and the voices,
the Earth could become in the space of three months
an earthly paradise.

Julos

Julos Beaucarne is a Belgian singer and songwriter.

S. M. MOHD. IDRIS

MOUNTAIN STREAM
IN GLACIER NATIONAL
PARK, CANADA

66 *Now that green has become the fashionable prestige color, we should be careful not to be diverted or misled by products, projects, technologies, or institutions that may proclaim themselves 'green' but in reality use this as a cover to continue to exploit both nature and people. Our fear is that the rhetoric of ecology will be used by the power structures to confuse and mislead. Policies that are designed by corporate interests or on their behalf are being drawn up in nice-sounding ecological terms such as 'sustainable development' and 'forestry action plans.' Environmentalists therefore have to continue to give deep interpretations and clear analysis of the ecological crisis, and to have critiques of the false solutions.* 99

S. M. Mohd. Idris is the Coordinator of the Third World Network, and the President of Friends of the Earth, Malaysia.

BARBARA PYLE

BATHING IN THE RIVER GANGES

66 *There is an old Chinese proverb that says:
'Unless we change the direction we are headed,
we might end up where we are going.'
We stand poised at a crossroads . . .
At a threshold of great opportunity.
Which road shall we choose?
The road to continued destruction,
or the road to peace with the planet?
Our planet will not be saved by any one big decision;
it will be saved by many individual choices and voices.
And our voices must be heard NOW.
It is truly our last chance to prove our merit as a species.
I believe we create and control our own destiny.
And I reject the possibility of living on a further degraded planet.
By our powers combined, we can make a better world.
So let us serve the planet well.
And get on with it.* 99

Barbara Y. E. Pyle

Barbara Y. E. Pyle is the Vice President of Environmental Policy for TBS Superstation. She has also worked as a photojournalist.

THE WAY FORWARD
CELEBRATING THE EARTH
JONATHON PORRITT

*The future will either be green, or not at all. This truth lies
at the heart of humankind's most pressing challenge: to learn to live
in harmony with the Earth on a genuinely sustainable basis.*

From the early 1960's onward, environmentalists have had a feeling that time is running out. Some of their earlier, gloomier messages were disregarded on the somewhat dubious assumption that for every problem there is an appropriate technological fix to be found. There is no shortage of appropriate technologies; we do indeed depend on them for the future. But it is the social and political context within which they are deployed that matters.

What we now know is that long before the oil runs out, or industry's precious raw materials become prohibitively scarce, the Earth's basic life-support systems (clean air, fresh water, self-renewing soils and forests) will have become exhausted or irretrievably degraded unless we can change our ways.

At the heart of every environmental problem, there lurks a political, economic or spiritual cause. That realization distinguishes today's international green movement from yesterday's environmentalism: one has to be constantly alert to the whole picture, incorporating ecological principles into every facet of government and international affairs.

To achieve any kind of reconciliation between our human aspirations and the constraints of a finite planet means quite simply that it is those aspirations that are going to have to change. True enough, we can learn to make far better use of the Earth's resources, constantly improving efficiency to get more from less. And we can indeed learn to make far better use of the one resource that is all but infinite, the sun. But however "environment-friendly" our new technologies may become, there will always be some diminution of the Earth's natural wealth, year in, year out.

MASAI WOMEN
(opposite) *One of the most important features of traditional societies such as the Masai is a sense of place and a role in the environment. This connectedness is celebrated in dances, songs, and rituals that are often regarded as strange, or "primitive," by go-getters in the West. Yet, looking at the dealers on the New York cotton exchange* (inset, above), *it is hard to imagine anything so primitive as the West's obsessive worship of the big buck.*

MESSAGES TO THE GODS AND SPIRITS
In less industrialized parts of the world, deeper values than the pursuit of economic growth give meaning to people's lives. Tibetans print prayers on scraps of cloth (far left), *which are left to bleach in the sun on the roofs of Buddhist temples. In Benares, on the sacred river Ganges, the sky lantern festival of Akash Deep* (near left) *is held every autumn. The lamps guide the spirits of the dead as they visit the living.*

JAN GRZESICA

66 *The exceptional position of man in the world of creation
gives him no excuse for treating the world of nature in an absolute
and irresponsible way. Man is a spiritual and physical being, and due to his
spirituality is transcendent to nature. Seen in unity with his environment,
man stands at the top of the whole hierarchy of the created world,
and through him alone the world achieves its proper value.
Such an understanding of human existence makes the relationship
between man and his natural environment more cooperative. Man in this world
is God's partner in the act of creation. To shape the natural environment wisely,
he should approach it with reverence. The aim of any economic or technical growth
should always be directed to the full development of the human person.* 99

Jan Grzesica is a Polish priest and author. He writes for the Catholic press,
and works to promote environmental causes.

HARVESTS AND FESTIVALS

*Though few people in
the West would choose
to winnow the grain for
their own bread, as is
still done in Nigeria
(near right),* many
*now regret the distance
that has grown between
them and the land on
which we all still
depend. We have even
lost that sense of the
passage of the seasons,
with our supermarket
shelves bearing fresh
produce from any part
of the world at any
time. In Thailand
(above right)* the
*harvest is still
celebrated at the New
Year. It is ironic that
much of Thailand's
most fertile land should
be devoted to growing
fruit and vegetables for
people so out of touch
with the Earth that
their own Harvest
Festival is little more
than an empty ritual.*

That brings us back to the tricky issue of our
human aspirations. "People want more," it is
argued, "and they always will." If so, the politicians' job is simply to meet those demands, not to
point out the error of our collective ways, let alone
to endeavor to "change human nature".

In the West, our heads are so filled with talk of
inflation, international competitiveness, exchange
rates, balance of payments, and so on, that we
sometimes forget the original political premise on
which this economic jargon depends: that if people have enough money (by virtue of producing
and consuming more), then they will automatically
be happy. They will be able to buy the goods and
services they require to meet their needs.

IDENTIFYING NEEDS

Against that apparent political consensus are now
raised the voices of all those who argue that this is
an unwise, inefficient, and even inhumane way of
meeting our needs; that money, in itself, cannot
buy happiness; and that we would be better
advised to concentrate on achieving real improvements in the quality of our lives.

There would seem to be two categories of
human need, overlapping each other, but very different in essence. There are those fundamental
material needs, which most people in the West

take for granted, but which many in the Third World can only dream of: food, shelter, warmth, clothing, health care, education. These are things that money can (and usually does) buy.

Then there is the host of less tangible, less material needs that money often cannot buy. These differ from one culture to the next, but include some or all of the following:

● Good work: not just being able to earn a living, but feeling fulfilled in so doing, and being able to serve others in the process.

● Security: being able to rely on and enjoy the affection, friendship, and love of others.

● Self-reliance: being independent, free of debt, with enough to meet one's needs plus a bit extra.

● Recreation: being able to have a good time in good company.

● Respect: feeling valued by others at home, at work, or in the community.

● Challenge: feeling that one still has things to do without being blocked at every turn.

● Belonging: fitting in, being part of an indefinable web of family and friends.

● Rootedness: feeling embedded in a place, reassured but not imprisoned by familiar sights.

● Inspiration: being taken out of ourselves or profoundly enlightened by other people, rare experiences, religious or spiritual values.

● Freedom: the personal liberty that is essential in striving to meet these needs.

Modern politics has never addressed these basic human needs, but simply assumes that the postwar industrial consensus will deliver them as an indirect consequence of getting steadily richer and consuming more and more. Such utter folly is almost impossible to countenance. Very often, the capacity of individuals and society to meet such needs is actually destroyed by devoting all our energies to getting richer. Ends have been terminally confused with means, and we are all the poorer for it. That for me is why modern politics has become such a blighted wasteland.

HIGHER AIMS

Over and above such a list of unquantifiable needs there are two further aspirations that seem crucial to any lasting process of transformation. The first is being able to celebrate, to rejoice in friendship, in special occasions, in important rituals, and in the beauty and mystery of the Earth. For most of

WATCHING THE WHALES (left) *One sign of hope for the future is that far more money is now being made from people traveling and taking vacations to watch living whales, such as this pod of killer whales off the coast of British Columbia, than from people buying slaughtered whalemeat. More and more people are seeking recreation by reconnecting with the Earth and its creatures.*

AUTUMN LEAVES CAUGHT IN A STREAM ON THE COLORADO PLATEAU IN UTAH (below)

EDUCATION FOR LIFE
These children at school in famine-stricken Ethiopia don't see themselves as the generation of the future, but as that of the present. They, and millions like them around the world, have work to be done right now – not least the task of persuading adults of their responsibilities to them and to the Earth itself. As environmental studies assume increasing importance, schools are turning out the first generation of children to be environmentally aware.

ALAIN HERVÉ

❝ *I spend part of my summer in the Chausey archipelago off the west coast of France. In winter, it is inhabited only by sea birds and rats and half a dozen men; in summer, by herds of tourists and boating people.*
Last summer we had an argument with some kids, 12 to 14 years old, who had been camping on a tiny rocky island. They came back and proudly told us how they had captured rats in cages, soaked them with gasoline, ignited them and let them run free. We told them they were criminals. They told us that rats were rats and ate the food they had brought in. We kept returning to natural rights and morals, each of us trembling with contradictory feelings, commitments, and knowledge. They were not criminals, we were not saints. My personal conviction is that till now man has been both a natural killer and a natural beautifier. It is not enough to say that we are ecologists, nature lovers, advocates of good feelings, pantheist poets. As ecologists, we must know that we are a plague on planet Earth, and that we are going to proliferate up to the point of destroying our own species. To get out of this lethal trap, we have only one chance. We do not need more technical contraptions, more scientific discoveries. We need to reach another level of consciousness. **❞**

Alain Hervé

Writer Alain Hervé is the founder of *Les Amis de la Terre* (Friends of the Earth, France).

us, the art of celebrating the Earth has to be relearned, often by reference back to art and literature. For authors such as Blake, Wordsworth, Goethe, Tolstoy, Emerson, and Thoreau, nature was truly alive, and our relationship with it one to be cherished and joyfully celebrated.

Once again, that spirit is beginning to flourish in our industrial culture. There is within it a profound spirituality that takes us far beyond the rather anemic, utilitarian version of stewardship currently popular with many Western politicians.

The challenge we face is not just a question of managing the Earth's resources more efficiently, or of learning to exploit the Earth's wealth in a rather less destructive fashion. Nor, at the other end of this spiritual scale, does it entail the outright worship of nature. Somewhere in between there lies a recognition of the intrinsic value of the rest of life on Earth, a feeling of reverence for its self-renewing complexity and beauty, and an often confused intimation that we are all, in the end, one.

A SENSE OF PURPOSE

The second aspiration that I feel is essential is to find a real sense of purpose in life. "We're here because we're here, so enjoy it while you can," hardly provides an answer to the great mysteries of life and to our role here on Earth. Politics has become disturbingly purposeless, as the goals of society or individual effort are progressively absorbed in that all-embracing process of achieving economic growth and getting richer. But growth for what? Richer to what end?

Fortunately, we have not yet become a totally purposeless, self-serving society. There are still people who devote their lives to others, giving freely of their time and their love. There is an ennobling purposefulness to this devotion, which even the most arrogant cynics find hard to dismiss.

But I do not believe that such an individually derived, counter-cultural sense of purpose can ever be sufficient to offset the tide of alienated materialism that now motivates the majority of people in the developed world. And I very much doubt that we can heal the human spirit without discovering and learning to live by a new sense of purpose appropriate to the age and the ecological challenges we now face.

That higher purpose must surely be the one referred to in the foreword of this book: to meet the needs of all people, to enhance the quality of our lives, and to protect the future of those who follow by living as stewards of the whole Earth, not just the parts that happen to be useful to us.

Those who maintain that it is impossible for politics to be geared to such a sense of purpose condemn us all to the toils of unsustainable consumerism. They also condemn the Third World to permanent poverty, for by their standards we will never be rich enough to begin the process of wealth distribution from North to South.

A different kind of politics must and will be built, and many thousands of organizations around the world are blazing a trail in this direction that others will surely follow. The anguish of the Earth and its hard-pressed people can now be heard loud and clear, even by those who persist in trying to shut out these voices.

Time is running out, and crucial decisions, with irreversible consequences, do have to be made between now and the turn of the century. Technologically, the greening of the Earth lies within our grasp; the only question that remains to be answered is whether or not the human spirit is adequate to the task.

THE DALAI LAMA

❝ Our ancestors viewed the Earth as rich and bountiful, which it is. Many people in the past also saw nature as inexhaustibly sustainable, which we now know is the case only if we care for it.

It is not difficult to forgive destruction in the past which resulted from ignorance. Today, however, we have access to more information, and it is essential that we re-examine ethically what we have inherited, what we are responsible for, and what we will pass on to coming generations.

Our marvels of science and technology are matched if not outweighed by many current tragedies, including human starvation in some parts of the world, and the extinction of other life-forms.

The exploration of outer space takes place at the same time as the Earth's own oceans, seas, and fresh water areas grow increasingly polluted. Many of the Earth's habitats, animals, plants, insects, and even micro-organisms that we know as rare may not be known at all by future generations. We have the capability, and the responsibility.

We must act before it is too late. ❞

His Holiness Tenzin Gyatso is the fourteenth Dalai Lama of Tibet, spiritual leader of the nation and the Buddhist faith.

AT ONE WITH THE WORLD
The raw beauty of a wild place such as New Zealand's Mount Cook can be breathtaking, but you don't have to climb mountains to experience the extraordinary power of the natural world. It's all around us, even in the midst of our polluted cities: you only have to want to see it, to be open to the inspiration that it can bring. The evolution of today's industrialized way of thinking away from the self-destructive greed that has characterized our rape of the Earth may take several generations. To our generation falls the challenge of mapping out that evolutionary climb with a new-found sense of purpose.

RECOMMENDED BOOKS

The following books offer a wide range of practical tips and sound common sense on the steps each of us can take – at home, at work or on vacation – to minimize our harm to the environment and to reduce our consumption of natural resources.

The Canadian Green Consumer Guide by Pollution Probe (McClelland & Stewart)

The Canadian Junior Green Guide by Teri Degler and Pollution Probe (McClelland & Stewart)

Good Planets are Hard to Find by Ronald Bazar and Romar Dehr (Earth Beat Press)

Looking at the Environment by David Suzuki (Stoddart)

Two Minutes a Day for a Greener Planet by Marjorie Lamb (Harper Collins)

MANEKA GANDHI

66 *In this short extract from a speech Chief Seattle made in 1854, I find an explanation to many of the threats to our planet:* 99

How can you buy or sell the sky, the warmth of the land? The idea is strange to us.
If we do not own the freshness of the air and the sparkle of the water, how can you buy them?
We are part of the Earth, and it is part of us. The rocky crests, the juices of the meadows, the body heat of the pony, and man – all belong to the same family. The shining water that moves in the streams is not just water, but the blood of our ancestors. If we sell you land, you must teach your children that it is sacred – that each ghostly reflection in the clear water of the lakes tells of memories in the lives of my people. The water's murmur is the voice of my father's father.
We know the white man does not understand our ways. One portion of land is the same to him as the next – for he is a stranger who comes in the night and takes from the land whatever he needs.

Maneka Gandhi

Maneka Gandhi is the Minister of State for Environment and Forests in India.

USEFUL ADDRESSES

If you wish to support the efforts being made to protect the Earth and its inhabitants, or would like more information about the environmental issues described in this book, please write to the following organizations.

Organizations in Canada

Canadian Nature Federation
453 Sussex Drive
Ottawa, Ontario
K1N 6Z4

Canadian Parks and Wilderness Society
160 Bloor Street East, Suite 1150
Toronto, Ontario
M4W 1B9

Canadian Wildlife Federation
1673 Carling Avenue
Ottawa, Ontario
K2A 1CA

Environmentally Sound Packaging Coalition
2150 Maple Street
Vancouver, British Columbia
V6J 3TS

Friends of the Earth
251 Laurier Avenue West
Suite 701
Ottawa, Ontario
K1P 5J6

Greenpeace
185 Spadina Avenue, Sixth Floor
Toronto, Ontario
M5T 2C6

Pollution Probe
12 Madison Avenue
Toronto, Ontario
M5R 2S1

Solar Energy Society
15 York Street, Suite 3
Ottawa, Ontario
K1N 5S7

World Wildlife Fund (Canada)
90 Eglinton Avenue East
Suite 504
Toronto, Ontario
M4P 2Z7

World Society for the Protection of Animals
PO Box 15
55 University Avenue, Suite 902
Toronto, Ontario
M5J 2H7

International Organizations

Alp Action
Bellevue Foundation
P.O. Box 6
1211 Geneva 3, Switzerland

Centre for a Common Future
Palais Wilson
52 Rue des Paquis
CH-1201 Geneva, Switzerland

Greenpeace International
Keizersgracht 176
1016 DW Amsterdam
The Netherlands

International Planned Parenthood Federation (IPPF)
Regent's College
Inner Circle
Regent's Park
London NW1 4NS, UK

International Rivers Network
301 Broadway, Suite B
San Francisco, CA 94133, USA

Rainforest Action Network
301 Broadway, Suite A
San Francisco, CA 94133, USA

Right Livelihood Award
P.O. Box 15072
S-0465 Stockholm, Sweden

United Nations Environment Programme (UNEP)
P.O. Box 30552
Nairobi, Kenya

Worldwatch Institute
1776 Massachusetts Avenue, N.W.
Washington, D.C. 20036, USA

World Wide Fund for Nature (WWF) International
World Conservation Centre
Avenue du Mont Blanc
CH-11996 Gland, Switzerland

Zoo Check
Cherry Tree Cottage
Coldharbour
Dorking
Surrey RH5 6HA, UK

FRIENDS OF THE EARTH INTERNATIONAL

Humanity is abusing nature on an unprecedented scale. The global extent of pollution, the extinction of species, and the irresponsible waste of natural resources have created an urgent need for an international response.

Friends of the Earth International coordinates the efforts of 43 national groups to win this battle. It was founded in 1971 as a network for the exchange of information and campaign coordination. There are now Friends of the Earth groups in 21 industrialized nations, 16 developing nations, and 6 Eastern European countries. Together they represent the environmental concerns of over 800,000 members. The exchange of so many different views, North and South, East and West, makes Friends of the Earth International a unique organization.

Friends of the Earth International (FoEI) is currently engaged in the following international campaigns:

● Tropical Rainforests: FoEI is fighting to reform the tropical timber trade and to protect the rights of forest dwellers.
● Ozone Layer: FoEI is working to strengthen international agreements to eliminate the use of ozone-depleting substances.
● International Dams: FoEI is campaigning to stop World Bank funding of destructive dams.
● Global Warming: FoEI is persuading municipalities to recognize their role in reducing carbon emissions, and is promoting the transfer of energy efficient and renewable energy technology between North and South.
● Marine Issues: FoEI representatives are lobbying for increased environmental protection at the International Maritime Organization, the London Dumping Convention, and the International Whaling Commission.

Each national group is autonomous, with its own campaigns, structure, and funding base. FoEI membership is not based on any political, religious, ethnic or cultural affiliations. Members are bound together by a common cause: the conservation, restoration, and rational use of the Earth's resources. The fundamental principles underpinning the work of FoEI include:

● A recognition that environmental problems can only be tackled effectively by international action at both governmental and non-governmental levels, and that citizen participation is a critical part of that process.
● An understanding that environmental problems cannot be approached in isolation from the social, economic, and cultural factors that influence them.
● A readiness to cooperate with other organizations to ensure the widest range of resources and views.
● A commitment to promote positive alternatives as part of any campaign to prevent further environmental destruction.

Representatives of the member groups meet as a decision-making council once a year. Together, they select the Friends of the Earth International campaigns, and appoint lead groups to campaign on behalf of the international network.

Friends of the Earth International, P.O. Box 19199, 1000 GD Amsterdam, The Netherlands

THE SAVE THE EARTH FUND

Proceeds from the sale of *Save the Earth* will be used to create a special Fund within Friends of the Earth International. Its purpose will be to support smaller Friends of the Earth groups in countries where fundraising is difficult, particularly in developing countries and Eastern Europe.

It will provide seed money for newsletters, membership drives, and basic office and communications equipment. Without this kind of infrastructure support, it is almost impossible for many groups to cope with the pressure on them. Some of the money will be used to help coordinate the campaigning activities of different Friends of the Earth groups on key global issues, ensuring a coherent presence at international negotiations, better campaign materials, and a stronger presence in those countries where environmental awareness has made little progress.

Decisions on the allocation of the proceeds from *Save the Earth* will be taken by the Executive Committee of Friends of the Earth International, which is elected by all the member groups on an annual basis.

MAIRI MACARTHUR

66 *Ten years ago, I went to my first meeting of Friends of the Earth International. I recall a babble of accents, a kaleidoscope of ideas and views and strategies. The spectrum of resources at our command ranged from modest to tiny. Could this small, motley crew help save the Earth? But I also remember the words of a Japanese member tumbling out so fast we had to ask her to slow down. She was pleading passionately, not for an issue in her own country, but for Pacific islanders, threatened by nuclear testing. Not just their crisis; ours, too.*

Citizens' groups such as FoEI can reach across geographical and cultural boundaries, to act together in a way that our governments have so often signally failed to do.

A phrase which, for me, captures the spirit of FoEI is 'amateur radical.' Radical because it goes to the root of things, to the poverty and injustice and oppression which are inextricable from environmental destruction. Amateur because it harnesses the energies and idealism of ordinary people. It reminds us that the power to change things does not lie solely with those who lay claim to it, but with each and all of us. And at the root of amateur is the word 'love.' 99

Mairi MacArthur

Scottish environmentalist Mairi MacArthur was the first Chairperson of Friends of the Earth International.

SPECIAL CONTRIBUTORS

Absalom, Jack 44
Adams, Douglas 100
Aga Khan, Sadruddin 44
Aleandro, Norma 49
Anderson, Theo 114
Asner, Ed 179
Attenborough, David 114
Atwood, Margaret 194
Batisse, Michel 18
Beaucarne, Julos 195
Bhagwat, Ravi 135
Binney, Don 93
Bragg, Charles Lynn 149
Branson, Richard 31
Brown, Bob 173
Brundtland, Gro Harlem 114
Cartier-Bresson, Henri 30
Cockburn, Bruce 49
Commoner, Barry 30
Cronkite, Walter 38
da Cruz, Humberto 152
Dalai Lama 201
de Wit, Cindy 78
Drew, Simon 190
Dumont, René 115
Durrell, Gerald 44
Ehrlich, Anne 119
Ehrlich, Paul 119
Filippini, Rosa 149
Fowles, John 45
Fujiwara, Eiji 190
Gahrton, Per 18
Gandhi, Maneka 202
Golding, William 148
Goldsworthy, Andy 173
Göncz, Árpád 107
Gore, Al 194
Grzesica, Jan 198
Harrison, George 38
Havel, Václav 92
Hemming, John 51
Hervé, Alain 200
Hueting, Roefie 161
Hughes, Ted 192
Idris, S.M. Mohd. 195
Jackson, Jesse 38
Jones, Caroline 138
Kelly, Petra 115
Krenak, Ailton 141
Kumar, Satish 132
Kuroda, Yoichi 51
Lackovic Croata, Ivan 18
Lerner, Alejandro 149
Long, Richard 45
Lovejoy, Thomas 77
Lovelock, James 19
Lutzenberger, José 29
Maathai, Wangari 60
MacArthur, Mairi 203
Macaulay, David 27
Mansholt, S. L. 100
May, Robert 77
McCartney, Paul 148
McKenna, Virginia 31

Menuhin, Yehudi 109
Miller, Joe 24
Milligan, Spike 115
Moberg, Eva 64
Moore, Patrick 148
Morin, Edgar 107
Morris, Desmond 115
Mundey, Jack 127
Murphy, Dervla 179
Ono, Yoko 45
Parsons, Brendan 180
Patterson, Freeman 82
Peterson, Russell 109
Pimenta, Carlos 66
Ponting, Clive 38
Potts, Gary 141
Puttnam, David 30
Pyle, Barbara 195
Redford, Robert 45
Reilly, William 92
Rifkin, Jeremy 92
Ripa di Meana, Carlo 29
Roddick, Anita 168
Rothschild, Miriam 83
Runcie, Robert 179
Russell, Andy 27
Sabato, Ernesto 105
Sagan, Carl 104
Sandbrook, Richard 66
Schiwujowa, Halina 30
Scott, Lady 165
Shepherd, David 73
Signorino, Mario 19
Singh, Karan 19
Steadman, Ralph 186-7
Strong, Maurice 29
Suzuki, David 19
Swaminathan, M.S. 68
Taplin, Guy 165
Tazieff, Haroun 149
Thomas, R.S. 92
Tolba, Mostafa 68
Turner, Ted 93
Tutu, Desmond 135
Uriburu, Nicolas 114
Ustinov, Peter 93
van der Post, Laurens 59
Vavrousek, Josef 148
von Weizsäcker, E. U. 31
Vorontsov, Nikolai 31
Williams, Heathcote 153
Williams, Robyn 194
Yablokov, Alexey 194
York, Susannah 34
Zelnik, Jerzy 104
Zydeveld, Chris 127

INDEX

A
Aborigines 139, 140
Academy of Science (Soviet Union) 170
Acanthogammarus victori 170
Aché Indians 137
acid rain 105, 107
acidification, lakes 105
Adair, Red 145
Addis Ababa University 169
Africa: grain production 65
    grasslands 57
    Okavango swamp 177
    poaching 21
    population growth 117, 118
    soils 63
    solar power 26
    tribal peoples 137
    tsetse flies 59
    urban growth 124
    water shortages 34
Aga Khan, Sadruddin 85
agoutis 76
agriculture: anti-desertification 37
    declining production rate 22
    genetic resources 69
    and global warming 98
    grain production 64
    grasslands 57-9
    irrigation 63, 67, 146, 168
    organic 67
    and population growth 65
    research 68
    rice 36
    "set-aside" policies 59
    "shifting cultivation" 63
    slash and burn 50
    soil erosion 63-9
    see also croplands
Ahmadabad 125,129
AIDS 48
air pollution 103-9
    acid rain 105, 107
    Alps 85
    carbon dioxide 22
    history 89, 90
    ozone depletion 90, 91
    smog 103-4
    Third World cities 127
    vehicle emissions 106
Alaska 101
"albedo effect" 49, 81
Albright and Wilson 163
Aleutian Islands 163
algae 163, 164
Alp Action 85
Alpine Convention project 85
Alps 82, 85
Amazon: cattle ranching 53, 61
    dams 171
    deforestation 47
    fish 147
    grasslands 61
    Indians 76
        defending rights (COICA) 54
    soil erosion 63, 64
    waterlilies 176
Amazonia 51
Amish communities 69
ammonites 71
Amoco Cadiz 17
Anatolean Plateau 63
anchovies, declining catches of 154
Andes 81-3
Angara River 170
Antarctic Ocean 143
Antarctic Treaty (1961) 86
Antarctica 43
    depletion of fish stocks 154
    factory fishing 144
    future of 86
    and sea levels 81-2, 86
    seal hunting 151
Antelope Canyon, Utah 43
anti-fouling paint 160
antibiotics 35
ants 60
Antwerp 163
Arabian oryx 72
Aral Sea 146, 169

Arctic 82, 101, 138
Arctic Ocean 153
Arizona 41
armadillos 77
arms expenditure 37
Arrhenius, Svente 89-90
Asia 57, 118, 124
Asia Waterfowl Census Project 181
Asian Wetland Bureau 181
Ataturk Dam 146, 172
Athens 104, 124
Atlantic Ocean fish stocks 152, 154
atomic bomb tests 16, 163
Australia: Aborigines 139, 140
    grasslands 61
    rivers 167
    solar power 25
Ayer's Rock 140

B
Bacon, Francis 184
Baikal, Lake 170
Baltic Sea 165
Band Aid 35
Bangkok 125
Bangladesh 81, 98
    1988 disaster 91, 96
    water supplies 172
    women workers 131
Barabaig tribe 140
Baringo Fuel and Fodder Project 60
barn owls 63
barnacle geese 185
BASF 163
bearded vultures 85
bears, brown 85
bee orchids 75
beef 50, 61
bees, carpenter 75
Beijing 146
Bellerive Foundation 85
Beluga whales 143
Benares 197
Bengal, Bay of 96, 112
Benin 134
Berry, Wendell 69
Bhatt, Ela 129
Bhil tribe 140
Bhopal 17
Bhutan 82, 83
Bikini Atoll 16
bilharzia 169
Bintuni Bay 181
biodiversity 71-9, 134
birds 75, 159, 161
birthwort 75
bison 61
black rhinos 42
Black Sea 152
Blake, William 200
blood flukes 169
Blueprint for a Green Economy 36
boglands 175, 176
Bolivia 75, 123
Bombay 124
Borneo 50
Botswana 177
Brahmaputra River 172
Brasilia 126
Brazil: air pollution 103
    floods 99
    grasslands 61
    Kayapo Indians 113
    population growth 120
    rainforests 52, 53, 54
    tribal peoples 139, 140
Brazil nuts 75, 76
breeding, fruits and vegetables 78-9
Britain: acid rain damage 107
    colonialism in India 132-4, 135
    drinking water standards 169
    foreign aid 193
    large blue butterflies 60
    nuclear weapons tests 90
    peatlands 178
    recycling 193
    sewage discharge into seas 162
    wetlands 175
        gravel workings 181
        Ramsar Convention 177
British Columbia 199
Broads, The 181

brown bears 85
Brundtland Report 37-9
Buddhism 184, 197
Burger King 50
Burkina Faso 134
Burma 21
Burundi 73
Bushmen, Kalahari 138-9, 183
butterflies 60
Byron, Lord 151

C

cacti 76
Calcutta: waste 125, 128
calico flowers 75
California 108, 146
Cambodia 33
camels 132
Cameroon 48, 53
Canada 140, 153, 163
cancer 48, 67, 107
carbon dioxide 90
   China's emissions 34
   greenhouse effect 22, 100-101
   increase in atmosphere 96, 97
   role of grasslands 60-1
   role of peatlands 178-80
   role of rainforests 49-50, 51
   vehicle emissions 106
carbon monoxide 105, 106
Caribbean 95, 99
Carroll, Lewis 163
cars see vehicles
Carson, Rachel 183
cassava 50
catalytic converter 105-6, 108-9
Catholic Church 118
cattle: Amazon 61
   methane production 91
   ranching: beef 50
   soil erosion 53
   tsetse flies 59
Central America 50, 53, 61
CFC's 90, 91
Chácobo Indians 75
chameleons, three-horned 43
Chao Phraya River 125
Charles, Prince of Wales 79
Chernobyl 17
Chesapeake Bay 160
Chicago 113
children: and family size 118-19
   mortality rates 35
   in Third World cities 128
   World Summit for Children 28
Chile 52
China: carbon dioxide emissions 34
   coal 101
   dolphins 172
   family planning program 118, 119
   loss of croplands 66
   nuclear weapons tests 90
   terraces 63
   water shortages 146
   wetlands 181
Chipko Movement 54, 83, 134
Chittagong 112
cities 66-7, 123-9
Ciudad Juárez 126
Clean Air Act 107-9
climate 49, 95-101
cloudforests 47
clover 75
coal 98, 101
coastal communities 159-65
coconut fiber 178
cod, declining catches of 154
cod icefish, declining catches of 154
coir 178
Cold War 37
Colombia 54, 118
Colomoncagua 112
colonialism 132
Colorado 81
Colorado Plateau 199
Colorado River 172
Columbus, Christopher 140
Comechorus baicalensis 170
Common Agricultural Policy 58-9
companies 191-2, 193
"compassion fatigue" 39
computer models 61

conifers, acid rain damage 107
Conservation Reserve Program 68-9
consumer action 193
contraception 48, 49, 117-19
Cook, Mount 201
Coordinating Organization for Indigenous Bodies in the Amazon Basin (COICA) 54
Copacabana 164
Copaiba langsdorfii 72
copper mines 21
coral reefs 162, 164
Coto Doñana National Park 180, 181
cotton grass 85
cotton-topped tamarin 54
cow dung, as fuel 135
cremation 66
crimson rosella 71
croplands 63-9
Crown of Thorns starfish 164
cryosphere 81
Cuajone 21
Cuba 118
Cumbria 163
Cuna tribe 138

D

daisies 77
Dall's porpoises 155
Damascus 172
dams 82, 85, 169-71
Darwin, Charles 77, 79
Dayaks 140
DDT 16, 175
deforestation: Earth Summit 28
   in mountains 81
   rainforests 47-54
   rate of 22
   soil erosion 131
   and soil quality 66
Descartes, René 184
deserts 36, 59, 138
Dhaka 125
diarrheal diseases 35
Dinka tribe 113
Dioscorea elata 49
disease 35, 59, 169
Dogon tribe 34
dogwhelks 159, 160
dolphins 155, 156, 172, 184
drift nets 155, 156
drinking water 147, 169, 172
droughts 95, 99
drugs, from rainforest plants 48-9
Dubos, René 15, 41
ducks, killed by pesticides 180
dung, as fuel 135

E

earthquakes 82
Earthscan 36
Earth Summit 28, 83
East Africa, water shortages 34
East Anglia 181
Easter Island 111
Eastern Europe 16, 37, 146, 189
The Ecologist 171
economic growth, and sustainable development 39
Ecuador: rainforest 50
   Waorani 140
Edéa 53
Egypt 146, 168
El Niño current 154
elephants 21, 57-8
elephant seals 151
Ellesmere Island 153
Emerson, Ralph Waldo 200
emperor penguins 86
Endau Rompin 180-1
energy: firewood 36
   fuel prices 100
   solar power: African village 26
     Australia 25
     Netherlands, street lighting 191
Environmental Investigation Agency 155
"environmental refugees" 33, 42
Eritrea 33

erosion: after deforestation 131
   mountains 81
   sediment in rivers and lakes 168
   soil 63-9
estuaries 159-61
Ethiopia 200
   "compassion fatigue" 39
   famine 33
   genetic diversity 69
   poverty 82
Ethiopian Highlands 81
Etosha National Park 147
Euphrates River 172
European Community: acid rain 105
   air pollution 109
   animal feed imports 50
   Bathing Waters' Directive 162
   Drinking Water Directive 169
   grasslands 58-9
European Parliament 155
Evans, Mount 81
Everglades 144, 160, 177
extinctions 22, 23, 71-9
Exxon Valdez 162

F

fallow land 63
family planning 117-19
family size 121
famines, Ethiopia 33, 39
FAO 154
farming see agriculture
Faroe Islands 155, 161
Farraka Barrage 175
Fearnside, Philip 61
ferns 175
fertilizers, pollution of seas 162-3
fiber optics 26
fire 95, 111
firewood 36, 66
fishing: Calcutta's sewage system 128
   depletion of stocks 152-6
   factory fishing 144
   fish farming 163-5
   size of stocks 22
   by tribal peoples 138
flame scallops 143
flamingos 147
floodplains 167-8
floods 81, 91, 95
Florida: Everglades 177
   Everglades water lily 144
   loss of manatees 72
Flow Country, Scotland 177, 179
flowers, pollination 75-6
flukes 169
food, and population growth 64-65
forests: acid rain 105
   Alpine 85
   effects in Europe 107
   mangroves 160
   watersheds 172
   see also rainforests
fossil fuels 90
France 90
Friends of the Earth International 104, 203
frogs, red-eyed tree 47
fruits 77-8
fuel, cow dung 135
Fuji, Mount 81
fungi, in rainforests 49
fur seals 151

G

"Gaia hypothesis" 41
Galapagos Islands 156
Galapagos tomatoes 76
Gambia 134
Ganges River 132, 172, 197
Ganges Delta: estuary 160
   Farraka Barrage 175
gannets 159
Garhwal Himalaya 134
genetic engineering 65, 73
genetic resources 69
Genoa, Gulf of 164
Germany 107, 161
Giant Triton 164
gill nets 155, 156

global warming 95-101
   "albedo effect" 81
   deforestation 49
   floods: 91, 95, 98-99
   peatlands and 180
   rainfall 81
   rainforests and 49-50, 51
   role of grasslands 60-1
   sea levels: 98
     ice and 81, 82
     low-lying islands 99
   temperature increases 97-100
   vehicle emissions 106
   Venice 28
goats 81
Goethe, Johann Wolfgang von 200
golden-lined frog 167
Goldsmith, Edward 171
gorillas 73
grain production 22, 64
grasslands 57-61
Great Barrier Reef 164
Great Lakes 170
Great Plains 63, 146
Greece 168
Green Belt organization 54
Green movement 25
Green Revolution 65, 134
greenhouse effect see global warming
Greenland 112
Greenpeace 163
groundwater 146
Guinea Bissau 134
Gujarat 129
Gulf War (1991) 37, 145
Gurney's pitta 21
Guyana 111, 139

H

haddock, declining catches of 152, 154
Haiti 128
halons 90
hamburgers 50
Hampstead Heath 191
Hansen, James 95
Hardin, Garrett 144
hardwoods 50, 53-4, 193
Harlem 129
hartebeests, Coke's 58
Harvest Festivals 198
Hawaii 76
herring, declining catches of 152, 154
Heyerdahl, Thor 143
Hibiscus rosa-sinensis 75
Himalayas 81, 134
Hinduism 184
Hispaniola 140
Hmong hill tribe 184
Holland 161, 191
Honduras 112
Hopi Indians 190
housing: loss of croplands 66
   Third World cities 123, 124
human rights 118
hurricanes 95, 96
Hussein, Saddam 145
hyacinth macaws 47
hydrocarbons 104, 106
hydroelectricity, in Amazonia 51

I

ibex 85
ice 81-2, 86, 98
ice ages 100
Ichkeul, Lake 175
Illinois 43
Incas 63
India: carbon dioxide emissions 101
   Chipko Movement, 134
   colonialism, 132-4 135
   Narmada Dam 171
   population growth 117, 118, 119
   rainforests 54
   rural resources 131-5
   Self-Employed Women's Association 129
   soil exhaustion 66
   Survival International 139
   tribal peoples 140
   urban growth 125
   water supplies 146, 169, 172
   wetlands 175, 181

Indian Ocean 159
Indians, North American 151
Indonesia: agriculture 36
    soil erosion 63
    terraces 63
    tribal peoples 139, 140
    urban growth 124
    water supplies 172
    wetlands 181
Indonesian Environmental Forum 54
Industrial Revolution 41, 89
infant mortality 118-19
Innu tribe 140
insectivorous plants 176, 178
insects 47-8, 75
Integrated Pest Management 67
Inter-Governmental Panel on Climate
    Change (IPCC) 51-4, 96, 98
International Institute for Environment and
    Development 36
International Planned Parenthood
    Federation 118
International Whaling Commission 153, 155
Inuit 112, 138, 153
Iowa 180
Iraq 37,145, 168, 172
Ireland, wetlands 175, 178
Irian Jaya 181
irrigation 63, 67, 146, 168
Islay 185
Israel 146
ivory, ban on sale of 21
Ivory Coast 52

J

Jakarta 124
Japan: drift nets 156
    global warming and 99
    kelp-farming 156
    "maglev" trains 25
    mercury poisoning 162
    Mount Fuji 81
    recycling 193
    slaughter of porpoises 155
    terraces 63
    wetlands 181
Java 124
Jordan 146

K

Kalahari Bushmen 138, 139, 183
Karachi 124
Katmandu Valley 192
Kayapo Indians 113
Kelabit tribe 139
kelp 156
Kenya: consumption 117
    grasslands 58, 59-60, 61
    rainforests 54
    soil erosion 168
    tribal peoples: Samburu 137
        Turkana 140
    water supplies 34, 146
Kerala 118
Kew Gardens 79
killer whales 199
Korea 156
Korem 39
krill 86
Kuwait 145

L

La Paz 123
Labrador 140
Lagos 125
lakes 82, 105, 167, 170
large blue butterflies 60
Latin America 35, 124
Law of the Sea Convention 153, 165
Lebanon 168
Lemma, Akililu 169
leopards 71
leprosy 77
Lesotho 82
Lima 126
lions 41
Live Aid 35
Liverpool Bay 162
loggerhead turtles 161
London 16, 89, 103

London Environmental Economics Centre 36
Los Angeles, air pollution 107, 108
Lovelock, Jim 41
Lumad tribe 140
Lutzenberger, Dr. José 54
lynxes 85

M

macaws 47
Madagascan sifakas 22
Madagascar 48, 52, 168
Madagascar periwinkle 48
Madhya Pradesh 185
Madrid 124
magnetic levitation ("maglev") 25
magnolia 41
maize 43, 79
malaria 175
Malayan Nature Society 180-1
Malaysia 47-8, 52, 181
    tribal peoples 139, 140
Maldive Islands, global warming 99, 159
Mali 34, 36, 134
manatees 72
mangroves 160, 181
Manhattan 90
Manila 123, 126
manioc 50
maple trees 42, 77
Marchon plant 163
marshes 175-81
Maryland 15
Masai Mara National Park 58
Masai tribe 58, 197
Matang 181
Matterhorn 85
Mauritania 134
Mediterranean 152, 164
"mega-cities" 124
Melpa tribe 137
Mentawai tribe 140
mercury pollution 162
methane 82, 91, 96
Mexico: grasslands 61
    population growth 118
    rainforests 48
    urban growth 124-6
    water supplies 172
Mexico City: air pollution 103
    housing 124
    population growth 125
    poverty 35
    smog 104
microchips 24
Middle East, water supplies 146, 172
military expenditure, "peace dividend" 37
milky storks 181
minerals, ocean bed 153
Minamata Bay 162
Mississippi Delta 160
Molina, Mario 90
monsoons 81, 131
Montreal Protocol 91, 97
mosses, bog 178
moths, pollination by 76, 79
Mountain Gorilla Project 73
mountains 81-5
Mozambique 65

N

Nairobi National Park: Black Rhino 42
    Coke's Hartebeest 58
Namibia 147
Narmada Dam 140, 171
Narmada Valley 139
Nasser, Lake 171
National Cancer Institute 48
National Geographic Society 170
National Research Council 67
NATO 140
Nebraska 180
nectar 75-6
Nepal 192
    lakes 167
    poverty 82
    reforestation 131
    terraces 63
    women workers 133
nets, fishing 155, 156
New Guinea 137

New York: air pollution 90
    cotton exchange 197
    population growth 125
    poverty 36, 129
New York Botanical Garden 79
New Zealand 76, 159, 201
Niger 37, 133, 134
Nigeria: harvests 198
    rainforests 52
    urban growth 126
    water supply 146, 147
Nile River 146, 168
nitrogen fertilizers 64
nitrogen oxides 105, 106
Nordhaus, William 100
North America: grasslands 57, 61, 63
North Dakota 15
North Sea: depletion of fish stocks
    154
    pollution: international action 165
        sewage 156
        tributyltin (TBT) 160
North/South divide 33-4
Norway 163
nuclear families 121
nuclear power, in Third World 112
nuclear weapons tests 90
Nugkuag, Evaristo 54
nuts 78

O

oak trees 77
oceans: fish farming 163-5
    minerals 153
    over-fishing 151-6
    pollution 143, 151, 162
OECD 193
oil: Amoco Cadiz 17
    Gulf War 145
    pollution of oceans 151
    Torrey Canyon 16
    wasted resources 24
oil-palm trees 47-8
Okavango Basin 175, 177
optical fibers 26
oral rehydration (ORT) 35
orchids, insect pollination of 75, 79
organic farming 67
Orwell, George 39
oryx, Arabian 72
Ouedraogo, Bernard 134
Our Common Future (Brundtland Report)
    37-9
Overseas Development Administration 193
owls, barn 63
oysters 160, 163
ozone 104-5, 107
ozone layer: depletion of 22
    harmful substances 90
    Montreal Protocol 91
    UNEP 97
    and skin cancer 164

P

Pacific Ocean 156
Painted Desert, Arizona 41
Pakistan 175
Panama 138
Papua New Guinea, rainforests 52
Paraguay 137
parakeets 71
Paris 119
parrots: hyacinth macaw 47
    Yellow-headed 28
pastoralism 132, 138
"peace dividend" 37
peatlands 175-81
Pemagatsel 83
Penan tribe 139, 181
penguins 86
peregrines 16
periwinkles, Madagascar 48
permafrost 82, 101
Peru: anchovy fishery 154
    copper mines 21
    defending rights 54
    rainforests: biodiversity 47
        urban growth 126
pesticides 67, 180
Pesticides Action Network 67
Phewa, Lake 167

Philippines: agricultural research 68
    nuclear reactors 112
    rainforests 54
    tribal peoples 140
    urban growth 126
    wetlands 181
photochemical smog 103, 104
photosynthesis 51
photovoltaic cells 26
phytoplankton 152
pilot whales 155, 161-2
pitcher plants 176
plankton 152
plants: in the Alps 85
    biodiversity 71-9
    drugs from 48-9
    extinction 22, 23
    insectivorous 176, 178
    pollination 75-6
    wetlands 178
    see also rainforests
poaching 21
Pocosin bogs 178
Poland 146
Polish Ecology Club (PKE) 104
pollack, declining catches of 154
pollination 75-6
pollution: heavy metals 162
    see also air pollution; water pollution
population growth 117-21
    demand for food 64, 65
    mountain areas 82
    rate of 120-1
    urban growth 123-9
porpoises, Dall's 155
poverty: in cities 36
    mountain regions 82
    and population growth 118-19
    Third World 34-5
power see energy
power stations, acid rain 105
Pro Familia 118
Programme for Social and Community
    Forestry (India) 134
ptarmigan 85
purse seine nets 156
Pyrenees 105

Q

Queensland 48

R

radioactivity, nuclear weapons tests 90
rainfall: acid rain 105, 107
    global warming and, 99
    monsoon: greenhouse effect 81, 131
    North Carolina 90
rainforests: and climate control 49
    deforestation 47-54
        Earth Summit 28
        rate of 22
    economic potential 48-9
    loss of species 76
    tree-planting campaign 51-4
    tribal peoples 137
Ramsar Convention 177, 181
recycling 189, 193
red-eyed tree frogs 47
Reformation 184
refugees 33, 39, 42
religion 184, 185
Reni 134
reservoirs 169, 171
rhino: black 42
    horn 21
rice 36, 99
Rift Valley 59-60
Rio de Janeiro, 99
rivers: dams 169-72
    estuaries 160-1
    floodplains 167-8
    pollution 146, 168-9
Rocky Mountains 81
Rondônia 53
Roosevelt, Franklin D. 171
Rowland, Sherwood 90
Royal Botanic Gardens, Kew 79
Royal Society 170
Royal Society for the Protection of Birds 161
rural resources 131-5
Rwanda 73, 117

S

Sahara 42
  droughts 99
  expansion of 59
  pastoralism 138
Sahel 36, 59, 134
St. Lawrence River 143
salmon 163, 167
Samburu tribe 137
San'a 83
São Paulo 103, 124, 125
Sarawak 52, 139, 181
scallops 143
Schelde Estuary 163
schistosomiasis 169
Schumacher, E.M. 111
Scotland 163, 177, 185
Scott Paper 139
sea birds 159
seacows 72
sea levels, global warming: 98
  Antartica 86
  ice 81
  Venice 28
seals 151, 152
seas see oceans
seaweed 178
Second World War 185
seeds, biodiversity 76-8
Self-Employed Women's Association 129
Senegal 134
serendipity berries 79
Serengeti plains 41
"set-aside" policies 59
sewage: Calcutta 128
  discharge into seas 156, 162
  from tourism 164
Shanghai 125
Shatalov, Vladimir 89
shell collecting 164
shellfish 143
"shifting cultivation" 63
shore crabs 159
shorelines 159-65
Siberut Island 140
Signy 86
Silent Valley campaign 54
silicon chips 24
Six S Association 134
skin cancer 164
slash-and-burn agriculture 50
sleeping sickness 59
slime mold 78
Slovenia 85
slums 123, 124
smog: 89
  Alps 85
  health risks 103, 104
  London: 1940's-50's 16
  Los Angeles 108
  São Paulo 103
soapberry 169
soil 42
  and deforestation 53
  erosion 63-9
  grasslands 58
  loss of fertility 64
  in rainforests 49
  Nepal 131
  sediment in rivers and lakes 168
solar power 25, 26, 191
Somalis 15
Somerset Levels 178
South America: cattle ranching 50
  population growth 118
  terraces 63
  tribal peoples 140
South Coast Air Quality Management District 108
South Korea 118
South Orkney 86
South-East Asia 118, 140, 124
Soviet Union:
  Aral Sea: irrigation and pesticides 146, 169
  factory fishing 144
  Lake Baikal 170
  nuclear weapons tests 90
  soil erosion 63
  steppes 57

soybeans 99
Spain 180, 181
species: biodiversity 71-9
  extinction 22, 23
  in rainforests 47-8
sphagnum moss 176, 178
spiny starfish 144
spiritual values 37
squirrels 77
Sri Lanka 118
Stalin, Joseph 169-71
starfish 164
Stockholm Conference on Environment and Development (1972) 97
storks, milky 181
strawberries 77
strelitzia 42
Sudan 42
  Dinka tribe 113
  droughts 99
  water supplies 172
  wetlands 175
Sudd 175
sulphur dioxide 105
sunbathing 164
sundews 176
superconductivity 25
Surui Indians 53
Survival International 139
sustainable development 37-9
Sweden 105
Swedish National Institute of Environmental Medicine 105-7
Switzerland 107, 112
  Alps 82, 85
sycamore trees 77
Syria: Ataturk Dam 146, 172

T

Tadavi tribe 140
Taino tribe 140
Taiwan 118, 156
takahe 76
tamarins, cotton-topped 54
Tambaqui 147
Tanzania 57-8
teak 54
technology, green 25-6
Teheran 125
termites 57-8
terraces 63, 83
Thailand: cassava exports 50
  deforestation 21
  grasslands 61
  harvests 198
  population growth 118
  rainforests: destruction 50, 54
  refugees 33
  soil erosion 168
  tribal peoples 184
  wetlands 181
Thames Estuary 160
"Thermoplastic Concept House" 191
Third World:
  alternative technologies 112
  dams 171
  drinking water supplies 172
  population growth 117-19
  poverty 35
  rural resources 131-5
  urban growth 123-9
  water pollution 147, 169
Thoreau, Henry David 167, 200
Tibet 197
Tigray 33
Tigris River 172
Timbuktu 185
Togo 134
Tokyo 125
Tolba, Dr. Mostafa 97
Tolstoy, Leo 200
tomatoes 76, 79
topsoil, erosion 63-9
Torrey Canyon 16
tortoises 76
tourism 82-3, 164
towns and cities 123-9
trains, "maglev" 25
Transmigration Programme (Indonesia) 124

trees: acid rain damage 107
  Chipko Movement 134
  consumer action 193
  hardwood 53-4
  furnishings 50
  tree-planting campaign 51-4
  yew 104
  see also rainforests; wood
tribal peoples 22, 137-41
tributyltin (TBT) 160
tropical forests see rainforests
trypanosome parasite 59
tsetse flies 59
Tuareg 138
tuna 152, 156
Tunisia 175
Turkana tribe 140
Turkey 63, 146, 172
turtles 161, 164

U

ultraviolet radiation 164
UNICEF 35
United Nations 26
  Conference on the Law of the Sea 153
  Earth Summit 28
  Family Planning Association 117
  International Drinking Water Supply and Sanitation Decade 147
  World Summit for Children 28
United Nations Environment Program (UNEP) 97
  grasslands project 61
  Mediterranean Action Plan 152
  Montreal Protocol 91
  protecting regional seas 165
United Nations Conference on Environment and Development (1992) see Earth Summit
United States of America:
  acid rain 105, 107
  air pollution 104, 107-9
  Amish communities 69
  atomic bomb tests 163
  climate changes 95
  consumption 117
  droughts 99
  grain production 64
  maize 43
  nuclear weapons tests 90
  soil erosion 67-9
  Vietnam War 145
  water supplies 67, 146, 172
  wetlands 177, 178, 180
University College, London 36
urban growth 123-9
US Congress, Clean Air Act 107, 109
US Geological Survey 170
Utah 43, 199

V

vaccination 35
Valle de Chalco 124
values 36-7
vegetables 78-9
vehicles: air pollution 103-9
  carbon dioxide 22, 107, 108
  catalytic converters 105, 106, 108-9
Venezuela 47
Venice 28
Vietnam 181
Vietnam War 145
villages, rural resources 131-5
Vistula River 146
vultures, bearded 85

W

Wadden Sea 160, 161
Wallace, Barnes 178
Waorani tribe 140
Ward, Barbara 15, 36, 135
Wash The 183
water 143-7
  drinking water supplies 147, 172
  irrigation 63
  rivers 167-72
  role of mountains 81
  shortages 34, 66-7, 146
  storage 131-2
  see also oceans

water pollution 143-7
  Mediterranean 152
  oceans 143
    continental shelves 151
  oil spills 16, 17, 151, 162
  rivers 146, 168-9
water table 146
waterlilies 144, 176
waterlily frogs 178
watersheds 172
weapons, "peace dividend" 37
weather see climate
weevils 48
West Africa, deforestation 50
wetlands 175-81
  loss of coastal 159-60
whales: 161
  Beluga 143
  killer 199
  pilot: slaughter, Faroe Islands 161-2
    campaign against 155
  whaling 151-2
wheat 65
white-fronted geese 165
White Revolution 134
wildebeest 58
willow trees 167
wimplefish 151
Wisconsin 42
wolves 85
women: employment 133
  India 131
  family planning 118, 119
  role of 121
  in Third World cities 128, 129
wood: firewood: effects of scarcity 66
  hardwoods 53-4
  furnishings 50
  international perspective 193
  Mali 36
Wordsworth, William 200
Worede, Melaku 69
World Bank 139
  and the Asian Wetland Bureau 181
  Indonesian Transmigration Programme 124
  irrigation schemes 168
  Narmada Dam 171
  Programme for Social and Community Forestry 134
World Biosphere Reserves 181
World Conservation Union 83
World Health Organization 35
World Summit for Children, New York (1990) 28
World Wide Fund for Nature: Asian Wetland Bureau 181
  Ramsar Covention 177
Worldwatch Institute 69

Y

Yangtze River 172
Yanomami tribe 139, 140
yellow-headed parrots 28
Yellowstone National Park 95
Yemen: irrigation 83
  pastoralists 132
yew 104

Z

Zaire 43
Zimbabwe: family planning 118
  tsetse fly control 59

ACKNOWLEDGMENTS

Special thanks from Jonathon Porritt to Julia Brown for all the typing and support.

Dorling Kindersley would like to thank the following for their assistance: Emma Ainsworth, Heather McCarry, Elissa Boxall, Debra Clapson, Sharon Clapson, Wendy Gibbons, Corinne Hall, David Hiscock, Mark Johnson Davies, Charyn Jones, Miren Lopategui, Deborah Rhodes, Brian Rust, Salvatore Tomaselli, Alistair Wardle, Clair Watson; and Hilary Bird for compiling the index.

Dorling Kindersley would like to thank the following illustrators: Richard Lewis (pages 52/53; 65; 98/99; 106; 125; 154); and Barry Jones (pages 76; 120/121; 146).

Dorling Kindersley would like to thank the following individuals and organizations for their help in researching this book: IUCN Plant Conservation Office, London: Steve Davis; Missouri Botanical Gardens: Peter Hoch; Worldwatch Institute, Washington: Peter Weber; Survival International, London: Charlotte Sankey & Polly Mathewson; SOS Siberut, London; Renewable Resources Assessment Group, Imperial College, London; International Council for the Exploration of the Sea (ICES), Copenhagen, and the Bulletin Statistique de Pêches Maritimes; Marine Laboratory, Aberdeen: Roger Bailey; Population Concern, London: Marian Storkey; Climatic Research Department: University of East Anglia; Julie Whitaker; and the staff at Friends of the Earth UK.

Dorling Kindersley would like to thank the following for their kind permission to reprint extracts from the works listed below: p 30 Neville Spearman Ltd for Alone by Richard E. Byrd, published in London 1958; p 30 Victor Gollancz Ltd and Pantheon Books, a division of Random House Inc., New York, for Making Peace with the Planet by Barry Commoner, published in London 1990; p 38 Genesis Publications for Save the World by George Harrison; p 41 Charles Scribners Sons, New York, an imprint of Macmillan Publishing Company, for A God Within by René Dubos, copyright 1972 René Dubos, published by Angus & Robertson in London 1973; p 45 Grapefruit for Earth Piece 1963 by Yoko Ono, published in the USA 1964; p 49 Editorial Sudamericana for Nosotros by Norma Aleandro taken from Poemas y Cuentos de Atenázor, published 1986; p 49 Golden Mountain Music Corporation for If a Tree Falls, words and music by Bruce Cockburn, taken from the album "Big Circumstance", published in Canada 1988; p 59 The Findhorn Press for Wilderness and the Human Spirit by Laurens van der Post, taken from Wilderness, published 1982, based on 2nd World Wilderness Conference; p 89 Queen Anne Press, a division of Macdonald and Co, Publishing Ltd, for The Home Planet, conceived and edited by Kevin W. Kelley, published in London 1988; p 92 Faber & Faber Ltd for Politics and Conscience by Václav Havel, taken from Living in Truth, edited by Jan Vladislav, published in London 1987; p 100 Pan Books Ltd and Harmony Books, a division of Crown Publishers Inc. New York for Life, the Universe & Everything by Douglas Adams, published by Pan Books in London 1982; p 105 Emecé Editores, S.A., for Hombres y Engranajes by Ernesto Sabato, published 1951; p 111 André Deutsch and Curtis Brown Ltd for Only One Earth by Barbara Ward and René Dubos, published in London by André Deutsch 1972, © The Report on the Human Environment Inc 1972; p 111 Blond & Briggs for Small is Beautiful by E.M. Schumacher, published in London 1973; p 119 Hutchinsonand Simon & Schuster, New York, for The Population Explosion by Paul & Anne Ehrlich, published in London 1990; p 138 The Age for The Holy Spirit of the Great South Land by Caroline Jones, published in Melbourne, Australia 1988; p 143 Unwin Hyman, a division of HarperCollins Publishers Ltd, for The Ra Expeditions by Thor Heyerdahl, published in London 1971; p 148 Nobel Foundation for William Golding's Nobel Speech 1983; p 153 Jonathan Cape Ltd for Whale Nation by Heathcote Williams, published in London 1988; p 183 The Estate of Rachel Carson for Silent Spring by Rachel Carson, © 1962 Rachel Carson published by Hamish Hamilton Ltd, London; p 194 Toronto Star for an article by Margaret Atwood, published in Canada 1988. The Publishers have made every attempt to credit reprint extract permissions in the appropriate manner.

Photographic Acknowledgments

The following abbreviations have been used:
t (top), b (bottom), c (centre), l (left), r (right)
BC (Bruce Coleman); DK (Dorling Kindersley); RHPL (Robert Harding Picture Library); HL (The Hutchison Library); MP (Magnum Photos); NHPA (Natural History Photographic Agency); OSF (Oxford Scientific Films); PP (Panos Pictures); PEPS (Planet Earth Pictures/Seaphot); SPL (Science Photo Library); FSPG (Frank Spooner Pictures/Gamma); SAPL (Survival Anglia Photo Library)

2 PEPS/Tony Bennett 3 SPL 5 (tl) OSF/Stan Osolinski (tr) NHPA/Anthony Bannister (cl) DK/Dave King (cr) DK/Philip Dowell (bl) DK/Colin Keates (bcl) DK/Jane Burton (bcr) DK/Steve Gorton (br) DK/Colin Keates 6 (tl) DK (tr) DK/Dave King (bl) DK/Jerry Young (bc) Zefa 7 (tc) DK/Kim Taylor (tr) Barbara Y. E. Pyle (bl) DK/Dave King (blt) DK/Kim Taylor (brt) DK/Dave King (blb) DK/Jerry Young 8 (tl) SAPL/M. Kavanagh (tr) DK/Peter Chadwick (bl) DK/Dave King 9 (tl) DK/Kim Taylor (tr) DK/Cyril Laubscher (bl) DK/Neil Fletcher (brt) DK/Kim Taylor & Jane Burton (brb) NHPA/Karl Switak 10 (tl) DK/Tim Ridley (tr) DK/Steve Gorton (bl) PEPS/Robert Jureit (br) DK/Dave King 11 (tl) RHPL (tr) Image Bank/Benn Mitchell (cr) DK/Philip Dowell (bl) DK/Dave King (bc) DK/Kim Taylor (br) DK/Jerry Young 12 (tl) DK/Karl Shone (tc) DK/Dave King (bl) Barbara Pyle (br) DK/Richard Smith 13 (tl) DK/Dave King (tr) Image Bank/David Hamilton (bl) DK/Harry Taylor (br) DK 14 PEPS/Jim Brandenburg 15 (l) SAPL/Nellaine Price (r) Colorific/David Yszak 16 (tl) (cr) (br) Popperfoto (cl) Ardea/T.T. Smith 17 (l) (br) FSPG (tr) Rex 18 (tl) BC/John Nash (bl) Zefa 19 (t) BC/John Shaw (b) DK/Cyril Laubscher 20 Colorific/Mary Fisher 21 (t) Ardea/Kenneth W. Pink (b) NHPA/Anthony Bannister 22 (tl) Colorific/Dirk Halstead (tr) FSPG (ctl) RHPL/Hanbury Tenison (ctr) MP/Abbas (cbl) SPL/NASA (cbc) DK (cbr) PP/Michael Harvey (bl) K.G. Preston-Mapham (br) DK/Steve Gorton 23 MP/Ian Berry 24 Zefa 25 (t) Zefa (c) SPL/Taheshi Takahara (b) SPL/David Parker 26 (t) MP/H. Gruyaert (l) SPL/Simon Fraser (r) Spectrum Colour Library 28 (tl) SAPL/John Harris (tr) Alex Arthur (b) Zefa 31 (t) MP/Steve McCurry (b) Colorific/Jim Howard 32 Colorific/David Burnett 33 Colorific/Heimo Aga 34 HL/Stephen Pern 35 (t) Colorific/Dirk Halstead (b) Colorific/David Burnett 36 (l) BC/Norman Myers (r) MP/Steve McCurry 37 MP/Steve McCurry 38 BC/A.J. Stevens 39 Colorific/David Burnett 40 PEPS/John Lythgoe 41 (l) DK/Philip Dowell (r) PEPS/Jonathan Scott 42 (tl) BC/S. Nielson (tr) OSF/Stan Osolinski (cl) BC/Gene Ahrens (br) BC/Peter Ward 43 (tl) MP/Michael K. Nichols (tr) MP/Burt Glinn (cl) NHPA/Jonathan Chester (br) SAPL/Jeff Foott 45 (bl) PP/David Reed (br) DK/Steve Gorton 46 OSF/F.J. Bernard 47 (tl) (tr) DK/Colin Keates (bl) SAPL/Keith & Liz Leiden (br) NHPA/John Shaw 48 (tl) OSF/Raymond A. Mendez (tr) OSF/Edward Parker (b) DK 49 (t) DK (b) OSF/Roger Brown 50 (t) PP (c) MP/Michael K. Nichols (b) OSF/Edward Parker 52 (t) BC/G. Zeisler (b) MP/Peter Marlow 53 (t) MP/Michael K. Nichols (c) MP/S. Salgado (b) PP/Paul Harrison 54 (b) NHPA/K. Ghani 55 NHPA/Stephen Dalton 56 PEPS/Jonathan Scott 57 (tl) OSF/Okapia (br) PEPS/Hans Christian Heep 58 (t) SAPL/Richard & Julia Kemp (b) OSF/David Fritts 59 OSF/Avril Ramage 60 SAPL/Dennis Green 61 (l) OSF/Michael Fogden (r) OSF/Roger Brown 62 Colorific/Lee E. Battaglia 63 (tl) OSF/Muzz Murray (br) DK/Geoff Dann 64 (t) MP/Dennis Stock (b) Holt Studios/Nigel Cattlin 65 (tl) Zefa (tr) DK/Andrew McRobb (b) PP/Ron Giling 66 DK/Geoff Dann 67 (t) HL/Melanie Friend (b) DK/Steve Gorton 68 Holt Studios/Nigel Cattlin 69 RHPL/Photri/M. Long 70 OSF/Rafi Ben-Shahar 71 (tr) DK/Philip Dowell (cl) DK/Peter Chadwick (b) DK/Colin Keates 72 (t) BC (b) PEPS/Rodney Wood 73 (b) MP/Michael K. Nichols 74 OSF/Stephen Dalton 75 (t) OSF/Kjell B. Sandred (b) OSF/J.A.L. Cooke 76 (t) OSF/Godfrey Merlen (cl) DK/Peter Chadwick (cr) /Rod Williams (b) OSF/John McCammon 77 BC/Jeff Foott 78 OSF/Andrew Plumptre 79 (t) HL (b) OSF/Scott Camazine 80 RHPL/Nigel Blythe 81 (tr) DK/Andrew McRobb (cl) OSF/Ray Richardson (br) DK/Andrew McRobb 83 (l) BC/Jaroslav Poncas (r) Holt Studios/Richard Anthony 84 RHPL/Jon Gardey 85 (tl) Colorific/Chuck Fishman (tr) OSF/Frithjof Skibbe (bl) BC/Bob & Clara Calhoun (br) OSF/Roland Mayr 86 (t) OSF/Doug Allan (bl) OSF/Kjell B. Sandved (br) PEPS/N. Cobley 87 NHPA/Peter Johnson 88 SPL/Phil Jude 89 (l) DK (r) OSF 90 (tr) Constantin Emile Meunier, Dark Landscape Musée d'Orsay, Paris Photo The Bridgeman Art Library (cl) SPL/Will McIntyre (cr) PEPS/Howard Platt (bl) RHPL 91 (t) SPL/NASA (cl) OSF/Aldo Brando Leon (br) FSPG 92 FSPG 93 BC/Frieder Sauer 94 OSF/Stan Osolinski 95 (tl) FSPG (b) Colorific/Shepard Sherbell 96 (t) Colorific (b) FSPG 97 (t) PP/Alain le Garameur (b) PP/Michael Harvey 98 (t) MP/Jean Gaumy (cl) DK/Colin Keates 99 (tl) MP/Michael K. Nichols (tr) FSPG (cl) Colorific/Carlos Humbertot (br) PEPS/Herwarth Voightmann 101 Colorific/Black Star 102 MP/Bruno Barbey 103 (b) MP/Abbas 104 DK/Peter Chadwick 105 (cb) BC Gunter Ziesler (br) Colorific/Steve Woit 106 (t) MP/Michael K. Nichols (b) DK/Stephen Oliver 107 MP/René Burri 108 (t, inset) FSPG (c) Zefa (b) SPL/David Parker 110 SAPL/Nick Gordon 111 (1) NHPA/G.I. Bernard (r) Alex Arthur 112 (tl) Colorific/Black Star/M. Grobet (cl) MP/Ian Berry (cr) RHPL (br) PP/Helden Jaan Netocny 113 (t) Colorific/Jim Howard (cr) SAPL/Richard Kemp (b) MP/Miguel Rio Branco 115 (t) PP/R. Berriedale-Johnson (b) HL/Crispin Hughes 116 RHPL/J.H.C. Wilson 117 (t) SPL/Francis Leroy (b) MP/Michael K. Nichols 118 (l) HL (r) Colorific/Alon Reininger 119 Colorific/Brian Harris 120 MP/Michael K. Nichols 121 (tl) (tr) (b) Zefa 122 MP/F. Scianna 123 (l) PP/Ron Giling 124 (t) PP/Ron Giling (c) MP/Abbas (b) HL/Liba Taylor 125 MP/Philip J. Griffiths 126 (t) PP/Ron Giling (c) HL/Anna Tully (b) Colorific/Alon Reininger 128 (t) HL/Sarah Errington (b) PP/Heldur Jaan Netocny 129 MP/Eli Reed 130 MP/Steve McCurry 131 (tl) PP/Tom Learmouth (br) PP/Cooper Hammond 132 RHPL/F. Jackson 133 (t) BC/Mark N. Bolton (b) PP/Ron Giling 134 (cl) PP R. Berriedale Johnson (cr) PP/Geoff Barnard 135 PP/R. Berriedale Johnson 136 NHPA/G.J. Bernard 137 (tl) DK/Dave King (tr) Alex Arthur (br) Colorific/Jose Azel 138 HL 139 (t) SAPL/M. Kavanagh (b) MP/A. Venzago 140 (tl) PP/Trygve Bolstad (cl) HL/John Wright (ct) Derek Fordham/Arctic Camera (cr) SAPL International/David Beatty (right of world map) HL/Granada TV (bl) RHPL (br) RHPL 141 Colorific/John Running 142 OSF/Kim Westerskov 143 (l) DK/Andreas von Einsiedel (r) OSF/Z. Leszczynski 144 (tl) Greenpeace/D. Culley (cl) PEPS/J. Brian Alker (cr) DK/Dave King (b) DK/Steve Gorton 145 (l) FSPG (r) FSPG (r) FSPG/Gilles Saussier 146 (l) OSF/Judd Cooney (r) Colorific/Black Star/Boccon-Gibod 147 (t) HL/Anna Tully (cl) OSF/Partridge Films/Michael Goulding (bl) SAPL/Jen & Des Bartlett (br) DK/Steve Gorton (cr) DK/Dave King (b) OSF/Ronald Toms 149 (b) DK/Steve Gorton 150 PEPS/John Lythgoe 151 (tl) (tr) DK/Steve Gorton (b) SAPL/Jeff Foott 152 (t) SPL/Dr Gene Feloman (b) DK/Dave King 153 PEPS/Jim Brandenburg 154 (tr) PEPS/K. Scholey (tl – Herring) (c – Anchovy) (bc – Haddock) DK/Steve Gorton (cr – Cod) OSF/Fredrik Ehranstrom (bl – Cod Icefish) PEPS/P. Sayers (br – Pollack) PEPS/Jim Greenfield 155 (br) Greenpeace/Coffey (background) DK/Steve Gorton 156 (t) Greenpeace/Morgan (b) PEPS/Robert Jurfit 157 OSF/Godfrey Merlen 158 OSF/Kim Westerskov 159 (tl) DK (tr) DK/Steve Gorton (b) OSF/Ben Osborne 160 (t) PEPS/John Lythgoe (b) Alan Watson/Findhorn Foundation 161 (t) OSF/C.C. Lockwood (b) FSPG/F. Xavier Pelletier 162 (t) PEPS/Warren Williams (cl) Rex Features (b) PEPS/Keith Scholey 163 (t) Greenpeace/Cels (b) Greenpeace/Morgan 164 (t) BC/Nick de Vore III (cr) PEPS/Linda Pitkin (b) DK/Steve Gorton 166 PEPS/G. Deichmann/Transglobe 167 (tl) DK/Philip Dowell (tr) DK/Philip Dowell (tr) DK/Philip Dowell (b) PEPS/John Waters & Bernadette Spiegel 168 HL/Bernard Régent 169 (t) SPL/Sinclair Stammers (b) FSPG/Novosti 170 (t) OSF/Doug Allen (bottom and two inset pictures) OSF/Richard Kirby 171 The Ecologist 172 (t) SAPL/Nick Gordon (b) Rex 174 PEPS/John Lythgoe 175 (t) DK/Steve Gorton (bl) OSF/Alastair Shay (br) DK/Steve Gorton 176 (tl) DK/Steve Gorton (tr) BC/Frieder Sauer (tc) DK/Steve Gorton (bc) PEPS/Gwilym Lewis (b) PEPS/Ken Lucas 177 (t) PEPS/John Lythgoe (bl) OSF/Tony Bomford (br) PEPS/J.R. Bracegirdle 178 (t) Ardea/John Mason (c) DK/Steve Gorton (b) OSF/Michael Fogden 180 FSPG/Pablo Ramon 181 BC/M.P. Kahl 182 SAPL/Mike Price 183 (l) SAPL/Chris Knights (r) NHPA/Anthony Bannister 184 (tr) PEPS/James D. Watt (cl) PEPS/Peter Stevenson (b) Colorific/Don King 185 (tr) RHPL/J.H.C. Wilson (cl) MP/Abbas (br) NHPA/Stephen Dalton 188 Colorific/Black Star/Charles Mason 189 (tl) FSPG (b) SPL/Andrew McClenaghan 191 (tl) (cr) Zefa (tr) SPL/Michael Abbey (b) RHPL/David Hughes 192 Colorific 193 PP/Marcos Santilli 194 OSF/Bates Littlehales 195 (tr) Barbara Pyle (bl) OSF/Stan Osolinski 196 PEPS/Jonathon Scott 197 (tl) Colorific/Joe McNally (bl) Mustapha Sami (br) RHPL/J.H.C. Wilson 198 (tr) PEPS/Peter Stephenson (bl) PP/Bruce Paton 199 (t) (b) SAPL/Jeff Foott 200 MP/Ian Berry 201 Zefa

Cover Photographs
Author photograph copyright Roland Kemp
Front Cover: Earth (European Space Agency - Science Photo Library); Butterfly (DK); Plant (DK / Steve Gorton). Front Flap: Earth (European Space Agency - Science Photo Library); Stag Beetle (DK / Dave King); Butterfly (DK); Vine (DK). Spine: Earth (European Space Agency - Science Photo Library). Back Cover: Fish (DK / Steve Gorton); Snake (DK / Jerry Young); Bird (DK / Richard Smith). Back Flap: Plant (DK); Frog (DK / Jerry Young); Plum (DK / Peter Chadwick); Banded Demoiselle dragonfly (DK / Philip Dowell).